BURMESE
LOOKING
GLASS

BURMESE LOOKING GLASS

A HUMAN RIGHTS ADVENTURE AND A JUNGLE REVOLUTION

EDITH T. MIRANTE

GROVE PRESS
New York

Published by Grove Press
A division of Grove Press, Inc.
841 Broadway
New York, NY 10003-4793

Published in Canada by General Publishing Company, Ltd.

Library of Congress Cataloging-in-Publication Data

Mirante, Edith T.
Burmese looking glass : a human rights adventure and a jungle
revolution / by Edith T. Mirante. — 1st ed.
p.   cm.
ISBN 0-8021-1457-1 (acid-free paper)
1. Human rights—Burma.   2. Burma—Description and travel.
I. Title.
JC599.B87M57   1993
323.4'9'09591—dc20   92-11122
                                                           CIP

Printed on acid-free paper

Design and map by Irving Perkins Associates

First Edition 1993

1   3   5   7   9   10   8   6   4   2

For my father, Albert R. Mirante,
and my mother, Irma S. Mirante, to join her cities of books

CONTENTS

Author's Note   ix

The Unsafe Path   3

Trouble in Arcadia   43

The Home of the Brave   69

The Land of the Tai   119

Down the Rabbit Hole   145

The Opera   191

Through the Looking Glass   207

A Radiant Obstacle   237

Kata   283

The Spider's Web   297

Afterword   327

Glossary of Ethnic Groups and Armed Forces   331

AUTHOR'S NOTE

All of the events in this book really happened, and all of the people really existed. Most of the dialogue is reconstructed from memory, but some is from tape transcriptions (my human rights interviews). I have changed many of the names in the book. The remaining "real names" are most often noms de guerre that people have taken for themselves; when rebels operate in Burma's war zone, they often take another name to protect relatives who may still be under government control. It is not at all uncommon for the regime to imprison the family members of rebel soldiers or dissidents, and to torture them for information. Because such practices are the norm in Burma, I have provided pseudonyms to protect the security of my war-zone friends and acquaintances, and also to shield the identity of the foreigners who were habitually ducking across the Thailand/Burma border.

I am deeply grateful to my writing *sensei,* Jay Wurts, who showed me how to refine a book out of raw material. My appreciation goes to Edward Lacey (a warrior poet) and Jim Morris (a poet warrior) for early assistance and encouragement, and to Lisa Rasmussen and Rand Mirante for their guidance into the maze of publishing. For their faith, help, and clarity, my thanks to these at Grove Press: my editor, Emily Heckman; Roxana Petzold, Amy Brown, Alan Williams, and Tim Schreiber.

This book was written at friends' houses in Bangkok, Chiang Mai, Hong Kong, and New Jersey, and at the Mae Kok Villa in Chiang Rai and the Cathay Hotel in Penang. My thanks for putting me up as I wrote it to Linda, Wolfgang, Pippa, Aye Saung, Mr. Dean, Mr. Sak, and my mother.

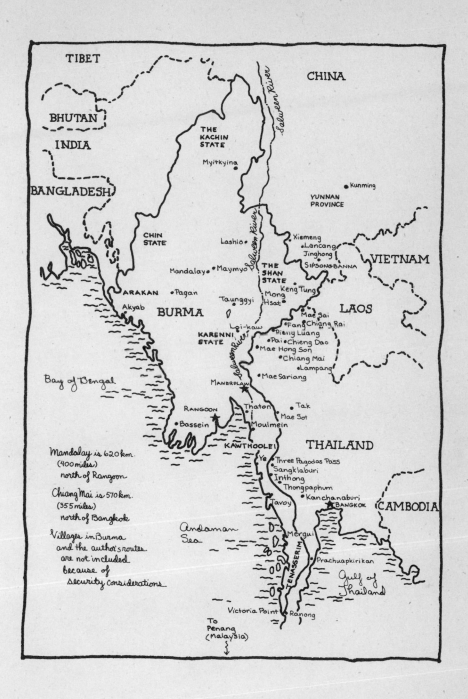

Our goal is not to take the safe path, which leads
ever downward into stagnation.
—Huggs McShane in an aerogram from Shanghai

But pleasures are like poppies spread—
You seize the flow'r, its bloom is shed;
Or like the snow falls in the river—
A moment white, then melts for ever . . .
    —Robert Burns, "Tam O'Shanter"

BURMESE
LOOKING
GLASS

THE
UNSAFE
PATH

⹀ 1 ⹀

My first pair of moccasins set me off on the unsafe path that would eventually lead into Burma. The moccasins were beaded deerskin, and my parents bought them for me at Teepee Town, a shop on Atlantic City's Boardwalk. I was two years old. I put the moccasins on in the store and wouldn't take them off. I walked out onto the Boardwalk, alone. I knew nothing of the tribes, but as I walked the

3

moccasins took me from the seashore to the forest and into the great prairies beyond. Beaded thunderbirds on my toes equipped me for adventure for the rest of my life.

My childhood, in the time of peace just after American troops left Korea, was full of history's wars. My brother and I played all kinds of war games, even ancient Scottish Clan Wars (in kilts, with wooden swords). In the overgrown backyard of our New Jersey house, we stalked through the underbrush with our toy Remingtons and Colts, ready for anything. The house had been a military hospital during the Civil War, and neighbors told us we had ghosts: soldiers who had died of malaria, dysentery, gunshot wounds, still moaning and suffering a century later.

History was our passion, and my childhood area of expertise was the Native Americans, their lore, their romance, their lost cause. My family looted the public library for all it was worth every week, and I brought home all the Indian books. I organized the neighborhood kids into my tribe. I was the feral kid who appears deep in the heart of suburbia from time to time.

Coming from an eccentric family must be one of life's great strokes of luck. My parents indulged their son and daughter in all the exotica of *Just So Stories*, *National Geographic*, *Ripley's Believe It or Not*, "Frank Buck's Bring 'Em Back Alive," and ceaseless trips to New York's Museum of Natural History. We toured Civil War battlefields in the Ford Fairlane and roamed New York's ethnic neighborhoods in search of perfect ethnic restaurants. My father, a Princeton honors graduate, worked hard selling Frigidaires and Speed Queen dryers in his appliance store. He wore Brooks Brothers suits, smoked cheap Italian cigars, and read verse in Latin and Old English. My mother, an Irish-American beauty, read and read until her books were stacked into a book maze, a book city in the attic that we called "the Library." Dinners were always interrupted by someone's running upstairs for a book to settle a dollar bet, prove a point, reveal some tantalizing fact.

On Sundays my mother and brother went to church, but I went to bakeries with my father, hunting the ultimate Italian rolls. Somehow I completely eluded the grip of Catholic indoctrination.

(My brother had been put through the wringer in a year of nun terror at the appropriately named Bender Academy, so after that it was secular public education for us both.) I despised school—it interrupted my reading with the horrors of algebra and geometry. I cultivated a "bad attitude," and by my teens I was considered a full-fledged troublemaker. I was particularly known for intervening when teachers disciplined other students, ending up in the principal's office myself. But then it was the 1960s, and a troublemaker seemed the thing to be, as much as at any time in history.

I managed to get accepted at Sarah Lawrence College, an enclave of independent intellectuality just north of New York City, and I began painting seriously there. I developed my painting style on my own because I was the only student who painted people and landscapes (abstraction still reigned in those days). I used acrylic paints that mixed with water and dried fast in strong skins on canvas. I painted at night. All night. I took some other courses, a little Japanese history, a little medieval architecture, and I spent an extraordinary amount of time flying and hitchhiking cross-country to rock concerts. I met the bands, danced on their stages.

I graduated in 1974 and went straight to California, where I lived among towering madrona pines in the canyons of Marin County, north of San Francisco. Marin had the winter I had always wanted, green and moist as a terrarium, and in those days it was a tough little rock and roll world, burrito stands and biker bars, before every last hill got fitted out with a condo. I painted pictures of grinning demons swerving the great cars of the fifties over back roads. I drank tequila, I danced, I collected things made from endangered species. Ivory bracelets clicked together on my equally pale arms, and in my long red-blond hair I wore Burmese tortoiseshell combs. I admired men for owning python-skin cowboy boots and tiger-skin rugs. I was familiar with collectors of all sorts of rare things: firearms, human-skull drinking cups, Nazi staff cars, vintage drugs. Dressed in black velvet and antelope leather, I slinked through dangerous neighborhoods with a legendary vampire guitarist, who called me "the little savage." I walked through the forest at night, knife in hand, protected by luck.

* *´ *

When the 1980s began, I began my travels to Asia's timeless lands. I went to Asia for the art. I liked a certain polished type of art, with cracks and flaws and bits of gold in it, which was to be found in several Asian countries. I started in Kyoto, then visited Bangkok and Kathmandu. Along with the art, I found the people, and among the people I found friends: punk-rockers, aristocrats, teachers, artists. I returned to California after two months in Asia and painted pagoda roofs into my pictures with the glimmering of mica-dust paint. The gallery that showed my work specialized in contemporary Californian art and Asian antiquities, and my paintings began to synthesize the two. San Francisco, called "Golden Mountain" by the Chinese, was not so far from Asia. One could hear all the right dialects in the streets. There was only water in between.

I was working in lucrative spurts as a market-research consultant for a design firm, and I moved to the "Golden Mountain." I rode horses in Golden Gate Park, I pumped some iron in a gym in the Mexican district, I slam-danced to noise on Broadway. But most of all I was drawn to things Asian, and I often found myself in Vietnamese cafés, or wandering the alleys of Chinatown. I liked the way the food combined so many ingredients, endless variations on spicy, sour, salty, sweet. I liked the way the shops sold things out of ancient dynasties amidst echoes of the 1920s, 1940s, and an unknown future. Ghosts flew in the fog and dragons twisted around red-lacquered pillars. Golden Mountain's refugees from a dozen Asian wars tossed a hundred herbs in smoking woks. At night, such corners of California *were* Asia, and I (Irish-Italian) was an Asian-Californian.

In 1981 I returned to the Himalayas, and then, en route to Thailand, I stopped in Rangoon, the capital of Burma. Rangoon had been nothing more than a steamy implication to me, some vague Joseph Conrad evocation of intrigue and palm trees. As Conrad had, I checked into the Strand Hotel, which had survived Burma's days as a British colony in gently moldy elegance. Tourists were only allowed a week in Burma (a country the size of France), and I spent mine looking at pagodas and talking with people. I hung out in the city tea shops with semi-hoodlums who wheeled and dealed on the black market. I committed my first violation of Burmese law by going to the Diplomatic Store to purchase several cartons of export-only Duya cigarettes, which the hoods bought from me to resell on the street.

Burma's rigidly state-controlled economy had become so strangled since the military dictator, General Ne Win, had taken control in 1962 that few cars had been imported after the tail-finned early sixties. "If you want to buy one of those cars, miss," a hood at The People's Patisserie told me, "the black market can take it apart and people will carry it over the mountains to Thailand, and it will be put back together for you in Bangkok, the old car good as new."

I asked about the smuggling route. "Oh, the border of Thailand is the fighting place, miss. Burma has many kinds of people. In this city we have Burmese people, and India and China people. Outside they are many kinds, who live in forests and mountains, and they are all the time fighting. This government sends the army to fight those ones all the time. To get anything nice you must go through the fighting place, because anything nice comes from the other countries. We don't have any 'Made in Burma' things like watches, calculators, radios, or even our shoes to wear."

The ceiling fans creaked painfully. We drank sweet, thick tea. Another black marketeer spoke: "Miss, you can go everywhere. We ourselves cannot do anything, cannot leave this country. I want to go anywhere but here. I want to go to Thailand, the United States of America, the outside world." He lowered his voice and we huddled over our tea glasses. "I hate my country," he whispered, "I hate it. Because of the Old Man it is not worth living here."

"Excuse me, the Old Man . . .?" I asked.

"Yes, the Old Man. General Number One. The one who does everything to give us the bad life. We are all matriculated students. Can we do anything? No jobs for us, no real money, only black market. If I speak about it, secret police can take me away. We speak, we die. The Old Man makes us live like dogs. My country is nothing now. The fighting ones in the mountains, maybe they are right. But we cannot do anything. Must stay here and work for the black market."

I realized that "the Old Man" meant the dictator, Ne Win. Limiting tourists to only seven days (restricted to controlled, central regions) may have been meant to send them away with superficial impressions of a quiet, tranquil land. But in my week I had managed to discover that Burma was not simply a romantic third world backwater but one that seethed with the suppressed resentments of its citizens against a virtually omnipotent military regime. From state-run factories incapable of turning out shoes or medicine to a vast network of secret police all too capable of torturing dissenters to death, Ne Win's army had Burma stuffed in its khaki pockets.

I could not recall ever seeing a magazine or newspaper article about Burma, and I was deeply disgusted by what I was learning about the country. At the same time, Rangoon and the up-country places, Mandalay and Pagan, exuded a gripping charm. The people tiptoed between army and police, rice-growing drudgery and starvation, but they did so with such grace, such wild creativity. They were hungry people with attics full of books, artists in ripped sarongs, beggars with degrees. In the overgrown gardens of decayed, abandoned British estates, the Burmese whispered and wept to me. They brought me into their terrible world as an automatic coconspirator. Power failures blacked out heartsick Rangoon and the rats fled the light of a candle given me by some criminal, jobless student. I found my way to the wide staircase of the Strand Hotel. How could I ever be the same again? One week was more than enough to pull me headfirst into all of Burma's pain, Burma's extreme beauty.

After my seven days in the Socialist Republic of the Union of Burma's worker's paradise, I flew on to Thailand. Art still ruled my life, and I met painters and antique dealers in Bangkok and the north's main city, Chiang Mai. I visited studios where venerable European artists showed me the proper way to drink Mekong, a

Thai rice whiskey: in a tall glass with soda, ice, and a squeeze of
lime. Theo Meier, a Swiss artist and long-time resident of Chiang
Mai, wrote the formula down for me in phonetic Thai, an incanta-
tion to be memorized. "You'll need to know at least that much Thai
when you come here to live and paint," Meier told me.

On the train back to Bangkok, I realized my direction was crystal
clear. Chiang Mai was the place to paint. A San Francisco art critic
had called my paintings "eerie" and "murky," which they certainly
were. I was sure Thailand's tropical mise-en-scène would infuse my
work with new color. I would return to live in Thailand, to the
orchid-adorned art colony right next to Burma.

I spent one more year in California. I took Thai lessons, rode in
the park, worked out, and learned to shoot guns and sail. I read
whatever I could find on Southeast Asian culture and politics.
Then, in September 1982, I left for Thailand, detouring to go
trekking in Papua New Guinea in the region of the dreaded Kamea
cannibals. (In the museum at Port Moresby, the only example of
Kamean culture was a necklace made from shriveled human fingers.) Intrigued by the tribe's taste for the bizarre, I went into their
remote territory to encounter them. There I learned that I could
walk over mountains in mud and rain, communicate with people
who knew no English (the Kameas liked the punk music in my
Walkman), and find common ground with those who had rarely
seen my kind before, as we broke barriers of language and history.

My training felt complete, although I didn't know quite what I'd
been training for. I had enough money saved up from market
research and painting sales to retire to Chiang Mai and paint full-
time for a while. At twenty-nine, I was free to do as I pleased. I had
no responsibilities. In San Francisco I had bemoaned the burden of
owning a good leather jacket: "You can't put it down for a minute,
you can't take it off and leave it over your chair when you're on the
dance floor. Unless you're actually wearing the thing, someone will
rip it off." "Remind yourself not to have children," a friend responded. "You can't even check them in the coatroom."

I had left my leather jacket in California, along with a couple of
boxes of books, some jewelry and paintings. Everything else I

owned was in the two duffel bags I had with me when I moved to Chiang Mai. I suspected that my lack of conventional commitments might prove an asset in meeting Southeast Asia's personal and political challenges.

⊐ 2 ⊐

I lived in Chiang Mai, a provincial capital that called itself "The Rose of the North" even though it was mostly a hodgepodge of dreary "shophouses." It was a flat town, surrounded by mountains that gave it a cooler climate than sweat-soaked Bangkok. Hidden amid Chiang Mai's concrete blocks were Buddhist temples of teak lacquered in the northern style, urban islands of serenity. Flame trees flared vermilion over the crumbling ancient wall and stagnant moat that surrounded the older district. Increasingly, Chiang Mai was becoming a tourist town, boasting fine souvenir craftsmanship, hill-tribe trekking tours, and hill-tribe prostitutes. It was also a cultural center comparable (in Thai terms, at least) to Kyoto or Florence. And it was the iceberg's tip of the Southeast Asian heroin trade.

All of that—flame trees, culture, climate, heroin—led to a particularly interesting expatriate population. When you met strangers at one of Chiang Mai's incessant Mekong-and-soda parties, you didn't ask them what they did. And you were particularly careful not to ask them what they *really* did. Identities revealed themselves gradually, if at all. Chiang Mai was home to narcotics agents (both pro and con), militant missionaries, sinister Rhodesian tobacco planters, secretive Japanese investors, alcoholic European artists, and ex–Air America pilots grounded there since the days when they supplied the CIA's covert war in Laos. Added to the mix were operatives of every insurgent group out of neighboring Burma and Laos, some of the world's top-echelon Chinese racketeers, and assorted Thai spouses and counterparts. Plus the ubiquitous agents of Thai Army Intelligence, an agency that all of the above considered an oxymoron.

Theo Meier had died, and his widow invited me to paint in his airy riverside studio. One afternoon, some of Meier's old friends stopped by. Among them was Jere, a pale shambling Dutchman who had been batik artist to the Laotian court before Laos's aristocracy had been done away with by the Communists.

"Since you're an artist, you should know about a place where I go," Jere said. "My other friends go also, and sometimes I set up my batik workshop there. It is a place not like anywhere else. We're going there soon, for a festival, the Shan National Day. Can you come along, too?"

"Of course I'll go," I said. "And where is this mystery place?"

Jere produced a map of Thailand, and with a piece of Theo Meier's charcoal drew a line snaking from Chiang Mai north, then sharply west. When it reached the border of Burma, Jere's shaky hand printed *Pieng Luang*. "Because it is winter and the roads are dry, we can go by truck. Before, I have had to go by walking. A long trip, sleeping in villages of the Lisu hill tribe on the way. But now the Thais are improving the roads along the border."

I recalled the Rangoon story of old cars being carried piece by piece over that border, and I was delighted to be headed for such a strange frontier. Pieng Luang was a gateway to Burma's Shan State. I had found out enough about Burma to understand that its geography had been its destiny. Over the centuries, several different ethnic groups had migrated into Burma, funneled along three great river valleys. The *Burmese* ethnic group established itself in the central plains. They built cities and monuments of stone and brick, as did the civilizations that arose to rival them: the Mons in the south, the Arakanese in the west, and the Shans in a vast, fertile plateau in the northeast. These four groups warred with each other for hundreds of years, while in the mountainous border regions fiercely independent tribes maintained their own separate cultures.

The Shans, a people related to the Thais of Thailand and the Laotians, were ruled by princes, who held fiefdoms large and small.

When Britain forcibly annexed Burma to its Indian Empire in the eighteenth century, the colonists made treaties with each Shan prince. British authority quelled conflicts (prince against prince and princes against other ethnic groups). At peace, the Shan people prospered. In 1948, Burma gained independence, and the fiefdoms, united as the Shan State, were guaranteed autonomy by the Burmese-dominated central government. But Ne Win's takeover of Burma in 1962 brought with it his plan to "Burmanize" the whole country. The Shan princes were stripped of power, and some were imprisoned or killed.

The princes and their families had been an educated elite, some of whom had very progressive, democratic ideals, which threatened Ne Win's military rule from the start. Many of these aristocratic idealists went underground, beginning an insurgency. Ne Win responded with ruthless anti-guerilla campaigns, and with efforts to suppress the Shans' language and literature.

In 1982, when I went to Pieng Luang, three different Shan armies proclaimed their opposition to Ne Win's regime and their support for Shan independence:

—Shan United Revolutionary Army, known as Sura.

—Shan United Army, called SUA.

—Shan State Army, called SSA.

I didn't know the difference between the three, but I knew that Pieng Luang was where the leaders of Sura, who included an aristocrat named Prince George, lived in a fortress compound, a law unto themselves. Pieng Luang was a stone's throw across the border to Mai Sung, the Sura headquarters on the Burma (Shan State) side. The name "Mai Sung" was from a Shan greeting that meant "Grow and prosper."

In a convoy of pickup trucks and Jeeps, we drove through a cold morning fog to Pieng Luang. The group included Thais, Europeans, and American residents of Chiang Mai. It was evening when our vehicles finally slipped into Pieng Luang, following an unpaved road past tightly shuttered teakwood houses and up a hill to the Sura compound. Guards in olive drab fatigues swung open a bamboo gate to admit us, and our convoy stopped at Prince George's house.

Prince George, a stocky Asian man in his forties, with an old green quilted nylon jacket wrapped over a V-necked sweater and blue slacks, stood waiting for us, blowing on his hands to warm them. As we climbed out, he greeted us in quaint, precise English— "Welcome, welcome. I trust your journey was agreeable?"—and shook our hands.

The prince had the worn good looks of a fading actor, but his manner was both gracious and sincere. His hair was combed from a side part, he wore a thin mustache, and I was reminded of Clark Gable on his last legs in *The Misfits*. Jere had told me that the prince had been educated at a school for the elite of the British Raj and had then attended a university in Germany. The prince's Western name, like those of many people in Burma, suggested an intense nostalgia for things British.

Sura had some women soldiers, and Prince George had married one of them. She was said to be politically ambitious, and my friends from Chiang Mai called her "Evita" behind her back (a back they said was covered with magic Shan tattoos of lions). She slouched by the door of the house, a mere teenager with cropped hair, dressed in a red sarong and yellow cardigan, holding her child, a baby boy with a striking resemblance to Peter Lorre. The boy sniffled and began to cry as we entered the prince's house.

I supposed the house would be considered a palace, but it lacked running water, electricity, and indoor plumbing. It was a low, unpainted wooden structure with a metal roof and dirt floors. We walked into the largest room, the guest room, where we would sleep on a platform that ran its length. The prince's small bedroom was at one end, and a dark medieval kitchen was at the other. A rickety bamboo outhouse perched at the back of the surrounding semitropical garden. In front of the house stood a dining table with a green vinyl tablecloth and some folding chairs, and soldiers stoked a fire beside it to keep us warm during dinner. Prince George lived simply, but what little he had was arranged to provide as much comfort as possible to his guests. We unrolled our bedding and went out to the welcoming bonfire.

We unwound from the long drive with a cocktail hour or two, and then dinner: rice, potatoes, pork, vegetables.

During dinner, Prince George apologized to us.

"I'm afraid that the festival is indefinitely postponed," he said. "It seems that our prognosticating Buddhist monks at the Mai Sung temple have judged the date we'd set for Shan National Day to be inauspicious. We hope you'll indulge us and wait for a few days."

Most of the Chiang Mai contingent decided not to wait. You couldn't tell with the Shans, they grumbled, it could be delayed for days, or for weeks. The Shans were fighting against domination by the ethnic Burmese, against General Ne Win's system of state control (the Burmese Army and secret police). They felt they would be better off having their own Shan nation than being lumped in with Burma's woes, but their own weaknesses hampered them every step of the way: a tendency to split apart like frenzied amoebas; reliance on soothsayers in saffron robes; and the constant lure of the drug trade. The Golden Triangle, where Thailand, Laos, and Burma's Shan State converged, was prime growing territory for opium poppies, the raw material of heroin. The Shan State had the largest opium crop in the world. We had passed fields of red and white opium poppies on the way into Pieng Luang, but Sura denied all involvement in narcotics.

Despite Sura's denials, mountain dwellers all over the area were producing opium. In the winter, the poppies blossomed and then dropped their petals, exposing heavy pods. Hill farm women and children patiently cut slits in each pod so the narcotic sap would drip out overnight. In the morning, the opium gum was scraped off, pod by pod. The accumulated opium would be sold to traders, who would pass it on to hidden forest refineries where skilled Chinese chemists processed it into successive stages of purity. Then, in the form of morphine or heroin, the product was turned over to crime syndicates for sale in Thailand, other Asian countries, or farther, overseas. Armed men escorted and protected the product every step of the way.

Although most of the guests returned to Chiang Mai when they learned the festival was postponed, I stayed on another day, along with Jere and a couple of the Americans. We went for a hike, and as we passed through Pieng Luang, I recognized the face on portraits that hung in the shops.

"They're big on Chiang Kai-shek here, aren't they?" I remarked.

"Pieng Luang belongs to Chiang Kai-shek's old Chinese Nationalist Army, the Kuomintang. KMT, for short," one of the Americans said.

"What are the KMT doing here?" I asked.

"They're here because Mao Tse-tung booted them the hell out of China in the fifties. They dug themselves in here, northern Thailand, and the Shan State, too, and got right into the opium business. With their connections to the overseas Chinese gangs, the KMT had it made in the shade for the drug trade. That's why they're here."

"How does Sura feel about the KMT drug trade?" I asked. "Didn't Prince George say yesterday that Sura is anti-narcotics?"

I was full of questions, but my friends fell silent. We climbed a hill that overlooked the village, to the top where a *chedi* (a cone-shaped pagoda) stood beside a wooden residence for Buddhist monks. An elderly, deaf monk braved a chilly breeze in his one-shouldered orange robe. We smiled to him and *wai*'d, a gesture of greeting and respect, hands pressed together with a slight bow. The *wai* was used by Thais, Shans, and Laotians, all people of the Tai ethnic group which had originated in China.

On our trip back to the village I asked Jere why the Sura rebels didn't get some journalists up to Pieng Luang to talk to Prince George and publicize the Shans' fight for freedom.

"They don't like journalists," Jere answered. "I brought one here a while ago, a Japanese guy. We went to the brothel in the village and he got really drunk. Worse than me, even. He gave one of the girls a five-hundred baht note—about twenty-five U.S. dollars—to go buy another bottle of whiskey for us. The girls only get thirty baht a throw and most of that goes back to the house, so this girl had just won the lottery. She was *gone*. The journalist freaked out completely. Like the Thais say, no money, no honey. No whiskey, either. He grabs another girl around the neck and shouts, 'Where's your friend?' But then he shuts up. The brothel keeper's pistol is pressed against the journalist's head. He knew what it was. That cold feeling."

"I think you always know what it is, against your skull, in the small of your back . . ." one of the Americans interjected.

"Anyway, the brothel keeper asked him very politely to leave the place. You know how polite the Chinese can be, even a Chinese Nationalist with his gun to a Japanese head. The Shans heard about the incident and decided that journalists are too much trouble. Inauspicious."

"I agree with them. All journalists are whores," an American said.

That night Prince George, Jere, and I drove across the border into Burma. As far as I could see was Sura territory, but I couldn't see very far in the dark, even from Mai Sung's own hilltop temple. I did not want to look any farther than the Sura headquarters pagoda, its *chedi,* anyway. The night was as cold as Hell frozen over, but it held a celestial sight: the *chedi,* with a round base and a whole cluster of spires glittering with electric fairy lights. It made me certain that there was something truly magical about the Shans. I had seen some humongous gold-plated pagodas in my time in Southeast Asia, but this ice-white one, ethereal on its drum base, enchanted me. It looked more the product of sorcery than masonry.

In the army camp just below the temple we joined a crowd of soldiers watching a movie projected on an outdoor screen. The soldiers stood (the ground was too cold to sit on), with blankets wrapped over their green uniforms. They smoked Shan cigars, tobacco wrapped in mulberry leaves, and the smoke rose into the projection path.

"This cinema show is called *Khun Sa, Opium Warlord*," Prince George told me with a drunken laugh. "You know about Khun Sa. Very famous. The King of Opium they call him. The Heroin Godfather. He is public enemy number one."

Khun Sa was indeed infamous throughout Asia for his conspicuous drug trafficking and control of heroin trade routes. He was the warlord of the Shan United Army (SUA), a great rival of my Sura hosts. The movie was loosely based on a Thai army attack the year before that drove Khun Sa and his private army out of their headquarters in a Thai village, back to the Shan State.

Now Khun Sa's SUA was skirmishing with Sura over control of smuggling routes—paths through the mountains where anything went, jade, rubies, heroin; paths for controlling the Shan destiny. Khun Sa was larger than life, and not just on the movie screen. Sura feared and hated him.

The movie made much of the Thai offensive against Khun Sa's stronghold (glossing over the payoffs to Thai authorities that had allowed Khun Sa to stay there for years before they bothered to kick him out). A scene showed Thai soldiers readying for the big battle. In real life, Sura soldiers looked at the onscreen weapons and nudged each other, giggling. The Sura troops had the same kind of weapons as the Thais, M-16 assault rifles, provided to Thailand by the U.S. and skimmed off for black market sale by Thai army and police officers.

A journalist appeared on the screen, a light-haired, foreign female one. A total figment of the scriptwriter's imagination, she interviewed Khun Sa. In real life, nobody interviewed Khun Sa. He was too aloof, too dangerous, and his Shan army also considered journalists "inauspicious."

Prince George and Jere decided the movie was boring, so we went inside a hut where some Sura officers were keeping warm with local moonshine. We joined them for a few drinks. The liquor, distilled from corn, had a repulsive taste and a kick like a mule's. Outside, on the screen, Thai helicopters hovered over Khun Sa's headquarters to strafe it and Khun Sa's men met them with machine-gun fire. The Sura soldiers watching the movie cheered all mayhem from either side.

In the hut, one of the Sura officers passed an envelope of brown powder to Prince George. He poured a little out onto his palm and tossed it back into his mouth. Jere, stupefied with Mekong and moonshine, declined the powder by listlessly waving his hand, but a Shan officer took the packet and ate some.

I was feeling a bit numb. I could hold my liquor well, but the rough moonshine did have its effect. The shoes I'd worn to Pieng Luang were flimsy Italian leather slippers, iridescent teal blue, with painted dragons. Now my toes were asleep in their dragon slippers, from cold or moonshine or both. The movie battle outside was raging. The Shan officers were gossiping in English about Khun Sa, something about murders at his old headquarters and assassinations in Chiang Mai, but I didn't catch much of it. I leaned on the table to prop my chin up.

"Here, miss, you take a little of this, and not drunk no more," one of the officers said, offering me the packet of powder. It smelled just like cinnamon. I put some in my hand, threw it toward my tonsils, and swallowed. A cinnamon taste. I blinked my eyes, sat up straight, and looked around. I was 100 percent sober. I could have recited the Thai alphabet backward and walked a tightrope through the Shan hills.

"Jesus. What is this stuff?" I said, each syllable perfectly enunciated.

"This is called *yah horm,*" the officer who'd given it to me said. " 'Good-smelling medicine' is the meaning in your English language."

"Instant sobriety," I said, very impressed. "Forget about heroin—the Shan State should export this 'medicine' to the world. This is great!"

Jere raised his head to disagree. "Why bother to get drunk if you're just going to take *yah horm* and ruin it? Anyway, nobody in Chiang Mai has ever been able to figure out what the stuff really is."

My Chiang Mai friends and I left the following morning. Prince George and his fellow officers saw us off at the gate of the Sura compound.

"Miss Edith, we are happy that you were able to visit our place and be introduced to the Shan nation," the Prince said. "We want you to know that you are most welcome here at any time. You needn't wait for a festival or an invitation. Like Jere, you are welcome to bring your art materials and use our land and people for your inspiration. There is much for you to paint here."

I wanted to return right away, and I made plans to go back with Jere, on foot, stopping in the tribal villages on the way. But Jere was in no shape for such a trip. Mekong and worse were making a wreck of him. On the day we were to depart, he didn't show up. I found him in the room he rented from a Thai family on the outskirts of Chiang Mai, lying in the dark. He told me that a few days before he had slipped in the bathroom and hit his head on the toilet. Thai toilets are shallow ceramic fixtures set low into the floor, to be used squatting, so that was quite a fall. He had passed out for hours—or was it days?—he wasn't sure. The Thai family finally found him, still unconscious, and fetched a doctor. When Jere came to, he was in bed in his darkened room, and he had felt around on the floor until he found a bottle of "white spirit," an illegally and ineptly distilled rotgut that packed far more of a punch than mere Mekong.

"I guess we're not going," I said.

Jere smiled dreamily, his eyes closed. "I had a Shan wife once. Not for very long. She attacked me with a knife. Those people are crazy. Watch out for them."

"Okay, Jere, I will," I assured him. As I left I could hear him calling out plaintively in Thai for someone to go to the corner shop and buy him another bottle of white spirit.

⹋ 3 ⹋

I did not know how to get to Pieng Luang by myself, so instead I went to Mae Hong Son, a town farther south on the Burma border. It was simple enough to get there, a twenty-minute flight in a small plane. The alternative was a relentlessly scenic eight-hour bus ride. Essentially the choice was between twenty minutes of excruciating airsickness as the plane bobbed through pockets of turbulence, or eight hours of milder, constant nausea as the bus weaved along the mountain roads.

The airstrip lay in the center of Mae Hong Son, which was built along a T of two main roads, one the highway from Chiang Mai. Most of the shophouses were made of smooth old polished teak-wood, and customers still took off their shoes when they entered the shops, a custom that had long since died out elsewhere in Thailand. Mae Hong Son was inhabited mostly by Shans, the branch of the

Tai race mainly found in Burma; the only Thais around were army and police personnel, and provincial administrators. In the mountains that ringed Mae Hong Son lived tribal people like the Lisus and Lahus.

I took a room at the Mae Tee, a Shan-owned hotel of 1960s design: blue concrete exterior, linoleumed lobby with a wide staircase to the two floors above. My bed had pink wool blankets. With its mountain ring, Mae Hong Son got frosty at night all year round, but Thailand was, of course, a tropical country, so heating was unheard of. Heavy blankets compensated.

A Chiang Mai friend who did agricultural development work with hill-tribe people had told me about a Shan woman named Nang Lao who sometimes guided foreigners around the border area outside of Mae Hong Son. I asked the young boys who staffed the Mae Tee front desk about her and she appeared in the lobby within an hour. She told me she had learned English to talk to the few foreigners who came to Mae Hong Son. "Maybe four or five are visiting each week," she said, "and another four live here. Two of them study things, one is a teacher, and one Peace Corps boy is building a bridge."

Nang Lao was short and restless. She walked faster than anyone else in Mae Hong Son. A lot was going on in that town—espionage, antiques smuggling, world-class drug deals—but all business was conducted quietly, at a leisurely, refined pace. Nang Lao, however, bustled along like she was in rush-hour Hong Kong, her long black hair flying out from beneath a huge bamboo peasant hat.

Her pace didn't slacken once we headed for the hills. She wasn't in the mood to play trekking guide, but she decided I could come along while she went to visit some border villages where she knew people. She didn't want my money but said I could buy a few things in the Mae Hong Son bazaar to take to the villagers. I purchased nylon fishing nets and malaria medicine. I hadn't even thought about malaria when I'd gone to Pieng Luang; it had been so cold there that no mosquitoes were around at all. But the border from Mae Hong Son south was infested with the anopheles mosquitoes that spread the disease. The malaria parasites that the infected mosquito injects into the bloodstream come in varieties—some deadly, some maddening, some just temporarily debilitating. Some strains were resistant to the standard, cheap, prevention measure chloroquine. In Chiang Mai, a doctor had told me to take chloroquine tablets plus a more powerful drug called Fansidar each week, to kill off the parasites as they swam in my blood. Such medication was too expensive for the border villagers. I bought jars of tablets that they could take when they first came down with the shaking and sweats that were malaria's symptoms.

For a few days I walked with Nang Lao and began to learn my way around the forest and the border. We stayed with the Shans in the valleys and in tribal villages in the hills. Nang Lao brought along a pistol because bandits infested the border area, *dacoits* who robbed and killed and slipped in and out of Burma. The gun was a nickel-plated automatic with no brand name, only a Thai serial number. We took turns carrying it. All along the way we met people with guns (hunters, smugglers, rebel Shan soldiers) as we followed trails from village to village. I liked being armed. The heavy gun was protection, but it was also a kind of totem of belonging in the frontier scene.

One afternoon, as we cut across a rice paddy, Nang Lao hailed a tall Shan who wore civilian clothes and had a pistol stuck in his belt. They chatted amiably in Shan and Nang Lao introduced him to me as a soldier from the Shan State Army (SSA), a Shan rebel group at odds with both my Pieng Luang Sura friends and the opium warlord Khun Sa's SUA. Before we continued on (he was headed for Mae Hong Son; we weren't), the SSA man flipped open a shoe box he was carrying to give us a peek at the contents. It was packed with wads of Thai money, purple 500-baht notes. As we walked on across the cracked earth of the fallow rice paddy, Nang Lao said, "That man brings the black market money to Mae Hong Son, to buy guns for SSA."

"What goods move through here on the black market?" I asked, kicking up dust as I walked, my sneakers changing from pale blue to brown. "Where does all that money come from? There must have been thousands of dollars worth of baht in there."

"That man's army, the SSA, they make the tax. Everything is coming to Burma this way. Everything you see in Mae Hong Son bazaar, your blankets, your T-shirts, your shoes, it is going to Burma. In Burma they make nothing good. Everybody wants all from Thailand. So they bring to Burma, they go by the SSA, and they pay tax to the SSA man."

"How about those people we've seen coming from the other direction, like those little old ladies leading the pack ponies, and the men with baskets on their backs?"

"Some things come from Burma, yes. The ponies are having some silk cloth, maybe some Buddha statue, old kind, nice lacquer or gold, from Burma temple. The men carry many Shan cigars in the baskets. Also, the cow and buffalo can come this way, to sell in Thailand, get good price. In Burma, sell to government only, and get no good price."

We often had to make way for herds of black buffalo being driven out of Burma by hill-tribe boys. West of Mae Hong Son really *is* the Wild West, I thought. "Does the SSA tax the buffalo coming out of Burma as well?" I asked.

"Oh, yes, SSA are getting a good tax on every cow. Every pony who carries silk cloth, they tax him too. Opium too, but not much around here. Most of the opium is coming in north of Mae Hong Son and up north of Chiang Mai, for the Chinese chemist men to make heroin from."

"When I was in Pieng Luang I found it strange that Sura, the Shan rebels, seemed to get along with those Kuomintang, KMT, so well. What could they have in common with a bunch of old Chinese Nationalist drug traders?"

Nang Lao laughed. "No, not strange. Sura, they work for the KMT. Down here is SSA, up north is Khun Sa's SUA. Sura is stuck in middle. Sura is afraid of Khun Sa, he is a big man, he wants everything on the border. Sura needs help from those KMT Chinese with their money. Or else Sura will get eaten up by big Khun Sa. The KMT is big business. Khun Sa is big business. Sura is only small business, guarding opium trails for KMT."

I started to object. "I don't think . . ."

"You should think. You go to Pieng Luang, you should be thinking about these things. These are the really things. I am Shan, so I know, and I want you to know."

That night we stayed in an unusual house, two stories enclosed by woven bamboo walls. The other houses in the countryside were built high on stilts with an open space underneath rather than a ground floor. A Shan *sayah,* a spirit doctor, lived in the two-story house, which was near a stream. The closest village was thirty minutes away, but its Shan residents often traveled to the *sayah*'s house for potions, charms, tattoos, and exorcisms. The *sayah* had a servant who cleaned and cooked, a young Shan boy about fifteen years old, from inside Burma's Shan State. The boy hopped around on one leg, the other having been amputated just above the knee. He cooked fish caught in the stream with greens gathered in the forest. When he had served dinner to the *sayah,* Nang Lao, and me, he settled down on a low bench in the corner to eat his own meal.

"This is not good for the boy, this hopping all the time," Nang Lao commented. "He needs a what-do-you-call-it leg."

"An artificial leg," I ventured.

"Yes, that. A new leg that they make in Bangkok. Tatmadaw got him in Burma." The Tatmadaw was the Burmese government's army. They were a well-disciplined force, totally indoctrinated for absolute loyalty to the regime. Their abuses of human rights in the war zone were neither random nor sporadic; they were carefully planned elements of Ne Win's counterinsurgency. Civilian populations were to be systematically terrorized into giving up all support for any insurgent groups. If that meant burning every last ethnic minority village out of Burma's frontier areas and scorching the remaining earth, well, the Tatmadaw was more than willing to do so. Its tactics were consistent, and much closer to the American frontier edict "The only good Indian is a dead Indian" than to any semblance of winning hearts and minds.

In his youth, Ne Win had been trained by Japanese fascists prior to their invasion of Burma, and his army behaved like the Japanese occupation forces, like packs of samurai gone berserk, demanding absolute obedience with automatic rifles. One of the Tatmadaw's favorite tactics was to capture ethnic minority villagers like the Shans or hill tribespeople and make them carry heavy loads of ammunition and other army supplies through the mountainous war zone.

"What happened to the boy?" I asked.

"Tatmadaw made him their porter-slave. They do it all the time to any man, woman, boy. They take them to carry their heavy things to the fighting. No good. Tatmadaw gives this boy no food then. He drinks some water, but bad water. Many porters are carrying the ammunitions for Tatmadaw. This boy got sick, like the running stomach. He cannot go along. Fell down. Burma soldier kicks him. 'Get up, lazy Shan.' Fell down again. 'Dirty Shan, you don't want to walk, okay you don't walk, then!' So the soldiers kick his leg again and again with the army boots until it breaks like a stick, one, two, three places." The boy was watching us from his bench, quietly pushing morsels of rice and fish into his mouth. "They leave him in the forest like that. Running stomach all over the leg breaks, with the bones showing, too. He is like a dead boy, then. But some hill-tribe hunters, they find him, cut off the bad leg, give him their own tea and rice. No doctor is there, nobody knows Shan language, so they brought this boy here to our *sayah*."

I looked over at the boy. He smiled and got up and hopped to a shelf to get the teapot for our after-dinner tea.

"That's really brutal," I said. "No wonder there's a rebellion."

Nang Lao rolled her eyes. "Of course. You think that on the Burma side two hours away from here they fight because of a Shan nation, because of politics things? No, mostly all are fighting just because of how the Tatmadaw is coming in and making them porter-slaves, always killing, hurting all the time. Burma government soldiers are always hungry for killing. They like it too much. See this boy, only one boy. Now he wants to be the rebel soldier for fighting the Tatmadaw."

We left the *sayah*'s place the next day to wend our way back to Mae Hong Son. The boy waved good-bye to us, wearing the black "boonie" hat I had given him (a brimmed cloth soldier's hat with a Shan tiger symbol on the front). Now he looked like some wounded

rebel soldier, not just another civilian victim, another porter-slave.
Nang Lao and I had not actually crossed the Burma border on our
trip, but I felt Burma's war had crossed over to us, in the form of
one Shan boy who suffered from it, and suffered all the more
because he wanted to go back to fight.

= 4 =

As one of Thailand's resident aliens, I had to leave the country
every three months to get a new nonimmigrant visa. Penang, a
resort island in neighboring Malaysia, was the closest place with a
Thai consulate. After I'd lived in Chiang Mai for three months, I
made a visa run to Penang, but the next time I decided to go to
Burma. A Burmese dissident, whom I'd met through an antique-
dealer friend in Bangkok, heard that I was going and asked me to
bring a package to his wife in Rangoon.

Burma's rules of escape were strict. Once out, few Burmese could
return, even for visits. They left everything behind: family, property, money. Getting a passport took months of investigation, brib-
ery, and a cabinet-level decision. Many Burmese opted for the
jungle route out, moving on foot through the ethnic minority rebel
areas like black market goods, and emerging months later in Bangkok, Perth, or London. I agreed to take the package. Able to come
and go as a tourist, I carried what I learned were documents into
Burma, past Mingaladon Airport's haphazard Customs inspectors,
and delivered them to N., the wife of the dissident.

In Rangoon, I found a superb bookshop near the National Museum. It was full of books abandoned by foreigners who had been
thrown out of the country when Ne Win took over in 1962. Ne
Win, xenophobic and obsessed with control, had devised a system
he called "The Burmese Way to Socialism," less out of a reverence
for Marxist theory than because state control offered his army

officers the easiest way to establish dominion over every aspect of Burmese life. Shops, factories, schools, even Buddhist monks were registered with the regime and had to answer for their every action to councils of army officers and Burma Socialist Program Party bureaucrats. Burma went from a parliamentary democracy with a free press and freewheeling commerce to an Eastern Bloc–styled police state overnight. Justifying his need for absolute authority by harping on the threat posed by frontier insurgents to national security, Ne Win then increased the size and power of the Tatmadaw year by year. Foreign influences were scorned as "neocolonialism." Ne Win did not want outsiders around to observe or interfere in his plans for Burma.

But in spite of Ne Win's vision of cultural purity—a population dressed (male and female alike) in Burmese sarongs, reading only Burmese books in the Burmese language—Rangoon's surviving intellectuals still thirsted for the whole world. The bookshop was bursting with literature from Kipling to Nabokov to Borges, and a long shelf held worm-eaten art books. Browsers in the back room leafed through historical tomes written in Portuguese, Russian, Italian, Urdu. I asked the proprietor, who wore a coffee-stained undershirt and checked sarong, if he had any books about the Shans.

"You want books about the Shans?" he whispered conspiratorily, as if I had told him I wanted rubies or opium or stolen jade Buddha statues. "Wait one minute, please."

He vanished up a back staircase and I heard him rummaging through what I imagined was a city of stacked-up books like my mother's attic library. He returned with *The Shans* by W. W. Cochrane, published in Rangoon in 1915, complete with photo captions like "Shans showing tattooing and rain covers." It was just what I wanted. I paid the man in U.S. dollars, which was just what he wanted. Ne Win's army economists had a very unrealistic idea of the worth of Burma's currency, pegging an official exchange rate of between seven and eight kyat to the dollar. On the black market something so solid and foreign as a U.S. dollar bill fetched around twenty kyat, and the kyat value slid steadily into the gutter.

I left Burma carrying some documents for the dissident, plus books and newspapers someone I'd met in the Strand Hotel lobby had asked me to bring to a magazine correspondent in Thailand. I had become a smuggler of information. It was one of Burma's most precious commodities. Foreign mail was opened and censored, as if the country was one big prison. The newspapers were Tatmadaw propaganda organs. Radio, and the one television station, existed to sing the praises of army, party, state. The Burmese, Chinese, and Indian people of central Burma were ensnared. Unless they ran—and ran far—they had no reprieve from secret-police control, block wardens, arbitrary search and seizure, detention without charges, and disappearance. The frontier groups like the Shans, Karens, and Mons at least had access to the borders and their own armed camps, and the hope that they could overcome the Tatmadaw by force. The people in the towns and cities, the Burmese ethnic majority as well as the Chinese and Indian minorities, seemed to have lost all hope. They muddled through with lowly black market schemes. Outside of the few government shops, anyone buying or selling could be breaking the law. Everybody broke the law. Some got caught. One never knew who might be next. Ne Win's system was a kleptocracy wherein the Old Man and his generals helped themselves to the spoils and the rest of Burma had to fend for itself. Ne Win stole like Marcos, tortured like Papa Doc, purged like Stalin, and dug his claws in like Ceauşescu. And he was clever enough to outlive them all.

For lack of a realistic currency, foreign trade or investment, and any management sense, industrial production in Burma had ground to a halt. The state couldn't even keep soap or shoe factories operating at a level to meet people's needs. Consequently the black market was the source for every conceivable consumer product, all smuggled from outside Burma. I saw vendors squatting on the pavement ready to run at word of police patrols. Next to them were squares of cloth with thumbtacks displayed on them, to be sold one by one as if they were jewels. I saw a black market trade in those little round erasers with brushes on the ends, and the miniature soaps from the in-flight lavatories of Thai International. The Thai airline pinned small orchid corsages on all its passengers, and when its flights arrived in Rangoon, children at the airport would beg for the flowers so their parents could sell the pins on the black market. It was a perfect welcome to Burma, one nation under Ne Win.

Burma's farewell, a week later, would inevitably be the impossibility of changing kyat back to hard currency at the airport bank's ant-infested counter.

Aside from forays to Burma and Penang, I spent eight months in Chiang Mai painting, and my new pictures were exhibited there in June 1983. Images of motion covered the canvases in the colors of Thailand's three seasons: cold (burgundy, charcoal, powder blue), hot (orange, yellow, burnt sienna), and rainy (celadon, violet, ultramarine). My paintings showed Chiang Mai girls on motorbikes, Lisu tribespeople in pickup trucks, Thai jockeys riding sleek racehorses, and a caravan of white Shan ponies near Mai Sung.

When the show was over, I left Thailand to attend my brother's wedding in New Jersey (via Borneo, the Philippines, Taiwan, and Japan). Arriving in the States broke, I took a temporary customer relations job at Tiffany in New York to earn my airfare back to Asia. I planned to travel in China on my way back to Thailand, so I took Chinese lessons in the evenings after work. On my lunch hours I would abandon Tiffany for the nearby IBM building, which had an atrium with café tables and clumps of captive green bamboo. There I would study my Chinese and contemplate the bamboo, a painful reminder of how far I was from Burma's wild bamboo. Outside the glassed-in atrium, aggressive fur-bearing Christmas shoppers fought their way toward Saks and Tiffany in filthy snow.

Before the winter was out, I made my way to China, where I put my language lessons to work. I took trains and talked my way from one end of the country to the other. By the time I reached the fabled city of Kashgar, near the Afghan border, I had become so fluent that another American observed, "You bullshit better in more languages than anybody I ever met." I made my way to Yunnan, the province of China that bordered Burma, and there I saw tribal people like those of Thailand and Burma's mountains. I wanted to visit Sipsongbanna, where the Dai people (relatives of Burma's Shans) were, but it was off-limits to foreigners, so I had to settle for some postcards of Dai temples to send to friends in Chiang Mai and Pieng Luang.

One of eight passengers, I took the once-a-week flight from Kunming, Yunnan's capital, to Rangoon. The other seven were overweight, middle-aged Chinese men traveling as a "sports delegation." Despite the limited passenger list, it still took Mingaladon's staff over an hour to locate our luggage, pass us through customs, and send us out to the waiting fleet of heavy Chevys driven by black-market-cigarette brokers.

I went directly up-country, by plane and "cooperative Jeep taxi" (a genuine World War II American Jeep crammed with passengers), to Maymyo, a mountain town above Mandalay, on the edge of the Shan State. In the days of the British Raj, Maymyo had been a hill station where weary colonists escaped the tropical heat, and during World War II it had been an Allied command center. Unlike most tourists, who would frantically try to see as many sights as possible, I spent five of my allotted seven Burmese days in Maymyo, which usually rated only an overnight stay at best. When I met local people in the bazaar they most often asked me two questions: "Are you British?" and "Are you leaving tomorrow?"

I stayed at Candacraig, a hotel that in the old days had been a home for British teak-company employees recuperating from job-related stress and fevers. Everything east of Maymyo was forbidden territory, but I saw Tatmadaw casualties from the frontier war being brought to military hospitals in town. In its present incarnation Maymyo was a Tatmadaw training center with an officer's school. I wondered was it here that they were trained in ways of torture and other forms of human rights abuse?

One day I met one of the officers. I had rented a horse, and after a day in the saddle, I rode up to Candacraig. As I dismounted, a Burmese man on the veranda called out to me in English: "You do look like a ghost of the Raj! So you must join me here for proper tea."

He told the waiter to bring another teacup, and I sat at his table. He introduced himself as an army major, in Maymyo for a lecture at the Tatmadaw staff college. One of Burma's privileged few allowed foreign study, he was a graduate of a university in the United States. He asked me where I'd learned to ride, so I told him about Golden Gate Park, and then we talked about China. I kept my mouth shut about the Shans and the war. Then, gazing across the hotel's lush lawn, the major said, "You know, Number One's daughter plays tennis here in Maymyo."

"I didn't know."

"Yes, I think she learned it when overseas. She went off to England to study medicine, but they had to send her back because her English was so poor. You see, her father had stopped all English instruction in our schools, to promote progressive Burmese nationalism. After she got sent back, all of a sudden our schools commenced teaching English again. That is how the mind of Number One works." He sighed. Like so many Burmese, he could speculate endlessly on the mind of Ne Win, the man whose name they dared not speak. Ne Win, a jowly, bespectacled man in his seventies, was something of a recluse, rarely seen by the public except on the golf course. His mind, his health, his family, were all subjects of endless, morbidly fascinated conjecture by those he ruled.

"The daughter came back," the major continued, "and now she runs the secret police. So she's a kind of doctor, anyway—pain specialist. The other ones, Number One's children by his many wives, they do as they please: pilot Burma Airways planes, take drugs, make drugs, sell drugs."

Burma Airways was a pathetic excuse for an airline, with shoddy maintenance, indifferent service, and frequent crashes. Now I was less eager than ever for the return flight to Rangoon.

"This country is only the country club of Number One and his family, and the old generals. I look at my life here and I am afraid. I am not a happy man, but there is nothing I can do, nothing at all."

I said nothing. I thought of suggesting he defect to the Shan rebels, but I decided the Shans would probably kill him just because he was a Burmese officer. I felt sorry for him, but he was part of the Tatmadaw, waging Ne Win's war against the Shans, Karens, and other frontier people with its widespread and calculated brutality, so I didn't trust him. As rebel sympathizer and document courier I could not even begin to mention what I knew of Burma. So I just let him pour out his discontent with the tea. He seemed to trust me, oddly enough, perhaps finding in me some reminder of his American education.

Back in Rangoon I visited N., the wife of the dissident whose packages I'd carried. A thin, genteel, young woman, she lived in one of the better-off neighborhoods. Her family had enough military connections to pursue various business interests, and to see that N. didn't escape over the border. She served me *khao soi*, chicken curry over yellow noodles, a dish I'd enjoyed in Pieng Luang and Mae Hong Son.

"Anything you want to see in Rangoon tomorrow?" she asked.

"Nothing in particular. Maybe the Museum of Natural History."

"Oh, very sorry, the museum will be closed."

"Never mind, I'll be back. Probably the next visa trip."

"I don't think so. I think you are having your last trip to Rangoon now. If you go around the border on the Thai side, plenty of spies will know your face. You're eating *khao soi* with Shan rebels in Pieng Luang, they know who you are. You can't do that and still get tourist visas for Burma. And even if you come here, they will watch you and everyone you are with. There might be a guilt by association."

I had known there would be a point when the Burmese authorities would get suspicious of me, but I thought I'd have a few more trips before being banned outright. It was depressing, to love Burma and not be able to visit, like some exile. Yet the thought of Pieng Luang compensated quite a bit. I still had so much of the Burma frontier, accessible from Thailand, to explore.

"I understand," I told N. "I'm sorry I won't be seeing you for a while. Maybe it's my last trip to Rangoon for now, but not forever. I'll be back in better times, when Number One is gone, right?"

N. laughed at my use of the term "Number One." Or perhaps at the idea of anything in Burma ever changing for the better.

⌐ 5 ⌐

After I returned to Thailand, I was again brought to the Burma border by an artist, this time to the southern territory of the Karen rebels. The Karens were a huge tribe who had migrated south from

the steppes of northern Asia, long before the Burmese and Tai
civilizations had appeared on the scene. The Karens had kept to
themselves and lived simply, peacefully in the mountains of Thailand and Burma, and in Burma's southern river deltas. Often
captured and exploited by other, more aggressive groups, the Karens still managed to maintain a way of life in harmony with nature
and were notable for honesty and egalitarianism. They were viewed
with some disdain by the Machiavellian princes and queens building cities in Southeast Asia. The first real respect the Karens got was
from British colonists and American missionaries, who found
something "stalwart, loyal, and true" about the tribe. Educated in
Christian schools and enlisted in Queen Victoria's army, the Karens
of Burma thrived. They began to think of themselves as a separate
nation. When their requests for recognition as such were denied by
Britain in 1948, when Burma became independent, the Karens felt
betrayed.

The Burmese military considered the Karens a threat to national
unity. When some Burmese soldiers massacred Karen churchgoers
at a Christmas service in 1948, the Karen rebellion ignited. And it
never stopped. The Karens believed the Burmese government
wanted to exterminate them and were convinced that the only way
to survive was to fight back. With their British Army background,
the Karens fought well, but the more they fought, the more vicious
became the counterinsurgency tactics of the Tatmadaw. Eventually,
Ne Win came to power, vowing to wipe the Karen rebellion off the
face of Burma. The Karens believed that meant annihilating their
tribe, and so they battled on, in a strip of jungle they called their
nation, backs against the Thai border, always desperate, always
wildly hopeful.

Brando P. Bryant was in Bangkok from Texas, by way of Tokyo.
He operated on the art-world fringe of conceptual art, mail art,
performance art, and avant-garde video. He knew the Karens
because he had worked on an international video project with the
theme of "borders." Bryant had made a video that began by crossing Tokyo's "border," the international departure terminal at
Narita Airport, with his camcorder left surreptitiously on all the

way through the metal detectors and customs inspections for a
suitcase-eye-view of departure. Arriving in Thailand, he headed for
a border—which just happened to be that of Burma—where he
met some Karen rebels. They were delighted to see a foreigner with
a camera. The Karens lived far from the opium region and had
nothing to hide. To them a visit from a journalist was not "inauspicious." Bryant began recording what he called "the Karen people's
struggle for self-determination." Now, six years into his Karen
video, Bryant was heading to a Karen rebel settlement just over the
Burma border from the Thai city of Kanchanaburi, and I accompanied him.

World War II's Bridge on the River Kwai was near Kanchanaburi, and we drove past it on our way into the border mountains. Bryant drove the Jeep like the devil while Roberto (his angelic
Filipino "art-ner" and cameraman) and I gripped the roll bars for
dear life. We left the main road and climbed, much faster than was
sane, a winding mud trail. Bryant had been a motorcycle racer
when he lived in Japan, and he howled like a wolf as he drove, mud
splattering his shaved head. Suddenly, with a screech of brakes, we
stopped short of a red-and-white bamboo pole that extended across
the trail.

WELCOME TO KAREN NATION KAWTHOOLEI a wooden sign
read.

"They call their rebel nation 'Kawthoolei,' " Bryant told me. "It
means 'Flower Land.' " We were in a place full of jungle blossoms,
quivering with butterflies and shaded by massive vine-draped trees.
This was the real jungle of "Bring 'Em Back Alive." In the Shan
State, higher elevation and large-scale deforestation had produced a
sparser landscape. Kawthoolei, though, was wet, and it shone in
infinite shades of green. It buzzed with insects and sang with birds.

Karen rebel soldiers (teenagers and a few who were no more
than children) appeared, lifting the bamboo barrier and waving us
through. Their uniforms were much shabbier than those of the
Sura soldiers at Pieng Luang, and their hair was longer. Physically,
Shans didn't look much different from the Thais and Chinese of
Bangkok and Hong Kong, but with the Karens I knew I was in the

presence of something else, a distinct tribe. One could definitely identify a Karen face in a crowd of Asians: a wide jaw, exaggerated cheekbones, huge eyes. A soldier's waist-length mane of black hair evoked for me the Cheyennes or Comanches, images from my childhood books, but that face could only be Karen.

The trail twisted into the village, where a contingent of Karen rebel military and civilian dignitaries welcomed us. The village was the administrative and strategic hub for the Karens' southernmost area of operations. We went to the primary school, where children in ragged, cast-off Thai school uniforms (white shirt and blue skirt or shorts) sang the Karen national anthem for us. They sat at their desks and their teacher asked them if they had any questions for the visitors from the outside world. They were too shy to speak, so Bryant said, "I have a question for you, boys and girls: What was your most embarrassing moment? What's your major? What's your sign? What's the square root of two thousand two hundred and ninety-two?"

Roberto was videotaping this, and he whispered to me, "Our Mr. Bryant is now into his Danny Kaye act."

For the next hour, with the teacher translating his rapid-fire English into Karen, Bryant regaled the children with songs and dances, admonitions about hygiene and nutrition ("brush your teeth," "eat your vegetables"), cartoons drawn on the blackboard, and animal imitations done on request. He even summoned girls to the front of the classroom to give them "manicures" with a metallic felt-tip pen. Grown-up villagers gathered to watch the show through the schoolhouse windows. Bryant was obviously the best thing to hit this war zone in ages.

The next day was a Sunday, so we went with the Karens to their sky-blue Baptist church. The congregation, about fifty strong, wore handwoven red-and-white tunics and sarongs, their traditional Sunday best. The choir sang old American hymns translated into Karen, which was a language of beautiful, silky tones, made for singing.

The first sermon was translated into English for our benefit by an elderly gentleman: "Our nation, the Karen people, have known

hardship and oppression and we have been driven from our own
lands to this poor jungle place. All we wanted was to be free to live
in our own harmless way. The forces of evil would not let it be. We
must fight for our faith, we must fight on. Every day the Karen
people are made the slaves of the Tatmadaw. Our Karen women
are defiled and villages are burned to ash. Every day we must trust
to the Lord to deliver us from all the evil."

The choir sang more hymns, and then an interminable series of
Bible readings commenced. Bryant, sitting at the front, fell asleep
with his hands clasped so it looked like he was in devout meditation. He awoke when his name was called from the pulpit. The
preacher asked him to say a few words to the congregation. Roberto
leapt up to videotape it.

"To me, this is all about prayer and adventure," Bryant said,
rising to the occasion. "You Karens are the rare people who understand both. You have your faith in prayer to get you through the
bad times. And you have the miraculous adventure of the Karen
struggle to rid Kawthoolei of its oppressors. I believe that you will
succeed in your adventure and your prayers will be answered."

"That was quite a good speech," I said to Bryant as we left the
church.

"Well," he drawled, "these people have been fighting for almost
forty years now, so they must have something that keeps 'em going.
Whatever it is, it sure ain't military success, and they're worse off
financially than ever before 'cause the price of their tin ore on the
black market has gone right through the basement. Maybe the
Bible-belting is what gets 'em through."

"That old-time religion," I said. "I had no idea the Karens were
Christian."

"Actually most of them aren't. They worship tree spirits and
family ghosts, or they're Buddhists the same as the Thais and your
friends the Shans. But the elite of the Karen revolution are Chris-
tians and don't let anybody forget it." He started singing "Praise the
Lord and Pass the Ammunition," only inverting the two verbs. I
hoped the Karens were taking it as a sudden burst of postworship
fervor.

Roberto pushed the soundtrack headphones off his thick hair and said, "The Karens say they went Christian because in ancient times, when they came down from 'the River of Sand,' in Mongolia or somewhere, they had this holy book and they lost it. So they ended up an illiterate tribe in Burma, always hassled and ripped off by the Burmese. But they had this prophecy that some day a white man in a boat with white sails would come and bring the book back to them. The book was about two people in a garden with fruit they weren't supposed to eat, and a snake and stuff like that. So when the Yankee missionaries—the Baptists—got to Burma, the Karens said, 'Hey, what took you so long with our book?' "

"So it's been 'Onward Christian Soldiers' ever since?" I said, prompting Bryant to burst into a new song.

We went on to a small riverside village and stopped at its schoolhouse for Bryant to do his Danny Kaye routine again. I left him and wandered into the teachers' office. Neat stacks of pre–World War II mission-school textbooks lay on a table. The American Baptists had created a written language for the illiterate Karen tribe, translated the Bible into it, published school texts.

"Nowadays it is very hard to get any kind of book in our language," a teacher sitting there said. "The government does not approve, so we have to make photocopies of these old books. Also we teach English so it can be the medium of instruction for high school and after. Unfortunately there usually is no after. Boys just go into our army then, and girls to work."

The office had a gun closet, since the male teachers were all in the Karen army and the female teachers worked for the Karen revolutionary organization. A stationary machine gun pointed out a window at the river flowing past. I was introduced to Daniel, a short, wiry man with sharp, friendly eyes and unruly hair. He was the director of education for the southern district of Kawthoolei, supervising all the Karen rebels' schoolhouses in the zone that hugged the Thai border south of the River Kwai. He shook my hand energetically and invited me to his house for coffee.

"This is Naomi, my wife," Daniel said, gesturing to a slender, serious-looking woman standing beside him. "She is the headmistress of the school system in this village, and an absolute genius," he added.

Naomi's seriousness dissolved into an exasperated grin. "Genius? I'm no genius. I'm only teaching Karen children to become geniuses."

Daniel whipped a magazine out of his army shoulder bag. "Look at this! A new *National Geographic*! I subscribe to it but it's usually late. They have to send it to our P.O. box in Thailand because we've got no mail service here. This tribe on the cover is from Africa, this is a *man* in the black lipstick and paint," he said, pointing at the glossy magazine. "It says inside that the men in his tribe spend all day putting cosmetics on their faces and fixing each other's hair. Really! You can see every amazing thing in this magazine. Everything in the world!"

That evening Daniel's riverside village got a dose of the outside world through Bryant's video show. The children's portion started out with Popeye and Betty Boop cartoons, and ended with a series of clips from Japanese monster movies. I wondered if it might be a bit much for children who had to walk home through the jungle in the dark. Roberto said, "At least the kids have flashlights and guns, just in case Godzilla jumps out of the bushes at them."

Next Bryant showed *Some Like It Hot* for the adult audience. Only a few people in the village were really fluent in English, but everyone seemed to understand what was going on. They laughed uproariously at Jack Lemmon and Tony Curtis in drag and seemed to appreciate Marilyn Monroe. Marilyn was, of course, beyond language. I supposed they'd all have to repent for *Some Like It Hot* next Sunday.

We stayed in the village two more days, and I interviewed some people for Bryant's videotape. Daniel spoke about Karen history. When I asked him why the Karens were fighting he quoted an early Karen rebel leader: "Because surrender is out of the question." It seemed to sum up their struggle. The Karens did not appear to be fighting out of a wounded sense of superiority like the Shans (a conquered civilization) but from gut fear for their survival as a tribe.

I asked the district's university-educated agricultural director about the crops the rebel village grew. "We want to irrigate the fields and have rice crops like in the old villages of the delta region," he said, "so we can have a bigger rice supply each year. But too many refugees keep coming to us from the frontline villages taken by the Tatmadaw. They come here because it is safer and close to Thailand. They think they can run into Thailand if the Tatmadaw comes here. Now we have no rice crops to trade, and we have hardly enough for our daily bread." He smiled sadly. "We have gone back to the Stone Age."

Naomi, Daniel's wife, showed me photographs of some of the "interior refugees" who had fled the fighting and Tatmadaw abuse but hadn't made it to another country. They were still in Burma— Kawthoolei's rebel zone—hiding in the jungle. The Karen educators tried to keep track of them, searching them out, keeping photographic records, boarding their children at the schools near the border. Each photo showed a family in front of its makeshift palm-leaf and bamboo hut. Few of the families were complete— they were missing fathers, mothers, or children, dead from war and its companions, disease and hunger. The children stood up straight and smiled for the camera no matter how malnourished they were, but the parents looked into the lens with anguish.

When we returned to Bangkok, Bryant and I made an effort to get some help for the Karen refugees. But we soon found out that the Karens weren't even considered real refugees, just "displaced persons." Even the fifteen thousand who made their way across the border and settled in camps near the Thai town of Mae Sot did not have official refugee status. It was the Thai government that decided who was and wasn't a refugee, and they felt they had enough of the official sort already in camps on their Cambodian and Laotian borders. More were coming in every day from Cambodia, Laos, and Vietnam, the countries of the big war. To them, Burma's was just a little war. Not even a war, an "insurgency." Not even an insurgency but "insurgencies": lots of insignificant little groups fighting a peaceful, neutral government for nonsensical reasons. The Burmese government defined its opponents as *dacoits,* bandits. Insignificant bandit activity didn't produce refugees; only big wars did. Or so went official government logic. And this was the logic that denied aid to those families in the palm-leaf huts and thousands camped precariously around Mae Sot.

Bryant and I visited the offices of various refugee relief organizations and they told us that the Thai government would not permit them to help the people from Burma. A few groups sent under-the-counter donations of basic supplies (rice, salt, and fish paste) to the Mae Sot camps, but large-scale, official aid never materialized.

⌐ 6 ⌐

When I had returned to Thailand from Tiffany and China, I had not gone back to live in Chiang Mai. I was tired of the Rose of the North, which was being overwhelmed by an exploding tourist trade. I rejected Chiang Mai in favor of Bangkok, a city that was so polluted, chaotic, and obnoxious that it defied tourism. In Bangkok, the tourists stuck like flies to clusters of hotels and go-go bars and rarely ventured far afield. I lived with friends at the city's edge. The "jungle suburb," as we called it, was the place where Bangkok terminated abruptly in banana and palm groves and ripe green undevelopment. A road stretched west to Kanchanaburi and the Burma border. Beside that road stood what might have been the last row of "town houses" east of India. I lived there amid the artifacts (Khmer bronzes, Balinese masks, old Burmese tapestries) of the antique dealer who owned the place.

I helped decorate the town house, and the antique dealer and his friends proclaimed me "Minister of the Interior" and let me stay for free. I had by then touched bottom financially. My money earned at Tiffany had run out, and the art gallery in San Francisco that represented my paintings had gone under. I did some free-lance art direction for advertising agencies, and I was an extra in Thai films and a television soap opera.

One February night, I went to the Foreign Correspondents' Club for a panel discussion on Afghanistan. I was curious about one of the panelists, a photojournalist, because he had written an article about the Shans for an Asian magazine. His name was Crispin Dunbar, but he was known simply as "Spin." A handsome, gawky New Zealander, he told of his travels with the Afghan *mujihadeen* to the forbidden city of Kandahar. As he spoke of giving first aid to a wounded Afghan child, my heart began to pound violently. True love hit me like sniper fire.

A week later at a university screening of an old documentary film about the Shan State opium trade, I was properly introduced to Spin by a mutual friend. Spin was dressed in the loose, drab clothing of a Pathan tribesman of Afghanistan. I was wearing my usual Bangkok gray and black: gray shirt, tight black pants, flat black shoes. We sat next to each other in little folding chair-desks. The mottled sepia film showed pony caravans of opium making their way through the infamous Golden Triangle, where the output of Thailand, Laos, and Burma's opium fields would be refined into heroin for the world junk market. Sepia-toned Shan soldiers were leading pack ponies through forests of teak and bamboo. I was struck by the realization that Spin and I were going to melt ourselves into that film. *We will go there,* I thought. Spin shifted uncomfortably in his seat. He had been positioned just like a Song dynasty statue of Kuan Yin: his right foot up on the seat with his right arm draped over the knee. I decided this was a good sign. Kuan Yin was, after all, the goddess of compassion.

Little folding chair-desks were not designed for the likes of Spin, who was six and a half feet tall. He looked very much like *The Phantom* of the eponymous comic strip, although he did not wear a hooded purple leotard or a mask. Like *The Phantom,* Spin called himself "The Ghost Who Walks." At thirty-five, he had haunted Asia for more than a decade, acquiring cameras, photographic skill, and little else.

Over the next month, Spin and I met frequently at his miserable hotel in Bangkok's hippie-tourist neighborhood. And we would run into each other in that city of five million, by chance, like the lovers in Cortazar's *Hopscotch*. Spin began to photograph me. He called me "The Dragon Lady" (out of the *Terry and the Pirates* comic strip), and he also called me "Blade," which was short for "Bladerunner," after a William Burroughs story about smugglers of surgical tools. He adored Beat literature and all kinds of aliases or noms de guerre. His favorite sport was illegally crossing international borders, an activity I was no longer unfamiliar with. We talked about the Burma border all the time, night and day, in his sweat-box room and at grubby canal-side food stalls. But Spin stayed in Bangkok, writing stories to go with his Afghanistan photographs, while I penetrated the Burma frontier again.

A show of my paintings was scheduled in Bangkok that spring, and I wanted to paint some Shan pictures for it. Along with Karen scenes I'd painted, they might interest people in the cultures and causes of Burma's rebel zone. Also, I was worried about the Sura people, since I had read some vague newspaper accounts of a massacre in Pieng Luang by the Rangers, a Thai paramilitary force. If I could get there and find out what had happened, I could get the information to journalists and human rights groups. So I took the train to Chiang Mai, which was on my way back to the Burma border.

TROUBLE
IN
ARCADIA

⚊ 1 ⚊

Up in Chiang Mai, rumors were rife. Ugly, too. Afternoons were spent trading them at Nit's Sandwich Bar, a preserved-in-aspic slice of 1950s Americana. The main room at Nit's had a row of booths upholstered in red and chartreuse tuck-and-roll vinyl. Tropical fish swam lazily in a glass tank, and uniformed waitresses lurked languidly in the room's corners. Nit's kitchen dished out

43

authentically Western food to a nontourist clientele heavy on
retired American military officers who had settled in Chiang Mai
at the end of the Vietnam War. Thailand was their second
choice—they would have preferred to live in a dream Vietnam at
peace, or an intact Cambodia, or a capitalist Laos. Thailand was
my second choice, too—I would rather have been in a Burma that
was minus Ne Win. Thailand's attractions were superficial: fruit,
flowers, the odd monument. But Burma fascinated me to the core.

The men at Nit's knew about Burma from intelligence operations they had run in the mountains of the Golden Triangle some
years before. Burma was tantalizingly intricate with numerous
ethnic groups, political factions, and shifting alliances. As the Ne
Win regime excluded foreign correspondents and stifled its own
press, information from Burma had become a black market commodity in itself. Hot rumors were prized like rubies and at Nit's we
built elaborate pagodas of speculation.

"Don't you want to go to Pieng Luang and find out what's going
on?" I asked my American friends, as we attacked dessert. "What
about the reports that the Thai Rangers, the paramilitary force,
massacred villagers at Pieng Luang? You can't make any sense of it
by reading newspapers like *The Bangkok Post*."

"I wouldn't mind, ordinarily, but I'm not taking my truck up
that road," said Kulok, an erudite retired intelligence officer. "If the
Thai Rangers are putting roadblocks up we wouldn't get through.
And those Rangers can be nasty characters. Plus, there's been a
spate of highway robberies on that route lately, a band of hill-tribe
dacoits on the loose. If you've got to go, take a *songtaow* [pickup
truck converted to bus service with seats in the back] from the
bridge. And check in with the Sura safe house."

"I didn't know there was a *songtaow* service to Pieng Luang," I
said.

"Yes, one goes up every morning," Kulok said. "And it's your
best option for reaching your objective. *Dacoits* usually don't bother
to attack the *songtaows* because only poor folks ride in them. And if
it's just you, the Thai checkpoints will probably let you through.
One little blonde lady has a far better chance than us old guys in our
trucks."

"By the way, Edith, Sura isn't called Sura anymore," said Trowbridge, an ex-CIA man who spoke all the local languages. "They have a new name: the TRC, which is the Tailand Revolutionary Council. That's Tailand with no H, as in the greater Tai race of Southeast Asia. The word *tai* means *free*. That's how our Shan rebels like to think of themselves, although everyone does have a price."

"Who's leading the Tailand Revolutionary Council?" I asked.

"Mo Heing, Sura's one-armed general. He lost that arm in action against the Tatmadaw back when he was a Communist insurgent. Since then he's seen the light and become quite the Buddhist holy warrior, exceptionally anti-Communist."

In the far north of the Shan State, along the China border, the Burmese Communist Party fought its battles. Ne Win's form of socialism had no appeal for them. The aging Burmese ethnic leaders of the Burmese Communist Party (BCP) revered Mao Tse-tung and commanded ten to fifteen thousand hill-tribe troops. They were one of the largest insurgent groups in the world. But like the Chinese Nationalist KMT, the Communist rebels had gotten involved in the drug trade; their territory was Burma's prime opium-growing region.

"Mo Heing has really stirred things up with his heroin bonfire," Kulok added. "His men captured a Burmese Communist Party pony caravan carrying a lot of heroin and burned the goods. A kind of Buddhist moral gesture. Part of his Buddhist holy war image, I guess."

"When I was at Pieng Luang, Prince George told me that Mo Heing was watching Charlton Heston in *El Cid* on video," I said. "Maybe Mo Heing is El Cid of the Shan State."

"Mo Heing as El Cid, not bad," the ex–radio officer called Ringer said. "But remember that Khun Sa's the Al Capone of the Shan State. And Khun Sa, the opium warlord with the big private army, is salivating over Mo Heing's territory."

Mo Heing's small Shan rebel force of about one thousand troops was under threat from all sides. Mo Heing had offended both the BCP and the KMT by destroying valuable merchandise—heroin. Khun Sa was moving closer to a takeover, and the Tatmadaw was an ever-present threat.

"The relationship between Mo Heing and his group's KMT backers is extremely strained right now," commented Kulok, digging his fork into marble cake à la mode. "He was supposed to hand the BCP heroin over to them, not burn it, for God's sake. So now Mo Heing is caught between the proverbial rock and hard place. If he goes it alone without the KMT, he'll last about five minutes before crafty old Khun Sa comes out of the woods and consumes him."

"If he hasn't already," Ringer said with a cynical laugh. "A holy warrior in the Shan State has about the life expectancy of a fat duck in a Chinese restaurant kitchen."

I went to the TRC safe house, a nondescript building in Chiang Mai's worst slum. All the rebel groups had safe houses (in Chiang Mai or Mae Hong Son or Mae Sot) to provide severely wounded or ill soldiers with a place to recuperate after treatment in Thai hospitals, and officers with a place to stay when they came across the border to buy weapons. Thailand's authorities knew about the safe houses, and every so often they would stage an "immigration raid," which was little more than a shakedown for extra bribes.

A Shan boy in a camouflage T-shirt and torn jeans met me at the front door.

"Greetings," I said in Thai, "I'm a friend of Prince George's."

"Yes, I remember you from our headquarters, a couple of years ago. You came to the cinema show then."

"I am planning to return to Pieng Luang, just me this time. Is anyone from this house going back there?"

"No, miss, we are all sick and injured. But the *songtaow* goes to Pieng Luang at eight o'clock tomorrow morning, leaving from the bridge."

"Is it a problem to get there? I understand there's been trouble with the Rangers."

"No, it is no problem at all," the Shan boy said with a smile. I found that reassuring, but not completely so. It could well mean, "Hell, if you want to go up there and get shot by the Rangers, it's no problem."

* * *

I had dinner with a British short-story writer who lived in Chiang Mai. He had been in Pieng Luang when the Rangers had entered the village. They'd told him to get in his truck and leave. I told him I was going there.

"Not with the Rangers in occupation. You'll be signing your own death warrant," the writer said, and I laughed. "It's not funny," he said. "They aren't like regular Thai Army troops. The Rangers are recruited from the worst slums and the poorest farmland in Thailand and dressed up in wicked black uniforms. They go out and waste anyone their commanders tell them to, and usually a few extra just for fun. They do the Thai military's dirty work on the borders—Cambodia, Laos, and now Burma. Don't go. They'll shoot you just for being there."

That night I listened to tapes on my Walkman before I slept. A song by U2, "The Unforgettable Fire," played, Bono crooning "Walk 'til you run, and don't look back . . ." That's just how I'll head for the Sura—the TRC—compound when the *songtaow* reaches Pieng Luang, I thought. What the hell am I doing? *Dacoits* on the road, trigger-happy Rangers in Pieng Luang, a drug war between the TRC and its rivals. Plus the usual war with the Tatmadaw. I had heard about a Malaysian journalist who had crossed from Thailand to Burma at Mae Sai (the only northern border post that was not insurgent-controlled on the Burma side) and had been arrested there by the Tatmadaw. He'd suffered a couple of years in a Burmese prison merely for violating the rule that foreigners from nonadjoining countries could only enter Burma through Rangoon's Mingaladon Airport. If the Tatmadaw were ever to catch me with rebel troops, the charges would be worse: espionage and subversion.

I turned up the volume on U2. I won't get killed, I convinced myself. I'll get to Pieng Luang and I'll revisit the *chedi* at Mai Sung and I'll find out everything about the Shans. I would come back from Pieng Luang and lay out my experiences before the guys at

Nits, the short-story writer, and Spin, like a gem smuggler displaying rubies, like a Rangoon street vendor with a box of black market
thumbtacks.

= 2 =

In the morning, at the *songtaow* stop by the bridge, I spoke with a
pair of young Buddhist monks who were on their way to meditate
at the monastery at Mai Sung, where the TRC headquarters was
located. Things were off to a good start, since having monks along
was considered auspicious for travel. Sitting in the front seat, they
would probably discourage *dacoits* from raiding the *songtaow* (it was
bad luck to attack a monk). I sat in the back with a few old Chinese
people and their bundles and cardboard cartons.

March was the hottest, driest part of the year in Thailand. Forest-
fire smoke billowed over parched hillsides as we drove past. The
hill-tribespeople were taking advantage of the dry weather to burn
away the forest, clearing new fields that would be fertilized by the
ashes. It was a traditional farming method that had been environmentally sound when the tribes had vast tracts of land on which to
roam. Now they were confined to ever-decreasing hill territory, and
their agriculture caused soil erosion and climate changes. The hot
season in Thailand was getting hotter and drier every year. Soon
there would be no more forests to slash and burn.

The road had been improved considerably since my visit two
years before and electric power lines were strung alongside it. The
dust that flew in the back of the *songtaow* changed color every few
miles. It reminded me of face powder in cream, tan, ocher, rose red.
An old man next to me joked, "Nobody will notice the foreigner
among us—now we all have the same light-colored hair from the
dust!"

The *songtaow* stopped several times to pick up Lisu tribespeople, the rice and poppy growers of the mountains. The Lisu women dressed in layers of vibrant blue and magenta cotton. Ribbons festooned their glossy hair and their mouths brimmed with red betel-nut juice. A teenage tribesman dressed in blue jeans climbed onto the roof and I noticed a pistol tucked in his waistband.

Traffic was sparse as we made our way through the charred hillsides. Four hours after departure, we encountered Pieng Luang's morning *songtaow*. When it pulled up next to us, our driver handed theirs an automatic pistol. To me the Chiang Mai–bound passengers looked like a gang of *dacoits,* with hats pulled low over their faces, bandannas over their mouths, and dark glasses. Then I realized that everyone around me looked that way, too. It was only antidust garb.

At the first checkpoint, an officer in an olive drab uniform with a purple shoulder patch that read "Border Patrol Police" greeted the driver and asked politely for us to leave the *songtaow* while his men searched the baggage.

The Border Patrol Police opened and closed boxes, unzipped and rezipped bags, and put everything back just the way they'd found it. They asked some questions of the Chinese passengers, but ignored me completely. We all got back in the *songtaow* and went on to the next checkpoint a few miles away where the whole process was repeated. Again, I was ignored. "No problem"—just like the boy at the Chiang Mai safe house had said.

After another hour, we arrived at Pieng Luang's new Ranger post. The other checkpoints had been neat little booths with lightweight metal roadblocks, manned by soft-spoken border men in clean, pressed olive drab. The Ranger post was something else entirely. It was a slapped-together shack that reminded me of tree forts I'd built as a child. Crude skulls and crossbones were painted all over it, and a big, cracked wooden heart was nailed up over the door. I decided to call it "Fort Broken Heart."

Some teenage Rangers with utterly menacing expressions surrounded the *songtaow* brandishing M-16 rifles. They looked like a South Bronx street gang. Their basic black fatigues were accessorized with all kinds of nonregulation gear: pirate headscarves, earrings, wristbands, brightly colored basketball socks. The Rangers had spiky punk haircuts, skull tattoos, and Rambo survival knives. They combed through the passengers' belongings—all except mine. And they didn't ask me any questions. We passengers stood stiff and tense until the Rangers let us board again. As we drove away, we slowly began to relax and smile at each other. Just one more BPP checkpoint and we would arrive in Pieng Luang. And we hadn't lost a passenger yet.

⌐ 3 ⌐

Pieng Luang was a string of small teak buildings surrounded by rice paddies in a narrow valley. It was a very quiet village. "Pieng Luang's like Little Italy in New York," my friend Ringer had said. "Nobody steals your car because you might be the Mafia don's nephew. In Pieng Luang nobody's going to pick pockets because they just might belong to a KMT general's friend." Old-fashioned Chinese music played on the Taiwan tape decks of Pieng Luang, Burmese Duya cigarettes were sold in the shops, and posters of James Dean—the great rebel without a cause—adorned the fronts of some of the old steep-roofed houses. In its mysterious little way, Pieng Luang seemed a crossroads for the trade and cultures of the Himalayas, China, and Southeast Asia. It drew me in as Asia had enticed me, with an atmosphere as familiar as a remembered dream, but as unpredictable as a hallucination.

The *songtaow* dropped off most of the passengers at the market in the center of the village before continuing uphill. I jumped out at the top of the hill and walked into the TRC compound, where the Shan guard seemed to recognize me. I went to Prince George's house, cutting through his garden of orchids, pineapples, and tomatoes. I stopped at the front door, where a sun hat trimmed with artificial roses hung.

"The hat belongs to Prince George's wife," a voice said in

English from behind me. "She's been in Burma prison almost two years now."

I looked around. A frail man, bespectacled and reeking of whiskey, had followed me from the garden. He was holding freshly picked tomatoes. I instinctively *wai*'d him.

"Oh, miss, no need to make this Shan greeting. I am just a Burmese man and of no high rank. I am only the servant of Prince George. And if I were a Shan, I would now have to press my own hands together to return your nice greeting and these tomatoes would become tomato sauce!" He shouldered the door open. "Please do come in. You are most welcome here. The prince is not at home now, but he will be back from Mai Sung this evening. Take a rest."

Two more of Prince George's retainers greeted me inside the house. One was a mildly retarded man whom I recognized from my first visit, and the other was a Shan teenager in a Mao cap who was playing a guitar.

"This one, Ping, he takes a guitar lesson every day," the tomato-picker said. "Quite good, too. He will entertain us all with a song after dinner. My own name is Maung, and this one is Pon. We are all the cooks for the prince. He says too many cooks spoil the broth, so we are his broth-spoiling men." They were also Prince George's handlers, there to protect him from his drunken self as much as possible. It seemed that those who fit nowhere else in the Sura structure ended up sheltered at Prince George's house.

Maung directed me to the only bed in the guest room, a cot in the corner opposite the sleeping platform. I settled in for a nap and looked around the room. The walls were papered with posters of Thai movie stars and horrid fluffy kittens; on one wall was a large picture of Rangoon's Shwe Dagon pagoda. A shelf trimmed in gold paper held a small shrine of Buddha images and jars of wildflowers. Framed portraits of the Thai royal family hung high on another wall, a reminder that these Shans liked to consider the King of Thailand their head of state, although the enthusiasm was not reciprocated. A framed batik portrait of an old monk, signed by Jere, hung near my bed, above Prince George's paperback library.

I slept for an hour in my corner bed, and when I awoke another guest had arrived. A middle-aged Shan man, slim, in a green uniform, had spread his bedroll on the platform next to the blankets of the broth spoilers. He introduced himself to me as a captain from the Shan State Army, a rebel group beginning to break apart under pressure from other factions and the Tatmadaw.

"Our revolutionary group is in turmoil right now," he said in precise English, "so I have traveled through the forests to General Mo Heing's headquarters to offer my skills as a training officer. I care only for fighting the Tatmadaw. And what has brought you here?"

"Well, I, uh, am here to learn about the Shans," I stammered.

"Oh, very good indeed. You are a journalist, then, perhaps?"

"No, not a journalist. Just a friend, really."

"I am happy to hear it. We need friends from outside. There are dark days ahead for us. The Tatmadaw presses us from one side; Khun Sa presses us from the other." He pushed his fists together, knuckle to knuckle, and sighed. "So I hope the outside world will hear about this from friends like you. Are you British?"

"No, American."

"Really? I thought that since you are a friend of our Shan people, perhaps you were from a British family that spent time here in the old days... Will you have some of the tea I brought from the central Shan State? The servants are brewing it now."

I joined him for tea in the garden. While we chatted Prince George arrived. His hair and quilted jacket were dusty from the ride from Mai Sung.

"Miss Edith! What a surprise to see you," he said. "Well, maybe I'm not too surprised. I might have known you'd come back to look after us when we were having troubles. Where are the others? Still down in Pieng Luang village?"

"They didn't think it was a great idea to come up in their trucks."

Prince George raised his eyebrows and laughed. "And I agree with them! So you came by yourself in the *songtaow*? You are awfully brave and we are very glad you're here. I am just sorry there's only my poor place for you to stay and no festivities. My wife is gone—imprisoned in Taunggyi because she tried to sneak back to visit her family. There has been no trial. The Tatmadaw just keeps her locked up. That's it."

"What about your son? Was he with her?"

"No, she left him here. He's with the neighbor lady right now, but he cries all the time for his mama."

Prince George excused himself to speak in Shan with the SSA captain until dinner, which consisted of rice and soybean cakes, peanuts and fried potatoes. Some men, whom I remembered as Sura officers, joined us, and afterward Prince George held court, pouring Mekong whiskey into the same glasses we'd used for tea. Conversation was in Shan, Thai, and English—the last for my benefit.

The TRC foreign minister, K. Sam, an earnest man in his thirties, arrived with a Thai magazine reporter in tow. K. Sam wore a traditional Shan suit instead of a uniform. His blue home-spun jacket closed with knots and loops, and the matching trousers were typical Shan baggies, which have a huge waist that is gathered at each hip and knotted in front. He adjusted his heavy black-framed glasses and peered at me. I wore a striped Shan sarong and a sweater, jacket, and leg warmers. I was probably the only person in the world who wore leg warmers with sarongs, but I kept finding myself in cold places that were supposedly tropical. "It's very nice that you wear our traditional Shan clothing," K. Sam said. "You two, American and Thai, are the only visitors to come here since the troubles with the Rangers."

"You still haven't told me what happened when the Rangers came up," the Thai reporter said to K. Sam. "Maybe you can tell us about it now."

"I can tell you," Prince George said, pouring himself another belt of whiskey. "It was the latest attempt by the Thais to control the KMT."

"The KMT used to be vital to Thai national interests," K. Sam told me, "to keep Chinese Communists out. Now they are not so vital. More like an embarrassment. They are not Thai, and they keep a picture of Chiang Kai-shek instead of the Thai king. They

speak the Chinese language, gamble and trade guns, trade drugs."
He gave a self-righteous sniff. "Pieng Luang was known as Las
Vegas! The Chinese hid their gambling casinos behind those
closed-up shophouse doors at night, and the Thai soldiers finally
came to clean them up."

"It happened very fast," Prince George continued. "Two hundred, maybe three hundred Rangers came in by helicopter with a
list of Pieng Luang's undesirable elements."

"A hit list?" I asked.

"Yes. And they went around with that list and gathered up fifty
Chinese men and brought them to the forest. Casino men, small
drug-trade men, small gun-trade men." Prince George raised his
arms and imitated the raking motion of an M-16 firing on full auto.
"They use plenty of ammunition, those Rangers. Everyone on the
list is finished."

"Frontier justice," I said.

"Like a cowboy movie," Prince George said.

While the Thai reporter was writing all of this down, K. Sam
said, "Some of the Chinese were so shot to pieces that their families
could only tell who they were by the shoes on their feet."

"Did the Rangers come up here to your compound?" I asked.

"They came, but no problem. This event was for the KMT only,"
Prince George said. "They showed up at our front gate and asked if
we had any illegal weapons. So we handed over a few guns. Just
some rifles we'd borrowed from the KMT for a parade. The Thais
have no complaints with us."

"We are of course *Tai,* the same as them," K. Sam proclaimed.
"And we both hate Burma. Two hundred years ago the Burmese
king's army destroyed the Thai capital, Ayutthaya. Thailand will
never forget that. They would rather have us Shan revolutionaries
on their border than any Burmese army. We have many kind
friends in the Thai military. No hard feelings. Quote me if you
like."

He moved a candle closer to the Thai reporter so he'd have
enough light to write by, and continued, "The Shan State is as big as
Cambodia, and bigger than many countries in this world. We have

every reason to be a sovereign nation, in close association with Thailand, our gateway to the sea. The KMT had better just get out of our way, and if it takes a Ranger mopping-up operation to do that, we're all for it."

⚎ 4 ⚎

The next day I woke up before anyone else and walked to the Pieng Luang market, which took place every day between the crack of dawn and seven A.M. I could not understand why markets like Pieng Luang's and Mae Hong Son's began so early. The Shan and tribal vendors were forced to travel in the chilly dark, to sell their wares to Chinese customers who had been up half the night running *fan-tan* games of chance.

The market straddled a short lane on a dusty main street. Under a palm-thatched roof, along two rows of wooden platforms, sellers sat with their goods. Across from the entrance, a Chinese coffee shop had just opened its heavy teak doors for business. So my reward for rising early was a cup of coffee and the chance to watch the market world come and go.

"Ni hao." I gave the Chinese greeting to the coffee shop proprietor. I noticed that a calendar with a portrait of the Thai royal family on it had been hung conspicuously in his shop.

"Here, please have these with your coffee," he said, bringing me a plate of bean-paste buns fresh from the big aluminum steamer that warmed and perfumed the shop. The coffee was true border coffee: Nescafé in a glass, with thick tinned milk at the bottom and extra sugar. The spoon stood upright in it.

I opened my sketchbook, took the cap off a fine-point pen, and began sketching bits and pieces of the morning scene: Shan ladies hawking their heaps of potatoes, red onions, garlic, weedy cilantro, spices, squares of sticky rice confections; a Chinese woman with a baby wrapped to her back in embroidered cloth; a Shan girl in a striped sarong and an oversized fatigue jacket haggling over the price of dried fish.

As I sketched, shopkeepers up and down the street were folding back the doors of their shops, revealing stocks of border goods to be smuggled into Burma for the black market: boxes of rubber sandals, kerosene lamps, bicycles, plastic dolls. A turbaned Shan man extolled the virtues of his plucked chickens. A Lisu man stalked by, large knife in hand, a wild glint in his eye. Whole families strolled around outfitted in insurgent camouflage. The morning fog lifted gradually and the mountain air felt crisp.

I asked the coffee-shop man about the Ranger invasion.

"Oh, they just took the bad men away and shot them," he said, smiling. "No problem. We can still make good business here. Just have to pay a little to the Thai soldiers for a while. They will go away."

I had the feeling that this attitude probably extended from the humblest shopkeepers all the way up to the highest echelons of the KMT drug syndicates. The unlucky fifty, whose families were mourning over bloody shoes, were just lower-rank gangsters, unessential to the business at hand.

Under the market roof people bargained over cabbages and mushrooms, selected oranges, and weighed pieces of pork on old hand-held scales. They remembered to buy beans or forgot to buy a bottle of fish sauce. A dark-haired teenage girl sat in the doorway of a shop tapping her foot to a Chinese pop tune and stroking a black cat. I realized that there was something radically different from the first time I'd been in Pieng Luang: nobody was shopping with an M-16 slung over a shoulder. In the old Pieng Luang every other person packed ostentatious heat. I supposed they were afraid of having their weapons confiscated by the Rangers. None of the boys in black was showing his face in the market, anyway. Maybe they were still asleep at Fort Broken Heart.

When I returned from the market, I went to visit the neighbor who was baby-sitting Prince George's son. She was a TRC medical officer whose husband was also in Mo Heing's rebel army. Their house was as small as Prince George's but painted powder blue and furnished with overstuffed armchairs, a beige vinyl couch, and a teak-and-glass coffee table. The medical officer, Nang Seng, spoke English.

"Sit down here. No, sit on the couch, more comfortable for you. Have some tea. Have some of these chocolate biscuits, they come from Chiang Mai."

She settled her short, plump body, wrapped in a tight lace blouse and sarong, on the couch next to me. Extracting a photo album from a clutter of Thai magazines on the coffee table, she showed me the pictures. "This is me back in Burma. Very young! Very beautiful! Can you believe it?" She turned the page. "This is me when I get nursing certificate in Burma. After that I joined the Shan revolution, because I am a Shan woman and I don't like what Ne Win and his Tatmadaw do to Shan people. No rights at all for us. I am in the revolution for twenty-three years now. I met my husband in the revolution. Look, here we are the newlyweds. Next page, my children. They go to school here, but when they are older I will send them to get a good education in Thailand. Burma, forget it. My children are good students. They listen to their mother, even the oldest boy. I raise them well!"

I was more interested in Nang Seng as revolutionary than mom, so between bites of chocolate biscuit I asked about the TRC's women soldiers.

"They are mostly for special security," she told me. "But sometimes they go to the front line. They are brave soldiers, but they make a lot of problems with the boys. The boy soldiers fall in love, want to marry the girl soldiers. Then they both want to run away with each other, thinking of themselves only, not the revolution. But a thing we Shans know: if a woman soldier shoots a man who has a magic tattoo against bullets, the tattoo won't work, the man will die anyway. So a woman soldier is very powerful that way. Nowadays I am teaching the TRC women first aid. If they go to the front line, no hospital there, so if you don't have first aid, maybe you are dead."

"Where is the front line?" I asked. "It seems like the TRC has enemies on all sides."

"Oh, the TRC has big enemies: Burma Tatmadaw, and Burma Communists, and KMT," Nang Seng said, nodding her head. "But now that we Shans are all united, we can win."

I stopped eating and stared out the window at Prince George's run-down palace. The prince hadn't said anything about all Shans being united, and neither had the TRC foreign minister, K. Sam.

"What do you mean by united?" I asked. "What about the SUA pressing down until the TRC has only the one narrow trade route left?"

"Well, now that the SUA's General Khun Sa has agreed to join our TRC, we can all cooperate together in the revolution. Have you had enough tea? I'm going to visit a friend in Mai Sung. Please come along. My son will drive us in our new Toyota truck."

I climbed into the front seat, realizing that a number of new trucks had supplanted the Shan compound's former fleet of aged Jeeps. Sura's sworn enemy, Khun Sa, had consented to join their TRC—the old fox consenting to guard the henhouse, I thought.

Mai Sung was a collection of thatch-roofed bamboo houses interspersed with rice paddies and pastures where ponies and donkeys grazed. Poppies were not grown there—the TRC had banned them in their own backyard. A cool breeze stirred a purple heatherlike flower that grew across the hillsides. The sun shone gently on a scene of calm and plenty. Arcadia, I thought, a land worth fighting for.

Nang Seng's son stopped in front of the TRC printing press: a bamboo shack that housed the mimeograph machine that soldiers used to crank out textbooks, nationalist propaganda, and Buddhist tracts—all in the Shan language. "This is what our Shan revolution is all about," enthused Nang Seng. "The Burmese pretend Shan civilization never happened. They want everything Burmese and make everybody use Burma language. Why *their* language? The name of the first Shan revolution movement was 'Shan Literacy.' Shan students wanted to teach Shans to read their own language. That's all. For this, Ne Win killed many."

Her son had wandered off to another bamboo shack, where a

rock band was practicing. A small generator powered the amplifiers and electric guitars, and a girl's voice rang out over the rhythm section. One of the guitar players was young Ping from Prince George's house. "They play revolutionary songs," Nang Seng said with an exasperated sigh. "My son likes it very much—wants to join revolutionary army to be Mr. Rock Star! Come on, let's go to the furniture factory."

The TRC had recently attempted to give honest industry a foothold in Mai Sung by starting a furniture factory. The idea was to make very expensive pearl-inlaid Chinese-style furniture for sale in Thailand. It was labor intensive work and was supposed to provide people from other parts of the Shan State with a job alternative to opium-poppy growing. The pilot factory, located by a small stream, was a large open-sided framework of wooden pillars and beams supporting a metal roof. Some men were sawing wood and a dozen women sat at a long table fitting mother-of-pearl chips into ornate wood carvings. When we entered, they rose and saluted Nang Seng, then sat back down and looked shyly at me.

"These are the women soldiers working on the furniture," Nang Seng announced. "Keeps them out of trouble!"

They looked quite young to me, perhaps fifteen, sixteen years old, and they wore sarongs with army shirts, army jackets, and "boonie" hats. Each had a pile of shell pieces and they all worked slowly, selecting the right ones to fit each section of wood, a painstaking jigsaw puzzle. The kind of furniture the Shans were aiming for would be finished with a dark stain to simulate ebony and bring out the gleam of the inlay. Such work fetched a high price in Bangkok. But these Shans had a long way to go in making their factory profitable. There were only a few pieces in the factory, half completed: a table and some cabinets. The furniture was ill balanced and rickety, with most of the inlay missing and no dark stain.

Nang Seng asked me to wait while she went off to see her friend in a house nearby. A soldier girl brought a bamboo stool (which showed better craftsmanship than anything else in the factory) and set a glass of tea on the half-done inlaid table. I thanked her with a *wai* and she *wai*'d back, then returned to her work.

I quietly rapped the table. It didn't seem to be hollow. Surely the Shans aren't doing all this fancy cabinetry just to stuff the interstices with heroin, I thought. That would be just too obvious. . . . I looked at an inlaid peony—or was it an opium poppy?—and traced the outline with my silver-lacquered fingernails. The Spirit of Opium, I thought, recalling how I'd attended a masquerade ball in California years before costumed as just that: an Art Nouveau wraith with red-and-white silk poppies entwined in my hair. In those days I had not only portrayed opium, I had taken it. It was the only drug I ever really liked. It had an artistic mystique, as in Coleridge's "Xanadu" and Colette's lounge lizards. It was such a cerebral high: you could figure out everything, lying there, but you could *do* nothing. So it was ultimately useless and I gave it up.

One of the grand old KMT opportunists, General Tuan, had come up with the quintessential self-justification for the drug business. A British newspaper had quoted him: "To fight you must have an army, and an army must have guns, and to buy guns you must have money. In these mountains the only money is opium." Flawless logic, except that once the late General Tuan and other armies got involved in the opium business, their political goals had fallen by the wayside. Why should you jeopardize your opium caravans by veering off to fight the Tatmadaw, or to invade Communist China? The KMT never fought for anything but drug trade routes. Getting the opium from the farmers, transporting it, refining it, selling it, all required acts of exploitation and compromise at every level. Anti-Communist Shans purchased raw opium in bulk from Communist rebel cadres. So-called rebel groups paid off the Tatmadaw to let their caravans pass undisturbed. KMT refineries processed BCP opium into heroin. Some revolution, I thought, gloomily drinking my tea at the rickety factory table.

At the TRC compound in Pieng Luang, the tea drinking continued. And as long as the tea flowed and the Mekong held out, conversations meandered restlessly. That night they covered the Irish, the Wa, and the art of tattooing.

I raised a glass of Mekong in a toast to Ireland. "Today is St.

Patrick's Day," I explained, "sort of an Irish National Day. I'm Irish-Italian American. If you're Irish, you're supposed to wear green. I wonder if my camouflage qualifies."

"The British used to call us Shans 'the Irish of Asia,'" K. Sam said, his heavy spectacles slipping down his nose. "Maybe because we like whiskey and songs, and we're rebellious."

"Ah, so *that's* what I'm doing here . . . ," I said.

"Your ethnic group and nationality matter little," Prince George said. "Anyone can come here to help the cause of freedom. I myself am no more a Shan than you are."

I looked at the Prince with his ratty old quilted jacket, slicked-back hair, and forlorn but amused eyes, the half-empty glass always in front of him.

"*You're* not a Shan?" I said, amazed.

"No, certainly not. I am the prince of the Palaung tribe from the central Shan State, where the tea comes from. Any ethnic group can join this revolution, or not, as they desire."

"My parents were part Chinese but being of the Shan State, I consider myself Shan," K. Sam said, looking chilled in his thin homespun jacket. "And Miss Edith, since you're Irish, what is your opinion on the IRA?"

"I think some of the IRA are just Communists," I replied, "and some of the IRA are just murderers, and some of the IRA are just not afraid to die for freedom and equal rights. It's the same as here, only it's been going on for a lot longer."

K. Sam translated that into Shan for some non-English-speakers at the prince's table. I only hoped the war in the Shan State wouldn't turn into an endless maelstrom like Ireland's. The fine romantic Irish cause attracted many Irish-Americans, and the IRA had all kinds of ways to use them. I was glad I hadn't gotten involved as American gunrunner, propagandist, or as cannon fodder. With the war in Burma, I could stand apart and make my decisions as an outsider. I could gauge and regulate my involvement. It was a war and a cause that I—not my ancestry—had chosen. My reasons were irrelevant. Just the fact that I was there with the Shans and their Palaung prince was all that really mattered to them.

"Not only does the Shan State contain Shans and Palaungs," Prince George said, "also the Akha, Lahu, Lisu, and other tribes live in the mountains, and in the far north of the State is the land of the Wa. Have you met any Wa?"

"I never have," I said. "But I've read about them in old books and I'm fascinated."

"In the old days, the Wa hunted heads," Prince George said. "The tribe had two types: Tame Wa and Wild Wa. Both needed fresh-cut human heads to make the rice crop grow—or so they thought. They lived in fortified villages, and the trails leading to them were 'skull avenues,' lined with heads set on high shelves cut into trees and poles. The Wild Wa went out and got the heads— anybody's head. It didn't matter whose. As soon as they decided to go head-hunting they just attacked the first person they saw outside their own village. As for the Tame Wa, they bought the heads they needed from the Wild Wa."

"Every army in the Shan State has Wa soldiers now," K. Sam added. "Especially the Burmese Communist Party, since they're based in the Wa area. But the Wa don't understand about Communism, they just like to fight."

"Head-collecting isn't fashionable with the Wa anymore, but killing still is," Prince George said.

A current of cold air made the candle flames flicker, and K. Sam shuddered and changed the subject. "Who made the tattoo on your arm?" he asked me.

"A man named Spider Webb," I said, pushing up my sleeve to display the black and green scrollwork just above my elbow. "In his shop he had two glass cases: one was full of tarantulas, and the other had iguanas crawling over a human skull. Maybe he was part Wa. He used an electric needle, very deep. It bled a lot."

"Our Shan tattoos are not electric," K. Sam said. "They are done by hand, slowly, including special medicines to protect us from ghosts and any malefactors. Our tattoos are formulas in the Buddhist language, Pali; or lucky animals like the lion and the two-headed lizard." He said something in Shan to an old soldier, who rolled up his shirtsleeves, revealing blue-black forearms. "This is the old-style tattoo," K. Sam said. "Solid tattoo, also covering the legs. Our grandfathers had it, but now not many have this kind."

The other soldiers looked at the old Shan's leathery forearms with admiration.

"This old fellow's skin may resist vaccination needles, knives, even bullets," said Prince George. "The solid darkness is an anti-penetration tattoo. It is the real thing."

The old soldier spoke, and K. Sam translated. "He wants to know what kind of medicine is in your black and green tattoo, Miss Edith."

"Only the medicine that brought me here, past Rangers and *dacoits*," I said.

- 5 -

The Border Patrol Police had installed a loudspeaker system in the village, and it blasted out marching-band music and civic pep talks (in Thai, which few people in Pieng Luang understood) at sunrise. The market goers, up for hours, ignored it. Up the hill, Prince George slept through it. At his palace, breakfast was at ten o'clock, accompanied by his favorite breakfast music. Every morning the same cassette was played, a Golden Oldies compilation featuring time warp hits like "Guantanamera," "To Sir, With Love," and "North to Alaska." I thought "North to Alaska" was the greatest hit for the Golden Triangle, real frontier music to start the day.

After breakfast I decided to raise the issue of the new TRC alliance—which seemed to be the only topic that hadn't been covered in our after-dinner conversation.

"What's the status of the SUA regarding the TRC these days?"

"The SUA has joined the TRC," Prince George said without hesitation. "No one knows it except you and that Thai reporter who's already gone back to Chiang Mai to file his scoop with his magazine. K. Sam let the cat out of the bag, but we haven't announced it officially yet. We've been negotiating with Khun Sa for months. We want all Shans to be united. When we broke with the KMT Chinese, Khun Sa decided to allow his SUA to join us. We're both Shan armies, so it's much more sensible than being with the KMT."

"So the good news is that all the Shan groups are more or less united now, for the first time ever," I said. "And the bad news is that you've got the world's most notorious drug kingpin in the TRC."

"Well, yes, but we are going to rehabilitate him," Prince George said, pouring a slug of Mekong into his tea glass.

Later that day, I went to the Buddhist temple at Mai Sung, on the back of the prince's motorbike, with Ping driving. Prince George had missed out on the recent upgrade of the TRC motor pool, as his alcoholism had caused him to total one too many Sura trucks. He was left with a little Honda bike and was usually chauffeured on it. The bike had seen better days, and it was a slow ride in the dust to Mai Sung. Ping wasn't wearing his Mao cap, so his long hair blew in my face all the way. It smelled like Thai shampoo, Sunsilk, the same cheap brand I used.

At the temple, the elder monks were giving novices an examination in Buddhist doctrine. Those of us who were not monks (women and soldiers) were permitted to sit and listen in an open pavilion attached to the monastery's main hall. The temple complex was atop two peaks, the main hall and *chedi* on one; the monks' dormitories and a new ordination hall on the other.

The monks droned in Pali, the Buddhist doctrinal language, which was incomprehensible to me. I decided to walk over to the other hill to sketch. Shan architecture—particularly the ecclesiastical—fascinated me. Shan temple designs were grandiose in concept (multitiered roofs sprouted gables, turrets, pinnacles) but the materials were prosaic: weathered wood, corrugated sheet metal, some pierced-tin trim. The effect of intricate structures built with mundane materials was nothing short of sublime.

In the palace that evening I played a long game of Scrabble with Maung, the Burmese broth spoiler. He put up a good fight. Like many of the Shans, Muang showed that English proficiency was perhaps one happy legacy of the British Raj. Being able to speak and read English gave them access to what was going on beyond their mountains. They read the copies of *Far Eastern Economic Review* and *Time* that Prince George received. The *Review* was the only international publication that consistently covered the war in Burma, and it covered it well. Their Burma expert was Bertil Lintner, a Swede married to a Shan photographer who had served in the SSA. *Time* was valued by the Shans as *National Geographic* was by Daniel: as windows to the outside world.

Having exhausted Scrabble and *Time*, I explored Prince George's bookshelf. I found a white-covered paperback wedged in among the spy novels.

What's this book?" I asked Prince George as I tried to work it loose.

"Oh, that's just our catalog of synthetic gems that can be ordered from Europe," he replied.

It was always "buyer beware" for gem deals in tourist Chiang Mai. But if any outsider made it all the way up to the Shan State's black market gateway, it might be easy to convince them that such fake rubies and sapphires were coming straight from the fabled Shan mines of Mogok.

And what about my gems of information? I wondered. The real thing or synthetic? I was long past trusting the TRC people to tell the truth, and yet the worst truths came so offhandedly—"Oh, yeah, here's our gem rip-off scheme," "Oh, yeah, here's our alliance with the world's biggest drug warlord . . ."

= 6 =

The next day the highest-ranking monk of the Shan State, who Prince George in his Anglophilia referred to as "the Archbishop," was to arrive at the temple. I went to the foot of the hill to sketch the

Shans who waited to welcome their august visitor. They beat deep
underwater sounds from bronze gongs and struck shimmering
flourishes with cymbals. A *sayah* danced, his face to the hot sky, his
arms flung out, his fingers bent back, mixing necromancy with
Buddhist devotions. A line of women dressed in peacock colors held
bouquets. Barefoot children played with plastic M-16s. Someone
had dressed a baby in a shirt adorned with hand-painted poppies,
the kind of shirt made for the tourist trade in Chiang Mai, where
opium kitsch was all the rage. Boys herded cattle toward the
slaughterhouses of Thailand. Young girls gossiped, their fair faces
shaded beneath immense bamboo hats.

The Archbishop arrived, seated under an ornate umbrella in the
back of a blue Toyota flatbed. He was accompanied by a dozen
monks in vivid orange robes, more musicians, and a TRC video
crew. The old man accepted bouquets and stretched his wrinkled
face into a beatific smile.

I climbed the hill to the temple complex, which was a festive
sight. Paper streamers flew from bamboo poles, and Shan national
flags (yellow, red, and green striped with a full white moon at the
center), orange Buddhist flags, and red, white, and blue Thai flags
fluttered. Soldiers lounged in the shade of trees chewing on their
cigars, rifles propped up beside them. Monks of all ages ambled
peacefully by, some carrying big black umbrellas to keep the sun
from burning their shaven pates. Some, the oldest, had limbs blue-
blackened with magic tattoos.

I slept a last night in my corner bed before returning to Chiang Mai.
In that bed I always felt like I was in the upper left-hand corner of
something bewitching. I felt the edge of Thailand, the beginning of
Burma, the Himalayan foothills, one angle of the Golden Triangle.
Surrounded by intrigue and danger, I slept in a safe place. I had
escaped the bad situation the British writer in Chiang Mai had
warned me about. My *songtaow* had passed the lair of *dacoits*
unscathed. The Rangers were no longer in a murderous mood, so
their painted death's heads held no menace. Well-garrisoned Mai

Sung seemed far out of reach of the Tatmadaw. The KMT held back, and Khun Sa had been won over. The streets of the mountain capital were as enchanting as ever, and I was sure I would come back again, no matter what roadblocks appeared.

And yet this Arcadia's enchantment, its ceremonies and processions, obscured the true nature of the bad situation: the unspeakable corruption of the Shans. They had always been romantics. Their literature, their architecture, showed the lofty dreams of an aristocratic past, a golden age of Tai civilization. And who was more corruptible than the romantic? I had begun to comprehend that such fine ideals required some filthy deals to keep them alive. I suspected I was capable of it myself, willing to get really dirty for a fine cause. The TRC showed me just how low you could go. They were buying their precious cultural freedom with heroin, the enslavement of countless others. They were so far from conventional morality, so far above the law, so removed from sordid deaths in squalid cities and even from the starving tribal opium farmers in the mountains just beyond us. How could anyone care about such things when there was the shining dream of the Shan nation to fight for? El Cid and all that. The Land of the Tai.

Safe and warm under thick counterpanes, I slept in my corner bed. I was remote from the rest of the world, in the Shans' own land. Their dreams were my dreams, and I dreamt that their war was my war. Deep in the black night, I awoke for a moment to the sound of bells. The sweet jingling of brass was all that betrayed the passage of a pony caravan, moving through Pieng Luang under cover of darkness.

THE HOME
OF THE
BRAVE

⹀ 1 ⹀

My friends from Pieng Luang and Kawthoolei wrote to me all the time, pages of elegant penciled handwriting that would arrive in thin mud-stained envelopes at my Bangkok house, telling me the news, sending me regards, inviting me back. Even in Bangkok's sensory overload, I found it hard to direct my attention anywhere but Burma's war zone. The border trips to Pieng Luang,

69

Kawthoolei, and Mae Hong Son had taught me the ropes. I could find my own way around on the border, and I knew how to contact the rebels when I crossed it. The Shans and Karens had grown used to foreign visitors who had a look at the war and left, never to be heard from again, but I was addicted to the border and I couldn't turn my back and walk away. I needed the secret world, with its AK-47-toting twelve-year-olds, its refugee schoolmistresses, its warlords. I had to know what they were doing, how they were surviving, who was dealing with whom. My paintings began over-flowing with the border world: the morning market at Pieng Luang, Karens in the night jungle, malaria patients.

I combined my Burma border paintings with my scenes of Bangkok in an art exhibit called "City Streets and Jungle Stories" that opened in Bangkok in April 1985. I was privileged to travel in both spheres: jungle and city, border and gallery, inside and out-side. I decided to go to the U.S. and put together another painting show, with only my Burma frontier pictures, to publicize the people of an Asian conflict unknown to most Americans. Before I left for the States I would penetrate Burma again, making sketches, collect-ing information. If I set off in early June, my Thai visa would give me three months to go from the Karen area west of Kanchanaburi to the Shans' Mai Sung, crisscrossing the Thailand/Burma border as much as possible in between.

The Thai press was running obscure, garbled reports about fighting between the TRC and Karen forces in a valley called Mae Aw, near Mae Hong Son. This development concerned me, and since I knew both groups I thought I might be able to function as some sort of liaison between them. I wanted to help the Burma rebels communicate with each other, as well as with the outside world. I wanted to learn more about their fundamental goals and needs. I would travel the border, seeking the whole picture of conflict as well as pictures to paint.

The main problem with my plan was the season: monsoon rains would deluge my entire route, pounding roads into mud sloughs, making travel hazardous and slow. The rains would also bring out swarms of anopheles mosquitoes bearing the malaria parasite. The

disease had already brought down Spin and he was now in a
Bangkok hospital, raving with cerebral malaria that had infected
him at a Karenni rebel camp on the Pai River near Mae Hong Son. I
brought him flowers and candied pineapple and told him how nice
it was "to see a crazy person get delirious." Much as I loved him, I
didn't really mind that he wouldn't be along on my border trip. An
unspoken kind of rivalry had developed between us. He was used to
competing with other journalists for territory, and I didn't want
him elbowing me aside to get his photographs. Deep down, I
wanted to go places he hadn't been and see things he hadn't
photographed. I had my own camera, an autofocus Minolta. Spin
told me what kind of film to load it with. He also said, "Blade, it's
dangerous up there. Bring your knife."

I always carried my folding Kershaw lock knife with me. I also
had an army surplus poncho, a pair of Wellington-type rubber
boots, and malaria pills galore (the chloroquine and Fansidar that
had kept the disease at bay without side effects so far). Now all I
needed was a map.

I went to Siam Square, a shopping center with excellent book-
stores, but I could not find a decent map of the border. The stores
sold tourist maps of Thailand, showing points of interest and cross-
country routes, but the area surrounding Thailand was blank white
space. I settled for one that at least showed the rivers—the Tenasserim, the Salween, the Moei, the Pai—that crossed the border.
Thailand was colored pink, green, and orange, while the surrounding terra incognita, including Burma, was bright purple. It would
have to do.

I stopped in at Mister Donut for a couple of double-chocolate
doughnuts, anticipating weeks of chocolate deprivation to come.
Alistair, a friend who taught English at a nearby school, joined me,
and I told him about the search for a map.

"But it's really quite romantic to go off to a place without maps,
isn't it?" he commented.

"I suppose so," I said, "but I'd prefer more detail. This is useless. I can't even tell if there's a road from Three Pagodas Pass to
Mae Sot."

"Three Pagodas Pass—now that's a romantic name. At least that's on the map."

"The Karen rebels are at Three Pagodas Pass, and so are a group called the Mons, who are related to the Cambodians. So I'll find out what they're like and what they're fighting for."

= 2 =

My trip did not get off to a good start. Thinking like a Shan, I would have called it inauspicious. I had written to Daniel, the education official I had met in Kawthoolei, telling him I would be returning, and he had written back, saying he'd meet me when my bus arrived in Kanchanaburi. But when I arrived, a young Karen man handed me a letter from Daniel that informed me he had gone to Bangkok for a few days. However, the sons of a Karen official would bring me over the border with them. If I wished to travel by river in Kawthoolei, perhaps I could buy some gasoline for the boat while I was in Kanchanaburi. (In the rainy season, boat travel was the best way to cover jungle distances.)

The young man who'd met me and his two brothers had a Jeep. Despite Daniel's recommendation, they charged me for the trip, and at an exorbitant rate. The taxi fare, along with three big containers of gasoline for the boat, wiped out half of my cash. But I didn't haggle or protest because I assumed they were representing the Karen rebels and that I was supposed to cover expenses, since I was going along for the ride.

After they drove around town loading the Jeep with supplies (rope, cloth, lanterns, tins of biscuits), we drove west into the mountains that separated Thailand from Burma. We climbed, engine straining, until we reached a jungle trail that led to a sawmill owned by my guides' father. The mill was set tightly in a canyon of mud. My guides, who spoke little English, explained that the Jeep needed engine work and we would spend the night there before heading on to Daniel's village.

We drove to a large teak house with a broad porch. Adjacent was a tin-roofed shed where sparks flew from the saw that cut jungle hardwood into planks for Thai purchase. The driver's young wife welcomed me from the porch, saying, "Please come up." I took off my muddy boots, and we sat drinking tea and looking at framed photographs of the boys' father, a Karen politician, meeting with various rebel leaders.

"He leaves the boys here to take care of the family business while he is in important meetings," the driver's wife said. "Now he is at Mae Aw because of the problems there." The father was a representative of the National Democratic Front, an alliance of rebel groups. He was a revolutionary diplomat traveling the war zone. Meanwhile, his sons were sawing the jungle into veneer with desperate zeal, trying to make enough money to get out and stay out of the war zone. The revolution had been going on since 1949; I could understand how some third-generation Karens might not be as gung ho about it as the first two.

The family had prepared a room for me, spraying it liberally with Shelltox insecticide and illuminating it with Bear Brand Tropical Candles. The war zone lacked electricity except for the few generators that mostly powered rebel sawmills. My bed, a mattress on the smooth wood floor, had wool blankets for the night cold, and my hosts had placed a loaded carbine near it, in case I had the urge to shoot something or someone during the night. In Kawthoolei, every room, every vehicle, had a firearm of some sort available.

It rained intermittently all the next morning. The Jeep engine resisted repair. Goats tiptoed through mud and sawdust. A pair of fuzzy black gibbons played in the porch rafters. I studied the NDF photographs, intrigued by rebel groups not yet encountered: Wa, Pa-O, Kachin. Other wall decorations were a broken grenade launcher and some posters of the poker-playing dogs indulging in their anthropomorphic antics. The poker-playing dogs genre of art was also popular in Thailand, especially in Buddhist monasteries, where the posters served to show the debasing effects of vice.

When the sun came out and the Jeep was fixed, we made the hour's drive to the village where Daniel and Naomi lived. Naomi met me at the school. The Jeep was parked down the road, and I watched a small crowd gather around it. My guides began selling the goods they'd bought in Kanchanaburi.

"They are the traveling shop," Naomi said as we walked over to her unpainted wooden house, which stood on five-foot stilts in a muddy garden of banana trees and pumpkin vines. "They charge a lot."

"I noticed," I said. "Cab fare here was a little steep."

Naomi looked aghast. "They charged you money? They weren't supposed to! They make the trip all the time, for their own business."

"Well, I got here and I have enough gasoline for a river trip, that's all that matters. It was only a little bit of money. It's nothing." I had acquired the Southeast Asian habit of the inverted *kvetch*: The more something upset one, the more vociferously one would deny that it mattered at all.

Naomi improvised an elegant dinner from jungle flowers and pumpkin vines. Kawthoolei's cooks had the knack of turning weeds and odd bits of vegetables into what sold in California as nouvelle cuisine. Creations like vegetable tempura and sweet pumpkin consommé turned up on everyday tables where poverty made meat scarce. Kawthoolei was the refuge and experiment of a whole class of educated urban Karens who had (in university or just afterward) come to realize that they could no longer live in Ne Win's captive nation. Arrest and torture convinced some; for others it was a lack of employment opportunities. It was hard enough for ethnic Burmese to get decent jobs; for ethnic minorities it was close to impossible.

The strange wartime merger of Karen doctors and engineers from Rangoon or Moulmein with Karen farmers and jungle hunters had led to the rise of utopian communities along the border like Daniel and Naomi's village. The city Karens tried to improve crop yields, housing, health care, education; the jungle Karens taught basic survival. It was all done in the name of the revolution, one Karen nation under God, part of a theoretical federal system with the rest of the NDF—but autonomous forever.

As we ate our dinner, we heard a Bible-study group in the schoolhouse reading the Good Samaritan story in English. I was wearing a khaki shirt and camouflage trousers, which had been a punk fashion statement when I'd bought them in San Francisco years before. Now I blended in not only with the tribe but also with its architecture.

"I like the camouflage on the schoolhouse," I said, thinking it was just a macho paint job for its own sake.

"We did it because of an air raid four years ago," Naomi said. "Some visitors think we painted it only for morale. The planes have never come back, but of course they could."

"How many planes attacked here?" I added hot water from a red-enameled Chinese thermos to the Nescafé in our glasses.

"Three planes came. I got the frequency they used, tuning it in on my radio set as they flew over the next village. I heard the men in the lead plane shouting, 'This is not the target! This is not the target!' and I realized that *my* village was the target. I grabbed my baby and ran into the jungle. This was when Simon was very little. The whole village was running and hiding in the jungle. You cannot imagine how fast our village can run and hide unless you've seen it happen! The planes came back and fired machine guns on the houses."

Naomi pushed a strand of her lank, sun-browned hair back, and spoke rapidly. "I lay down on the ground under the jungle leaves with my body covering Simon. I just waited for a bullet to hit me. I thought, now a bullet is going to go into my back. It was all over in a few minutes and after the planes went away we found bullets everywhere. Tomorrow I will show you where the bullets went through my schoolhouse."

"Were there any casualties?"

"By a miracle, nobody got killed. But I was so afraid anyway. I could not bear to stay in my house during the day, when the planes could see to attack, so every morning before sunrise I took a boat across the river with my baby, to hide in the jungle. I only came

back at night. After a week I decided it was safe to stay in the
village. That night little Simon cried out, 'Mama, I can't sleep, the
house has a big snake under it.' I thought it was only his imagination, but I got a flashlight and looked under the house and there it
was. He must have seen it moving through the cracks in the floor. It
was a python, as long as this room." The room was nine feet across,
not an uncommon length for a Burmese python. "When I saw the
snake I screamed, and some men came and killed it. Daniel was
away at Manerplaw, Karen central headquarters. One of the men
who killed the snake was a teacher from my school. Very soon after,
this teacher got typhoid fever, and instead of crazy things he spoke
the truth. He said he was a spy for the Tatmadaw and he had tried
to kill my son by putting him in a well—but some people came
along so he had to stop, and he had called in the Burmese air raid by
sending out a message on one of our own radios. He said two other
spies lived in the village, and he named them."

"What happened to the spies?"

"They almost escaped, but our soldiers captured them. When
they were executed by gunshots, the two bled very much. All the
blood ran and ran from the bullet holes. But the other one, the man
who killed the snake, he did not bleed at all." Naomi stared into the
milky bottom of her glass. "Since then there have been no more air
raids. Everything is camouflaged."

Simon was already asleep in Naomi's bedroom as she went in,
holding a candle. I slept in a bamboo-walled guest room that had
been added on after the main wooden house was built. An M-16
and a pair of carbines hung on the wall within reach of my
mosquito net–draped bed. The pillowcase was embroidered: "I
Will Praise the Lord." Fireflies blinked around the room.

In the morning a hundred Karen schoolchildren mustered in front
of the bullet-pocked schoolhouse.

Naomi said, "The teachers are very happy that you've come to
our place on your visit to the revolutionary groups, and they ask
that you will make a speech for the students, something for their
morale. I will translate, if you don't mind."

After singing the Karen national anthem, the children stood at attention while I addressed them.

"I have come from very far away, from America, to be here with you, the children of Kawthoolei," I began. "Sometimes you might feel alone because of suffering and oppression, but you are not alone. Even as far away as America, you have friends who care about you. The courage and faith of the Karen people are a shining inspiration to the whole world." Then I talked a bit about Valley Forge, how the American rebels were so poor that they wore rags on their feet in the snow, but they survived and won against the oppressors anyway. And I told them how grateful I was to be a guest in their beautiful country, Kawthoolei. The teachers broke into loud applause when I finished and the children followed suit. I took my tentative first few Minolta pictures of them.

Of course the rest of the world did not care about the Karens at all. Burma was neutral and its civil war was beneath the interest of the superpowers. The outside world's attitude about the three-generation war was "let it bleed." The war zone had no Red Cross relief, no UNICEF aid. A few missionaries cared about the long-since-converted Karens, as did some intrepid French and British doctors. Thai-Chinese dealers in teak and tin ore cared about Kawthoolei's resources. But to the rest of the world, the war in Kawthoolei was as unknown as snow was to the jungle school-children.

While Naomi taught classes and supervised teachers, I sat in a beach chair in the open front room of her house, reading Lucien Bodard's memoir of Yunnan and Indochina, *Le Fils du Conseul*, in French. I had brought books in French because my French reading was slow, so the books would last longer, cutting down on book weight. But I hadn't brought a French dictionary, so I skipped lots of words and wound up reading just as fast as I would have in English. I welcomed the interruption when some soldier-teachers came by to talk.

Communications problems within Kawthoolei were severe, they told me. This district, the southernmost part of Burma that stretched way down along the Tenasserim River, was a month's jungle march from Karen headquarters at Manerplaw. Military command was ill coordinated, especially during the monsoon. In the past, war came to a virtual standstill in the rainy season, but in recent years the Tatmadaw kept up attacks all year round. Decades ago, Ne Win had sworn to "exterminate" the Karens (perhaps meaning just the rebels), and their continued existence seemed a personal affront to him. He had seized power pledging to return the whole country to law and order, but these tribal ruffians defied him just by hanging on in the mountains.

A gentle teacher in a commando beret said, "We will hold off the Tatmadaw militarily, we always have. The real difficulty is the economic situation. The price of tin is down so low. Karen government did not expect this, so we have no reserve currency, not even reserve rice. Very hard to get ammunition because our black market currency is exhausted. We try to sell our corn in Thailand, and our cashew nuts and honey from jungle bees. But now everything here goes to feed the refugees who keep arriving more and more. The Tatmadaw make press-gang sweeps through villages before launching their offensives. People fear for their lives and run to our revolutionary place. When we had money from tin, we could take care of all. Now our Karen government can only give rice and salt to the refugees." The Karen revolution was running on empty.

Daniel arrived in the evening. Daniel, the dedicated revolutionary, the raconteur, the connoisseur of the bizarre who read *Soldier of Fortune* and got upset when the facts were wrong, who showed me the "weird tribes" in his mildewed copies of *National Geographic*. He arrived with a handful of tiny plastic robots for Simon and great enthusiasm for my river trip.

"We'll take the boat upstream," he said. "Some refugees are living near the front line and I want to count their children and tell the parents they can send them to school here. I'll show you the route on your map."

I unfolded my Thai map. Daniel laughed and said, "That is no bloody map for your mission! It shows the river but nothing else—a big purple nothing! Wait a minute." He ducked into the bedroom and emerged with a silk map that had belonged to some World War II aviator. As I spread it open, I was suddenly transported into a page from *Terry and the Pirates*. The map was foxed with a few brown blotches, but was clearly legible. Daniel pointed out roads built by prisoners of the Japanese imperial forces (now paths that ran beside the river) and showed me villages and places where river rapids disrupted travel.

"The river is high now, and good for boating, but parts are extremely turbulent. Can you swim?"

"Not well."

"I can't swim at all. If the worst happens and the boat tips over, just grab the side and hang on. But don't worry, we'll have excellent crewmen."

I showed Daniel my planned route north from Kawthoolei. He gave me the names of Karens to visit near Three Pagodas Pass and in Mae Sot. He told me I would probably have to backtrack through Thailand, perhaps all the way to Bangkok, to get from Three Pagodas Pass to Mae Sot, because no border roads between the two were usable in the rainy season.

"You can borrow this map for the rest of your mission," Daniel told me. Thrilled with it, I folded the soft silk map and put it in my shirt pocket.

The longer I spent around the Burma war zone, the more interested I became in World War II's China-Burma-India theater of operations. "The war in Burma *is* World War II," I often told people who required a simple explanation of what it was all about. "The Karens and other tribes backed the British and Americans against the Japanese invaders. The Burmese had helped the Japanese, thinking it would be a good way to get rid of the British colonists. The war supposedly ended. The Japanese left, the Americans left, even the British left—but the Burmese and the ethnic minorities kept right on fighting." Burma had always had ethnic rivalries, but outright warfare had stopped until World War II brought it all boiling to the surface again. Everything that had happened since—military takeover of the government, the collapse of the economy, the rise of drug warlords—was all part of the ongoing frontier war.

In the war zone, I felt more like my parents' generation than my own. There, people thought of an American as a friendly Yank soldier helping them to drive away invaders. The only books that spoke of the conditions I was observing in the eighties were about the legendary Allied/tribal units like Merrill's Marauders and the Chindits from World War II. The insurgents' Byzantine schemes and power plays sent me into the dark atmosphere of Milt Caniff's pirates.

Simon had been sent home sick from the primary school and was awake all night, fevered and vomiting. A medic came over from the small hospital on the edge of the village to check on his condition. In the morning, Simon played with his new robots, but he refused to eat. Naomi started giving him spoonfuls of an elixir called Woodward's Grippe Water and everyone hoped the boy wasn't having a malaria attack. Kawthoolei was a great place for the disease. Many of the Karens living in the mountains were from the Irrawaddy Delta and Burma's coastal towns and they lacked the resistance of the jungle Karens. After the first infection, the parasites could stay dormant in the bloodstream and recur spontaneously, producing fever seemingly from nowhere, sapping strength. Also highly susceptible was the Tatmadaw. Burmese soldiers were hit so hard by malaria that mosquitoes were known as "the Karen Air Force." I often wondered how so many people could be sick all the time and still manage to fight a war.

Rain pelted down. We stared at the rain. "We'll leave in a day or two," Daniel guessed. I read *Le Fils*. Daniel went into the rain for meetings with teachers. When he returned, we drank border coffee.

"I don't like the fighting at Mae Aw," I said. "If the outside world perceives this war as a pack of squabbling factions, they're going to continue to ignore it. And that means the Ne Win government will continue to be accepted as legitimate. Obviously everyone can't be really unified and agree all the time, but I'd think outright battles could be avoided. It's a big waste of men and arms and makes everybody look bad."

"The action at Mae Aw," Daniel said, stirring murky clouds of milk in his border coffee, "is because of the Wa. The Wa were serving as the KMT soldiers, escorting their drug caravans on a very good trade route that goes from Taunggyi to Mae Aw. Khun Sa's TRC got fighting the KMT over that route. Since Wa soldiers were involved, and the Wa are part of our NDF alliance, we Karens had to go and help the Wa."

"So the Karens are in the position of helping the KMT drug army, even though the Karens have never had anything to do with the drug trade . . ."

"I'll admit it's uncomfortable. But it's good to fight Khun Sa. That man never fights the Tatmadaw, he is only interested in attacking other groups so he can move his drugs around on new routes."

"Well, I *have* noticed that since Khun Sa came into the TRC, all the Tatmadaw attacks on Mo Heing's army seem to have fizzled out. But maybe that's just because the Burmese are afraid of the TRC's increased troop strength."

Daniel chuckled. "Don't you know about the Ka Kwe Ye?"

"Not much. A kind of government defense force. What does that have to do with Mae Aw?"

"Ne Win started the Ka Kwe Ye in the 1960s to get the Shan State warlords on his side. He got the big men to promise not to fight the Tatmadaw and in exchange they could keep order in their own areas. That meant they could have their own armies for trading drugs. They just had to pay the Tatmadaw a percentage. Khun Sa was a Ka Kwe Ye man, and so was Maha Seng, who is the leader of the NDF Wa group now. Maha Seng has come over to the revolutionary side, but Khun Sa still plays his game with the Tatmadaw."

"Maybe now that he's joined with Mo Heing, he might get into the revolution, too."

"You'll see. As you continue on your mission, you may see the situation. Khun Sa is a trickster. Sometimes it looks like he will change. He makes his patrons angry—Thais throw him out, Burmese arrest him. But he always bounces back. We can forgive that he trades in drugs. We understand how it happens when the poppies are all over the place and they need money. We Karens live where the poppy doesn't grow, and we have tin and teak instead. What we do not forgive is that Khun Sa will help the Tatmadaw instead of fighting it."

"It sounds like the Wa are caught in the middle of all this. The wild card in the war."

"They are wild, all right. We had some in our district; they must have run away from a KMT camp in the north. They were lost and our soldiers took away their guns—Taiwan rifles—and gave them food and blankets. Then we got a message from Manerplaw that they were from the NDF Wa group, so we gave them back their weapons. They joined us for a battle against the Tatmadaw. The Wa held one hill, Karens held two others. At night we saw the Wa men dragging logs up the hill. Well done, we thought: fortification. Then we found it was not fortification—they were making a big bonfire. They danced around it. Those Wa don't care about anything, but they scare the Tatmadaw!"

After three days, the rain let up enough for the boat trip. We embarked at noon in a narrow craft powered by an Izusu truck motor. The Tenasserim River writhed past thick jungle fringed with tall plumes of free bamboo. Rising water engulfed trees at the banks. Our boatman, a middle-aged man with a canny smile, was an ace navigator. A teenage soldier perched on the bow to call out warnings of obstacles ahead. His left hand was wrapped with iodine-stained gauze. He sat stiffly, diverting his concentration from the river only to blow his nose through the bandage once in a while. The rest of the boating party consisted of me, Daniel, and the bow boy's sister. The sister didn't speak English, but I learned that her name was Rebecca and that she was a student nurse who would distribute malaria medicine to refugees along the river.

Cruising the Tenasserim, eased back on a pile of supplies and weapons, I was comfortable except for an M-16 stock that jabbed between my shoulder blades no matter how I shifted. We traveled at a perfect speed: not too slow to lose a sense of urgency, not too fast to observe the jungle shoreline. Black-and-white hornbills took flight from tall dipterocarps as we passed by. The boat's motor buzzed steadily. We rode quietly, alert, waiting for what each turn in the river would bring.

Our first stop was an old Karen village beside the World War II road. We walked up a muddy path from the river and crossed an open square where cows grazed in front of a white wood-frame church. Daniel pointed to a flagpole. "The Japanese left that when they retreated," he said. "Now the villagers fly the Karen flag. The monument next to it is to Karen soldiers who died in the struggle against the Burmese chauvinist government." He led the way up the steps of a wooden building that stood among the village's bamboo houses. "We will put up for the night in this Karen government office," he announced.

Rebecca and I went to a bamboo raft near the boat to bathe. In Southeast Asia, a daily bath was considered a necessity. It refreshed, cooled off the day's heat, and with generous applications of powder (Johnson's baby powder, medicated talc, or ground *thanaka* wood) kept jungle rot at bay.

Balanced precariously on the raft, I slipped a blue sarong over my military clothes. The cloth tube of the sarong covered everything as I slipped out of what I'd been wearing all day. I held the sarong with my teeth to unzip my trousers. Rebecca went through the same procedure and, finished, we knotted our sarongs under our armpits. The river was too deep to stand in, so we leaned off the raft and scooped up water with plastic bowls. We scrubbed away grime and rinsed with the cool brownish water. We washed our hair with Sunsilk and toweled off. I wrapped a red sarong around myself and I dropped the wet blue one. I put on a clean shirt, wrapped the top of the red sarong around my waist, and headed back up the bank to the village. Rebecca, now in a dry light blue sarong, lost her balance leaving the raft and grabbed the still-hot exhaust pipe of our boat engine. She swore (however a Karen Baptist girl swears) as an angry scarlet welt marred her palm. At the office building, a soldier painted her burn with gentian violet and bandaged it. Rebecca held her purple-stained bandage next to her brother's red gauze one and they laughed.

We boaters went to a Karen official's house where we ate dinner in the dark when our candles started attracting flying bugs. The Karens ate their rice and curries with their right hands, but a tin spoon and fork were laid out for my use. Back in the office building, benches and tables were pushed out of the way. I had a bed (a wooden platform with a mosquito net) while the others slept on the floor, lined up against the wall. For some reason I dreamed I was Snow White.

The songs of soldier boys woke me, soprano war chants. Naomi had told me that primary education was compulsory in Kawthoolei, but as soon as it finished at age twelve or so, many boys immediately joined the army. I had seen soldiers even younger than that, strange children of eight or nine, cool-eyed cigar smokers. They were said to be war orphans, fierce in combat.

When we left the village we brought another crew member with us, a young soldier who wore a green plastic necklace with his patched uniform. It rained all day, and the new boy bailed water from the boat. We sheltered ourselves and the supplies with ponchos and sheets of green vinyl. The bow boy, with a cape of plastic around his shoulders, shivered and sneezed as the boatman steered us over a stretch of rapids.

The seesawing river smoothed out after a couple of hours, and we stopped where a big teak house was visible from the boat. The people in the riverside village collected tin from the Karen mines to sell in Thailand. When the price of tin boomed, they had built fancy wooden houses with carved porticoes. Now there was no money. The villagers went hungry in their fine teak houses. Their children no longer went to school, and they fought with each other and screamed. Their good Thai clothes were now tattered and their hair was cut off in anti-lice crew cuts.

That night, Daniel and I drank the Nescafé we'd brought with us and he chewed betel nut. The juicy red wad in his mouth didn't stifle his recitation of disillusionment. His revolution didn't understand him. The Karen leaders were old men, unresponsive to Daniel's generation.

"Our leaders are honest and moral, but they have forgotten good strategy," Daniel said and leaned over a teak railing to spit excess betel juice into the yard below. "They use trench warfare with pitched battles. They do not listen to anyone who tells them we need guerilla warfare, sabotage. To them it is not proper war. So we are the big stalemate, only fighting to survive. I tell you, we can't win if we stay in our trenches. The old men at headquarters say 'Not to lose is to win.' They are wrong. Look at this place. What kind of future is here?"

"What do you think is going to happen?"

"Oh, we will win," Daniel said with frozen optimism. "But not yet. The next generation to fight this war will get it right. The *fourth* generation."

It rained all night and in the morning it was still raining. I had mosquito bites. The children ran around the house pounding the teak floors and each other. Scruffy black pigs rooted in the yard. I drank coffee and ate broken, gummy rice for breakfast. At noon we got back on the river, which was rising into flood, and the rain felt cold. The boat walloped over the rapids in the downpour. Hours passed by in a green haze.

In the afternoon, the river thrust up waves and whirlpools, roaring until it drowned out the noise of our engine. We stared fixedly ahead. Only the boatman was smiling. I realized that if we capsized, swimming would be impossible. Not even the strongest would survive. But at the same time I savored the roller coaster ride and the lush jungle and even the rain in my face. The bow boy shouted and waved his bandaged hand, sighting a rushing vortex like a tunnel in our path. We hastily pulled ashore.

Our stop turned out to be the new refugee settlement. The Tatmadaw occupied their old village, a few miles upriver, on the other side of the vortex. About a dozen families had sought refuge in the small jungle clearing. Rain glistened on the palm-thatched roofs of their bamboo huts. The old, established village they'd abandoned two months before had boasted schools, a church, a Baptist library, and orchards. Now they huddled in a dank glade by the flooding river. They had left their year's stock of rice when the Tatmadaw approached their village. The jungle wasn't going to give them anything easily.

We unloaded bags of rice and salt for them. Rebecca gave out malaria tablets. The refugees—women, children, and old men— were in the jaws of the fever diseases: malaria, dengue, typhoid. The young men were all off fighting near the occupied village. Camouflage clothing hung on bamboo walls, uniforms awaiting husbands who might not return alive. The children were cleaner and healthier than those at the tin-smuggling post, but how long could that last? A couple of weeks before, one of the giant trees had fallen and crushed a little boy to death. As soon as we arrived, Daniel began arranging for some of the children to come to his village as boarding students. They showed him, with charcoal on scraps of rice bags, how well they could read and write. Daniel would send boats back to fetch them. Their mothers looked grateful—the children would be safe.

We stayed in the hut farthest from the shore. It belonged to an emaciated man in his seventies and his family. The old man lit a kerosene lantern and we talked above the sound of heavy rain.

"We Karens have always been afraid of the Burmese," he said, his voice creaking, his hands trembling. "When the Tatmadaw came this last time, we took only the first things we could touch. The lantern, a small ax, this pullover. I had to leave my Bible and hymn book. Disgraceful. We ran to the river and took boats across. The whirlpools were too strong to go downriver by boat, so we walked through the jungle to this place. The Tatmadaw can come at any time, so my daughters are afraid. Still, we are happy that you have come to see us. Perhaps you could photograph us, to show the outside world how we are stranded here."

"Will you be safe from the river here?" I asked.

"Soon we must try to find a better place," the old man said. "If we can send the small children to the safe school, we can go into the jungle again and start a new place, plant orchards, build another church."

We headed back the next day so Daniel could dispatch boats to pick up the refugee children. I spent a few more days in Daniel and Naomi's village, waiting for transportation out. The sawmill guys were otherwise occupied (not that I could afford them), and all the other Jeeps were in complete disrepair.

I read Daniel's old copies of *Soldier of Fortune* and *Newsweek*. I could feel a cold coming on. Simon was still sick, still being dosed with Woodward's Grippe Water. Daniel had a slight fever and took a gumball-sized Chinese pill that came in its own little box with a label promising that it cured amnesia as well as fevers. From meal to meal, Naomi served tender green pumpkin vines—deep-fried, stir-fried, boiled, braised, breaded and in soup. Daniel slew a scorpion with a pair of pliers. I watched an anopheles mosquito whose legs were caught in candle wax struggle as the flame approached it.

Eventually Daniel and another man got a Jeep started and we rode a few kilometers to a rushing stream that we had to ford on foot. Another Jeep was waiting, conveniently enough, on the other side. Daniel started it up with great difficulty. We skidded through thick mud all the way to the Karen district headquarters that I'd visited before with Bryant. I noticed that some new houses had been built there: extremely nice teak chalets, mostly two stories, with walls placed at unusual angles and interestingly set-in windows. Inside I saw lofts and high ceilings and real staircases with carved railings.

I visited the region's commander, a colonel, to report on my "mission" (as Daniel had me calling it). I told him I would be learning about the situation of the groups on the border so I could help to inform the outside world and also enhance communication among the rebel groups themselves.

"Very good," the colonel said. "It's a very good idea." He wrote

out a laissez-passer in Karen script on flimsy paper and endorsed it
with his signature and an official Karen Army rubber stamp. It
identified me by age and nationality, and said that I was allowed to
enter Kawthoolei freely and should be accorded whatever help I
needed for my mission. It made me feel very official.

That night I stayed at the house of the district governor, who was
away in Mae Sot on teak business. On a table in his spacious, airy
living room I found the explanation for his headquarters' interesting architecture: a copy of *Building Vacation Homes and Cabins*
(published by California's *Sunset* magazine). In it were the plans for
all the chalets. The Karens are nothing if not adaptable, I thought.
They build cabins suitable for Tahoe or Vail at their rebel stronghold. They grow American pumpkins in the jungle and turn them
into Karen cuisine. They have American Jeeps and American
hymns, and they transform it all with the culture of their own tribe,
unique on the face of the earth.

⌐ 3 ⌐

To get to Three Pagodas Pass I went first by truck from the
Kawthoolei border back to Kanchanaburi, where I then caught a
bus to Thongpaphum. The Karens went inside Thailand to get
from one part of Kawthoolei to another, as there were no decent
roads on the Burma side. Thongpaphum was a misty little town
whose one main street was lined with shops selling goods for black
marketeers to bring into Burma. I stayed overnight in the shabby
wooden hotel, in a room overlooking the street. A tiny note in
English was glued to the door: "Don't carely fire in a this room."

I was the first passenger to show up for the morning *songtaow* to
Sangklaburi. I had my usual Thai breakfast of rice soup and iced
Coke while the driver waited for more passengers to show up.
Being first, I nabbed the coveted shotgun seat. Five miles out of

Thongpaphum, the pavement ended. The landslides had narrowed the road and the mud was bad. Hours after grinding through deeper and deeper ruts, we finally came to a large concrete bridge.

The Thai driver informed me that the government of Thailand had finished building a huge dam at Sangklaburi about a year ago. The old town had ended up underwater so the residents relocated to a new version of Sangklaburi, built on bluffs high above the flood plain. They'd been compensated financially for their old homes. Some used the payments to open shops in the new Sangklaburi; others had gambled it away.

"My *songtaow* can't go any farther," the driver said. "All passengers must please go by boat now."

Our motorboat moved carefully through the weird flood zone that was once the town of Sangklaburi. The yellow tops of rotting palm trees poked up from the murky water. Maybe this is what the jungle boat ride at Disneyland is like, I thought, never having been there. A gigantic Buddhist monument rose from a far shore—a *chedi,* not Thai, not quite Khmer in style. I aimed my Minolta at it. "Mon people are building that," the boatman said. We drew closer and I discerned bamboo construction scaffolding around a pyramidal brick tower.

Just after the boat passed the Mon temple, the new town of Sangklaburi appeared: bamboo huts, teak houses, and concrete shophouses laid-out across bluffs rising high from the flood, with a rain-swept panorama of Burma's border mountains for a backdrop. From Sangklaburi I went (as directed by Daniel) to visit a family of Karen Baptist missionaries. This required another *songtaow* ride on another crumbling mud road. They welcomed me with coffee and curry, a hot bath (water heated on a wood fire; there was no electricity yet in their border village), and a soft bed with white linens and a mosquito net. And more kindness and interesting conversation than any traveler dare hope for.

The family of Karen missionaries had been involved in politics in Burma and was in exile on the Thai side of the border under threat of assassination. The patriarch's grandson had just joined the Karen army. The older family members spread the gospel and dispensed medical care to Karens and Mons from both sides of the border. Their houses were full of English-language books and newspapers. Dressed in a sarong and British Army pullover, the patriarch sat in his sling chair. He kept busy using a red pen to underline passages in the Bible that struck his fancy. He showed me the business cards of journalists who'd visited him en route to Three Pagodas Pass. "I ask them to keep the names of my family a secret," he told me. "Burmese spies come and shoot at our house sometimes."

Another veteran of the revolution came to the patriarch's house for coffee. Uncle Benny was a big man in his sixties with a dignified bearing and a terribly mischievous glint in his eye. "Do you want to hear the story about the rhinoceros?" he asked me.

"Of course, Uncle Benny, please tell me."

"Deep in the dark forest inside Kawthoolei, not long ago at all, one man saw the tracks of the rhinoceros." Uncle Benny's voice became a hoarse whisper. "Big, deep tracks. Must be one big rhinoceros, the man thinks. He keeps walking. Then he sees a tree the rhinoceros had rubbed against. Marks show very high up on this tree where he rubbed his hide. Must be one tall rhinoceros, the man thinks. But it wasn't just the broken bark there, but gold dust! High up on the tree, gold dust. The rhinoceros, his hide was covered with gold dust because he had been in a stream that was full of gold. Do you believe me?"

"Yes, of course," I said. Uncle Benny's stories always included places where he'd pause and check to see if you still believed, I was to learn.

"We Karens got to find that rhinoceros now. If we can find him, then we will find the stream of gold. With this gold we can buy heavier artillery and surface-to-air missiles. And helicopter gunships. What we need to win the war."

It was too wet for the Karens to be out searching for gold-dusted rhinos, so I didn't join their El Dorado hunt. I stayed for several days and it never stopped raining. I wanted to hike through the mountains to Three Pagodas Pass, but as long as it rained there was no way out of the village by foot or even truck. I was coughing badly, trying to deny (to medical missionaries) that I had bronchitis.

Three Pagodas Pass obsessed me. The name alone was wonderful and it was the point where World War II's River Kwai "Death Railway" crossed into Burma from Thailand. The railway had been forced through the jungle by the Japanese at a cost of thousands of lives: Allied prisoners of war and enslaved local peasants. A narrow-gauged track still ran out of Kanchanaburi and trains still crossed a trestle over the river, to the delight of tour-busloads, but the functioning line now ended well before Thongpaphum and Three Pagodas Pass.

Three Pagodas Pass was not in the guidebooks. It was a black market Wild West town, always ready to erupt in violent conflict: Karens and Mons against the Tatmadaw, Karens against Mons, Mons against Mons. In the dry winter season just past, the Tatmadaw had approached within a few kilometers of Three Pagodas' bazaar and shelled it. Although they were driven back, the area still was not considered secure. Tourists didn't often go there, but the border watchers did, and they savored the experience like gourmets discovering a great little restaurant hidden in the French countryside.

It kept raining and I kept coughing, the fist of bronchitis clenched in my lungs. I drank Nescafé, talked to everyone I could, and read books about the Karens written in the 1920s (when British authors cared about them). The Karens asked me about other rebels of the world: Tibetans, Moros of the Philippines, the IRA, the Kurds. Armenia came up, and the patriarch asserted that Mount Ararat was located in Armenia. When one of his daughters challenged this fact, he went off and came back with a *National Geographic* map of biblical lands to prove his point. It was just like being back home with my own bookish family.

After I had been in the village for a week, it stopped raining and a big-wheeled *songtaow* returned me to Sangklaburi. The next day I took a *songtaow* to the Songklia River. The rest of the journey to Three Pagodas Pass had to be made on foot. I crossed the river on a pontoon bridge of lashed-together bamboo. A collection of dirt-floored shacks waited on the other side for anyone who wanted to change Thai currency for Burmese kyat (or vice versa) over a glass of Burmese tea. I kept walking a mud path that led across a logging road into the jungle. Smuggling porters carried loads in both directions. When the path forked I asked one of them which way went to "Chedi," using the Thai word for pagoda.

About twenty minutes from the river, I caught up with a nonporter who was walking to "Chedi." A Thai, he was wearing a counterfeit Dior golf shirt, a golf hat, and a Karen sarong. By way of introduction he produced from his Shan shoulder bag an identification card. He flashed it so quickly I didn't have time to read it, but I did get a look at his photo in a full-dress uniform with a chest full of medals. That didn't mean anything: Thailand was uniform happy and even the postmen had campaign ribbons. But this was no civil servant. He had served in the Vietnam War, he said, and more recently on the Thailand/Cambodia border, where he could still occasionally fight Vietnamese. Rolling up his shirtsleeve he showed me a cobra tattoo. Above the snake, English letters spelled out "QUEENS COBRAS." Snakeman was built like a brick facility, so there was room for the entire phrase in large print across his right bicep. The Queen's Cobras had been the original Thai combat force sent to Vietnam.

Snakeman, as I called him, told me he was going up to Three Pagodas Pass to "check on something," and he hadn't been there before either. He didn't ask me why I was going, but he seemed to know. He said, "I'm pleased to walk with someone who knows the hill tribes around here." I could tell he was a Thai Army Intelligence officer. The golf shirt was the dead giveaway, like an FBI man's shiny black shoes. Mufti-clad Thai intelligence operatives sported this studied casual look. They would hang around with insurgents in the jungle in the shirts they wore to play golf back at their Thai Army bases.

We slogged through the mud. I was wearing my rubber boots, which helped. Snakeman took off his rubber sandals, which would have been swallowed up, and hitched up his sarong. We climbed straight up a spongy hill, where you had to pull your whole leg out of the mud each time you put your foot down, and at the top was a small Mon village. Teak houses faced what had probably been a road in the dry season but was now a mud gully. Slowly we followed narrow footpaths that had been tamped down on the sides of it. After the village, the gully became a road again, laced with streams that we crossed on stepping stones. We kept up as quick a pace as possible, trying to reach Three Pagodas Pass before it started to rain again.

I was relieved to have Snakeman's company because of my lousy sense of direction. The previous winter I had gotten horribly lost on an afternoon's jungle walk in Malaysia's Cameron Highlands. I had wandered in circles, enjoying the natural splendor so much that I inadvertently managed to climb the same small mountain twice, and I was utterly disoriented until I emerged by chance in the garden of a hotel at dusk. The Cameron Highlands was where Jim Thompson, the legendary OSS man who had revived the Thai silk industry, had gone for a stroll on Easter afternoon in 1967 and had disappeared without a trace. So I had joked that on my hike I hadn't found Thompson but I'd found what happened to him—he was still climbing and reclimbing the same mountain.

In Three Pagodas Pass the path was arched with green bamboo, and limestone mountains jutted above. Three hours after the Song-klia River, Snakeman and I reached the Thai border post. Through an eccentricity of geography, the post stood on a piece of Thailand that extended—a small peninsula—into Burma. We had been walking through Burma since the river. I said good-bye to Snakeman there, and continued on.

⌐ 4 ⌐

Three pagodas were visible next to the Thai Army post. They were no more than seven feet tall, the three of them all lined up in a row looking just like white Parcheesi counters. I had expected something more along the lines of the dramatic Mon *chedi* of

Sangklaburi. But unimposing as they were, I was happy to see the three pagodas—I had arrived at last.

I took a path downhill into the bazaar. One-story shophouses lined the road, their open fronts spilling out goods for the black market. The buildings were patched together from scrap wood and bamboo, their peaked roofs of thatch or corrugated metal. Palm trees shaded them. I made my way through the rows of dilapidated buildings. Each shop held shelves and tables full of plasticware, cosmetics, toys, canned food—all for porters to bring deeper into Burma.

Uncle Benny had given me the names of two people I might stay with, since Three Pagodas had no hotel. I kept walking until I came to a Karen customs post, about a kilometer into the bazaar. Karen soldiers in tiger-stripe camouflage uniforms and broad-brimmed hats sat in the customs hut, adding up the day's taxes charged to the smugglers. I approached the most senior-looking one and showed him my Karen laissez-passer. He looked at it approvingly and at me inquiringly. I told him, first in Thai and then in English, "I am here to see Mr. Ai Riz." Then I tried it very slowly, since the officer didn't seem to understand either language, "Ai . . . Riz." Then I tried the other name. "I am here to see Mr. Joshua." He recognized that name, repeating it and motioning for me to follow one of the soldiers, who slung on his AK-47 and threw an olive-drab rain cape over it. We walked for a few minutes through a grassy field. It started to rain, and we arrived at a small wooden house that stood on stilts.

The soldier called Joshua's name. A skinny old man poked his head out the door, saw me, retreated inside, and then came rushing out unfurling an umbrella. "Please, please, do come in and make yourself at home!" he cried. "How good of you to come all this way in the rain. Are you British? No? American? Your people helped us in the last war, too. I have many things to discuss with you. Do come in." The soldier headed back to the customs post.

"You must be Joshua, then," I said. "Uncle Benny told me to look you up. The other man he mentioned is Mr. Ai Riz, but the soldiers didn't seem to recognize his name."

Joshua laughed. "Not a man! The name is Iris. She's a Karen nurse married to some Mon fellow. I'll take you to meet her, but you had better stay here. It's just my daughter and me now. My poor wife died last year. She was a wonderful cook for all the foreign visitors who stayed here. I'm sorry I can't provide more hospitality. I want to start a hotel here, with a swimming pool. And a museum about the Death Railway—we have many artifacts from that time. I was the first one to settle here. I saw it after the war and I thought, good location, this. Then it was only the jungle and the railway. Now it is the most famous black market."

A broken digital watch hung loose on Joshua's bony wrist, his spectacles were taped together, and his few teeth were scattered in his gums, but he had splendid military posture and eyes full of dreams. He had served in the British Imperial army during and before World War II. His daughter, Nina, a twenty-year-old with huge, perpetually anxious eyes, was retarded. His son, a bright young man who suffered from chronic malaria and shell shock, lived in an adjacent house with his wife and their new baby son named Liberty. A few times each year, when the Tatmadaw approached, the civilians of Three Pagodas Pass had to take refuge in the jungle on the Thai side of the border. "I always manage to save the guest book," Joshua told me. "Here, you may take a rest from your travels and read it at your leisure."

Joshua played host to the dozen or so foreign visitors who made it up to Three Pagodas each year. The guest book showed that about half were exceptionally intrepid tourists, and the others were journalists and other border fanatics. The "Comments" section was full of malarious ravings, especially from repeat visitors. Under "Nationality," one ten-year habitué had penned "United States of Malaria." The pages contained gemlike border essays on the Karen revolution, tigers, Joshua's late wife's cooking, tin mines, the music of frogs at night, and the grave of Jim Thompson. People came to Three Pagodas, met Joshua, fell under a spell, and returned again and again.

Joshua immediately provided me with a routine. Each morning we went to the bazaar for coffee and rumor collection, then we

found someone to tell us stories. Naps and reading in the afternoon,
a bath from a big ceramic jar of rainwater, dinner at some terrible
restaurant in the bazaar, then early, contented sleep.

We went to a Bengali shop for glasses of milky, pinkish tea and
rotis (Indian pancakes) drizzled with condensed milk and sugar. As
we finished our tea, Joshua said, "Miss Edith, do you want to know
about the first airplane hijacking? Karens were among the first
people in the world to take an airplane. One of the soldiers here can
tell you the story."

At the customs post, Joshua collected a sergeant major, thirty
years old, with sun-reddened shoulder-length hair. We brought
him to a nearby coffee shop and he chewed on an unlit cigar as he
spoke. Joshua translated his Karen, undoubtedly adding embellish-
ments of his own.

"My father hijacked the airplane," the sergeant major began.
"This was in 1952. It was a Burma Airways plane, going from
Rangoon to Akyab on the west coast of Burma. The pilot was
British, the copilot, Burmese. My father and two other Karen
revolutionaries pretended to be passengers. They strapped .38s to
their legs so they wouldn't show under their sarongs. Also, they had
one hand grenade. They meant to steal the plane and use it to start
up the Karen Air Force. After the plane had been flying for twenty
minutes, they went to the cockpit. British pilot says, 'What are these
fellows doing here?' and Burmese copilot says, 'They come and
catch our plane.' They show revolvers and pilot is not afraid, but
when they show the grenade, he says, 'Oh, we will go anywhere you
tell us.' "

I took out the silk map and asked the sergeant major to show me
where they brought the plane.

"About here, on a beach," he said, pointing his cigar near Bas-
sein, west of Rangoon. "When the plane landed, the Karens were
very sad because nobody was there to meet them. Many Karen
soldiers were supposed to be there, with a Karen pilot for the
airplane, but the hijackers had done their work three days later
than they were supposed to. You know how we Karens are, always
late, always on 'Karen time.' So the soldiers had given up and
moved on."

"What happened to the plane?"

"Well, they search all the passengers and the luggage and find that a government man on the plane is carrying very much money—700,000 kyat—to Akyab for official business. So they don't feel so sad anymore. In fact, they are very happy. So they give the passengers coconut water to drink and let the plane take off again: Good-bye, everybody. They put the money in a boat on the beach and one man sleeps in the boat to guard it. Two others sleep in a hut on the beach. During the night, Communist rebel soldiers come and capture the Karen man in the boat. With the money! But the other two have escaped, and they get to a Karen camp. Karen troops come and surround the Communists, so they have to surrender back the hijack man and the money."

"Why weren't any more airplanes hijacked?"

"They tried again, but it was not as successful as the first time, so they decided it is not a good tactic."

In a world full of terrorism, the Karens stuck to fair play. They weren't much for the stuff of headlines—hijacking, hostages, assassinations, civilian targets. They blew up the occasional railway car, lying badly about it afterward, but mostly they stuck to trench warfare and guerilla forays against military targets. The war was a stalemate, fought from hill to hill in jungles full of land mines. The Karens and other rebels hardly ever struck at anything of real importance, like Tatmadaw bases, airports, or cities. It was all very well that the Karens weren't terrorists, but their lack of aggressive strategy seemed to be condemning their grandchildren to the same endless war.

The Karens were admired for their tenacity, but their tactics often tripped them up. They did not get any kind of foreign aid, but their enemy, the Burmese military, was not foreign backed either. Ne Win was too xenophobic to accept aid with strings attached, so he lacked the matériel (bombers, helicopters, napalm, Agent Orange) to really do the job on the Karens. Meanwhile, the Karens were dependent on the Thai arms market for their weapons, spending their tin money for expensive guns at rip-off rates. Neither side ever took the offensive initiatives necessary for victory.

Joshua and I walked in the rain under his black umbrella. We

visited what he called "Chinatown," where most of the shops were
owned by demobilized KMT Yunnanese or urban Chinese who'd
fled Rangoon's institutionalized discrimination and violence. We
stopped in at the district office of one of the Mon factions, where a
few soldiers, enervated by malaria, sat beneath a Mon flag: a gold
flying duck and a little blue star on a red background.

Visiting Joshua was a free-fall through time. He told me stories
of the Wild Wa and their "skull avenues," which he'd seen as a
young private on an expedition to the Burma/China border in 1937.
The details of army life, his comrades in arms, his British officers,
were vivid. One day as we walked in the jungle a few kilometers
from the bazaar, he broke his brisk stride to turn and ask, "Did you
see the picture *Things to Come?*" Did he mean the H. G. Wells
science-fiction classic about the futility of warfare (made fifty years
ago)? Yes, that was the movie. "I saw it when I was in the army.
Quite good," he said. We marched on.

Joshua warned me that the foliage beside the path covered Karen
land mines. They were meant to cripple rather than kill, so the
Tatmadaw would have to use two soldiers to carry the wounded
man, putting three out of action instead of just one. Reportedly, the
idea didn't work all that well, as the Tatmadaw tended to simply
abandon their wounded soldiers in the jungle. Joshua and I walked
to the sound of bamboo, the stems knocking hollowly in the wind.
Long-haired, bleary-eyed soldiers trudged past us, back to Three
Pagodas from the front line. Smugglers strode doggedly into the
danger zone, goods strapped to their backs.

The big commodity moving from Three Pagodas' bazaar to the
interior was Aji-no-moto, a monosodium glutimate powder manufactured by a Japanese company. A huge demand existed for it
among the Burmese, who were convinced that it made their food
taste better, which may have been true, especially when people were
so poor that they often ate rice without any meat or vegetables.
Strong men and women smuggled Aji-no-moto in big metal tins
lashed together in stacks. When it reached Burma's towns and
cities, it was often adulterated with rice flour. The Aji-no-moto trail
was a weird parody of the heroin trade in the north; a white powder

that's not good for you, but people think they need it to enhance their lives. Foreigners were making the bucks on it—Chinese on the heroin, Japanese on the Aji-no-moto. And both powders were adulterated—to add to the profit motive.

I finally met Iris, who operated a dispensary at her house in the bazaar. Plump and pretty, she wore her hair flipped up on the back of her head with a brass barrette. In her well-schooled English she told me of her problems convincing the local Karens and Mons that malaria was transmitted by mosquitoes.

"They believe it comes from eating bad fruit," she said. "I ate some rotten old fruit to prove them wrong, but they just said, 'Oh, Iris, you are having the medicines, you can cure yourself of it anytime.' They won't change their minds, so they don't use mosquito nets and I have to run around with quinine to cure them. It is really too bad."

Iris told me conclusively that there was no direct route to the Mae Sot area. "In this season no truck or Jeep can get through, even on the Thai side of the border. You'll just have to retrace yourself to Bangkok, and then you can easily get a bus to Mae Sot." I decided that it might not be so bad to return to Bangkok (south on my way north), get some money from the bank, read my mail, maybe see Spin. I had a lot to tell him, tales of the Tenasserim and Three Pagodas Pass.

Joshua arranged for me to walk down to Sangklaburi with some Mons. He accompanied me as far as the *chedis,* where I took a picture of him standing by the Parcheesi counters with his black umbrella. He refused payment for my stay with him, so I took most of the money I had with me and put it in an envelope that I marked "World War II Museum Funding Contribution" and he accepted that. "Bring the photograph when you come back," he called as I set off.

My Mon companions traveled with an ox cart that held their goods—eight rice bags. After hours of plodding through mud in light rain, we got to the Songklia River. The Mons hired porters to carry the bags across to a *songtaow* that waited on the other side. The porters strained to lift the bags and carry them over the sagging pontoon bridge. It became obvious that the contents were heavier than rice. Riding in the *songtaow* with the cargo, I touched one of the bags. It felt like it contained large, smooth rocks. The Mons were going to great trouble and expense to bring eight bags of rocks out of Burma in the height of the rainy season. It seemed the Mons had gotten their hands on raw jade. From Burma's northern mountains, in the Kachin State, the precious rocks were smuggled to border towns where they would be cut and polished. When we reached Sangklaburi, the bags were unloaded at a shop that sold the same prosaic wares as the other shops in town: rope, boots, blankets, thermos bottles, flashlights. It was also the only shop in Sangklaburi where I'd seen jade on display, fine jade, the color of bamboo leaves and mountain mist.

⚊ 5 ⚊

I spent another night in Sangklaburi's clean new hotel, and another in Thongpaphum's seedy old hotel. I had disliked the food at Three Pagodas' bazaar (dull ingredients stodgily prepared), so I was terribly impressed with the Thongpaphum hotel restaurant's typical Thai-Chinese noodle soup—a clear broth, al dente yellow noodles, a few slices of pork, rings of scallion. What have I done to deserve such soup? I wondered. What have I done to deserve any of this— traveling the Tenasserim with a silk map, Uncle Benny's stories, walks with Joshua? I placed no stock whatsoever in karma, the Buddhist concept of doing good things so one would get something good in return. Maybe I was working on the opposite of karma, the idea that because of all the fantastic things that happened to me on the border, I would have to do something in return. I had noticed that some visitors wrote wistful comments in Joshua's guest book like, "I had not known about the Karen people before I came here. I feel sorry for their suffering, and I feel bad that I can't do anything about it." But there was always something one could do. I could do something to help. Not by trying to be a Karen, but by remaining an outsider and using my access to both worlds. The war in Burma was now my war. Now I would have to do something more than just observe it, I would have to play a part in it.

Uncle Benny had told me about a border village called Inthong, not far from Thongpaphum, with a Karen camp and tin mine. I took a *songtaow* there. The road snaked through wet bamboo, the most beautiful road I'd seen in Thailand, up into the mountains, until it ended at an eerie mining village. The gold roof finials of a Buddhist temple formed blurred silhouettes in the cold fog. From their outlines I knew I was still in Thailand because only Thai temples have such finials. I showed my Kawthoolei pass to a couple of Karen soldiers who had ridden up in the *songtaow* and they brought me to a shop run by a young woman named Noi.

Noi had the last shop in Thailand. Across the road stood a Thai Border Patrol Police post, where police and villagers whiled away the hours playing cards for money. This was the last "casino" in Thailand. In Noi's shop, shy Karen commandos with Cheyenne ponytails and British pullovers paid for cans of Eiffel Tower sardines and tins labeled "Please Drink Black Tea Powder Number One Brand" with wads of kyat.

Noi, wearing a pink jogging-suit jacket over a pink sweater and batik sarong, put aside a Thai fashion magazine when I entered. I introduced myself to her in Thai and she invited me to stay with her family (they lived in rooms in back of the shop). She lent me a warm polyester jacket because even indoors Inthong was clammy and cold. "In the dry season," Noi told me, "tourists come up here for the day to look at the view that goes all the way to the Andaman Sea."

After dinner, Noi and her numerous siblings, who ranged from elementary-school age to adolescent, sat wrapped in blankets on sofas and armchairs under monstrous mounted deer heads, watching video. The tape was a bootleg of a Mandarin sword fight series called *T'ang Dynasty*, and much to my delight, the show's sponsor happened to be Tang orange drink mix. Just as the video was getting exciting (an assassin was climbing through the window of the sleeping prince's pearl-inlaid bedchamber), the power went out. A package of Bear Brand Tropical Candles was fetched from the shop, and one was lit and stuck in its own wax on the table in front of me. The older kids went outside to pound on the generator. The little ones got to stare at me from the shadows. The smallest and bravest of them actually dared to initiate a conversation with me, the alien.

"A ... B ... C ... D ... E ... F ... G ...?" she ventured. I remembered that when I was not much older than she, I'd read a science-fiction story advising that the proper behavior on meeting a visitor from outer space was to start counting, so the being would know that you were sentient, too. Noi's little sister apparently thought along those lines.

"H, I, J, K," I replied, leaving her the best part, which she handled with aplomb: "Elemenopee!" I thought of the title of a video that Brando P. Bryant had made about a Thai tourist attraction, the Crocodile Farm: *What's a Sentient Being Like You Doing in an Incarnation Like This?* The other children were looking at her in awe, as you would if your kid sister started holding forth in classical Persian or spouting sagas in Icelandic. I fed her another line, "Q, R, S, T." She paused. A deep breath. "U, V, W ..." And just before "X", the lights went back on, the assassin backed out of the window rendered harmless by rewind, and the children blew out the candles.

In the morning, an English-speaking Karen officer offered to show me the Karen customs post. We walked downhill from the border, and I saw that the Thai villagers used the Burma side as a garbage dump: the rocky slope was speckled with pink, yellow, and blue plastic trash bags. (In logged-out, overdammed, ultrapolluted Thailand, one could find a plastic-strewn garbage heap anywhere, and now I saw that Thai garbage dumps even extended into neighboring countries, just as rapacious Thai logging operations were chewing their way into the Burma border jungles.) The Karen officer wore a long, dark cape and a beret. He looked like Macbeth in the fog. The shrubbery could have been camouflaged Karen guerillas. The Andaman Sea was invisible, as were India and Arabia. Even most of the garbage dump was obscured by the fog.

We spent the rest of the morning waiting for transportation out of Inthong and I was surprised when a *songtaow* finally pulled up. Noi's mother was in it, and she happened to be heading for the southern district headquarters of Kawthoolei. She unloaded some cartons of goods for the shop and got back in her seat. Some other passengers climbed in and we departed. One of the riders was a handsome young Mon insurgent whom the caped Karen introduced as the Mayor of Ye. The Mon spoke some English and he explained that he was not the mayor of the actual city on the Andaman seacoast, but the mayor of "the city in exile." He spent the first, most scenic, part of the trip vomiting out the back of the *songtaow*.

I was beginning to understand the Mons. Those I had met at Three Pagodas had been vague about how long they'd been fighting, how many they were, and just what territory they were fighting for. Part of the problem seemed to be that two Mon factions, due to a rabid personality conflict between their leaders, fought each other with a vengeance, doing the Tatmadaw's job.

At the Sangklaburi shop with the jade, I had seen a brochure for "Mon National University" with a curriculum, staff, and student body drawn from Mons living in Burma, Thailand, Cambodia, and Vietnam. It turned out to be 100 percent imaginary. The university was for "the Mon people of old Empires of Dvaravatti, Thaton, Hariphunchai, Hamsavaddi"—ancient Mon domains. Thaton, for instance, flourished in the third century B.C. and was conquered by the Burmese in 1057. Was there perhaps an Etruscan Liberation Party, I wondered, or a Mayan Revolutionary Front? Or were the Mons the only ones out there fighting for an empire that had vanished centuries ago?

The Mons had introduced much of Southeast Asia to Buddhism, built great cities and monuments, sailed the oceans. They spoke a distinctive language full of rolling R's, loud dissonances, and lyrical nuances—like Scottish mixed with Cantonese and Welsh. But Ne

Win had declared the Mons "assimilated": to be a Mon in Burma was to be obsolete. So the Mons fought on more than one front. They fought the usual war with M-16s and grenade launchers, and they also fought a war of the imagination. To preserve their identity and visions of imperial glory, they set up a parallel universe of "exile," keeping government and art and learning intact in this realm of the mind until such time as their guns and rockets would bring about its reestablishment in the physical world.

When the *songtaow* made its turn toward Kawthoolei, I got out and hitchhiked into Kanchanaburi, where I caught a bus to Bangkok. I was too late for the express, and by the time my bus got to Bangkok it was almost ten o'clock at night. A police roadblock was set up on the outskirts of the city. The bus was stopped, the driver got off, and to my astonishment, the police arrested him. This left us passengers stranded and irate. Some major inverted *kvetch*ing was going on as, sweaty and tired, everybody insisted that *it didn't matter*. A few soldiers on leave from the border got off the bus to investigate. I expected more trouble, since animosity often flared between Thai police and soldiers. But the driver took out his wallet and started shelling out his on-the-spot fine for whatever offense he may have committed and we continued on through the neon city to the bus terminal.

Back in my jungle-suburb town house, I read weeks' worth of mail and the *Bangkok Post*. I exchanged my mildewed laundry for clean clothes, packed a sweater and blue jeans for the cold weather of the north, and ditched the French books for Peter Fleming's *Brazilian Adventure*. I went to the bank and swung by Mister Donut. A letter from Prince George had requested books on Asian art motifs, so I bought some at Siam Square. The bus to Mae Sot would leave in the evening, so I still had time to see Spin.

By midday the photojournalist, clad in his usual Pathan rags and reeking of Tiger Balm, lurched out of his tenement and down the alley, looking for something to eat, and perhaps a story. I tracked him (that medicinal smell) through the tourist slum he inhabited, and appeared before him in "The Claustro Corner," one of his favorite low-budget, low-ceilinged greasy spoons. He rose courteously and leaned over the table to kiss me on the mouth.

"Well, the Dragon Lady has returned," he drawled.

"Yes, but not for long. I'm going to Mae Sot tonight on the Bus from Hell. Serves me right for doing this in the rainy season, I guess." I ordered limeade. The Claustro was known for its fruit drinks and Spin was buying.

"But you got to Three Pagodas! What's it like?"

"Oh, it's amazing. You have to go there. A wonderful old Karen—a British Army veteran—will take care of you. He told me fantastic Wa stories. Lots of Karen troops were around, and Mons, too. And I think I've begun to figure out the Mons. They're not just fighting for survival like the Karens, they're fighting for a Mon renaissance."

"Interesting. What's the weapons situation like over there?"

"*Beaucoup* AK-47s and Chinese RPGs. They come from Chinese arms shipments for their Khmer Rouge. Thai dealers get into the Cambodia-bound shipments and skim some off to sell to the rebels in Burma."

We talked on about guns and jade and malaria, and I told the story of the golden rhino. At the other tables, hippie backpackers suspended their own conversations about dope and diarrhea to eavesdrop. I had gotten my first rolls of film developed, and I showed the prints to Spin: Karen commandos, Three Pagodas bazaar shopkeepers, trucks stuck in mud. Spin flipped through the pictures and gave me a look that made my skin crawl.

"Blade's composition is a little off. Is that all you took?" Like all professional photojournalists, Spin shot in mass quantities.

"Yeah, well, I'm not really used to it yet . . ."

"Never mind, they're not all that bad. I would never go off on a trip with a camera I'd never used before . . ."

I changed the subject by taking out the silk map. When it was

time for me to leave, Spin walked me to the bus stop. Defying a
Thai taboo on public displays of affection, he surprised me by
sweeping me up a foot in the air to kiss me. Passersby slowed their
pace to watch.

I arrived in Mae Sot the next morning, after an uncomfortable night
on a speeding over-air-conditioned bus. I took a taxi to the home of
a Karen officer. I showed my laissez-passer to the officer's wife,
Gloria, a smooth-skinned matron with an upswept hairdo. She
wore traditional Karen dress: a striped sarong and embroidered
tunic. She looked at the pass with a distinct lack of enthusiasm.
"Well, what is it you want to do while you're here?" she asked
distractedly.

"I would like to visit the refugee camps and then go to Karen
headquarters at Manerplaw."

"The roads really are bad now. You can't get to Manerplaw.
Perhaps one of the refugee camps. Why don't you check into your
hotel and I'll send someone over later to let you know if it can be
arranged." I was dismissed.

It was obvious that she was busy. Her women's organization was
effectively in charge of the refugee camps, where food distribution
and health and education programs were Karen-administered.
Gloria also had to meet with the foreigners who came to Mae Sot:
reporters, missionaries, aid workers. From her large, comfortable
house she sold Karen handicrafts and textiles from Burma's frontiers to raise funds for the camp. I noticed the sarongs on display.

"Have you got any Kachin sarongs?" I asked. "The black ones
with the embroidery?" She found a black Kachin sarong for me to
buy and the atmosphere warmed up a bit.

"I'm sorry we can't do more for your mission," Gloria said. "But
we are so busy with the camps right now. More refugees keep arriving and the weather is so bad. But I think that tomorrow when I go to
Wangkha camp for a women's group meeting, you can come along."

The next morning we left for Wangkha camp in a *songtaow*
accompanied by other women from Gloria's organization. Their
husbands made enough money in the tin, teak, and cattle businesses

to afford houses in Thailand, Thai immigration payoffs, and education for their children in Thai schools. The women devoted most of their waking hours to work on behalf of the Mae Sot district's fifteen to eighteen thousand other Karens who were not as lucky.

"Thai farmers give us some bad land that they can't use for farming," Gloria explained. "And the refugees build their little huts there with bamboo and leaves from the Burma side of the Moei River." Thai authorities, I learned, would not allow the Karens to use any materials from Thailand, so they risked their lives going back and forth under Tatmadaw shelling to get bamboo. A few Christian groups would provide rice and fish paste, and French doctors established a clinic. For everything else, the Karens were on their own.

The road ended about a mile from the camp, which we reached by a plank-walk through a swamp. I expected to see a fenced, prisonlike place, but instead we arrived at a neat little village of low huts with brown leaf roofs. The huts stood along muddy lanes, and some had flower gardens growing around the front doors. One long shack sold soda pop, batteries, soap, and toys.

"The Thais came here with this shop," Gloria said. "Some of the refugees hire out as cheap labor for Thai farmers, so the Thais opened this to make sure they have things to spend their little money on."

Gloria introduced me to Skaw Ler Taw, an elderly Karen revolutionary who edited an English-language magazine. His white hair stood up from his high forehead in a crew cut, and while the women attended their meeting he shuffled along on ballooned feet and showed me around the camp.

"Hypertension caused this miserable swelling of my feet," he said. "But there is so much work to do I have to ignore it. The refugees aren't here because they like Thailand or expect to get on a jumbo jet and go to America like the Vietnamese. The Karens only want to return to Kawthoolei. Every one of them would go back in a minute, if they could. They came here expecting to stay two months, and now it's been two years. The Tatmadaw keeps shelling and raiding our trading posts and villages on the other side of the river. There is no going back for the refugees now."

I admired Karens like Skaw Ler Taw and Gloria for the disciplined way in which they cared for their endangered people. They made me aware that there was much more to surviving the war than weaponry. The Karen volunteers provided a safety net for thousands of civilians, and I thought this was perhaps the Karen movement's finest achievement.

It took me ten and a half hours and three stupefying bus rides to get from Mae Sot to Mae Sariang. I checked into Mae Sariang's only hotel, a gloomy three-story edifice. A large hole gaped in the ceiling of my top-floor room, but I was too tired to go downstairs and request another. Cheap Thai hotels usually had holes drilled into the walls, perfect for room-to-room voyeurism. I carried a roll of gaffer's tape, useful for all sorts of things, including taping over peepholes (with the option of peeling back the tape if it sounded like anything really interesting was going on next door). The yawning gap in this ceiling was beyond tape, though. I climbed up on a table and shined my flashlight into it. Seeing nothing but dust-coated rafters, I decided it was harmless, and I slept undisturbed.

In the morning I felt something crunch as I slid my left foot into its Chinese Wellington. The crunch was a two-inch cockroach, now deceased. Either it had fallen out of the ceiling hole straight into the boot, or it had scaled the boot's slick side. I decided to be more careful about shaking my boots out before I put them on—especially in the jungle. If a roach could make it, so could a scorpion.

At the morning market I asked about transport to the Salween River. There wasn't any, not that day in the rainy season. If I couldn't get to the Salween, then I couldn't get to the Moei River, and Manerplaw was near the confluence of the two. I was a month and a half into my three-month visa, and rather than wait around in Mae Sariang for transport to Karen headquarters, I decided to continue north, where other rebel groups awaited on the Pai River.

I took a bus to Mae Hong Son, got a room at the Mae Tee for the night, and went to visit a young woman I had met briefly on my first visit to Mae Hong Son. Emma was the daughter of a British diplomat and a Shan princess, and she had grown up in England.

After university she had gone off in search of her Asian roots and had ended up teaching English in Mae Hong Son, and learning Thai, Shan, and Burmese. A kind, quiet soul, she was tuned in to all the crosscurrents of political intrigue on the border. We became friends immediately, sharing a taste for chocolate ice cream cones and Shan factional scandals.

Emma showed me how to get to the Pai River base, home of the Karenni rebels, by hiring a longboat with an outboard motor, which buzzed along the Pai River between jungle cliffs until it stopped at a settlement of stilted houses. The Karennis were a Karen-related tribe, called red Karens because of their clothing. Those who weren't in red wore olive drab, and I asked one of them to show me the way to the house of Arnold We, the Karenni rebels' foreign minister, whom Spin had visited a few months before.

Arnold We sat on his bamboo porch. Shirtless, with a bowl haircut and an aquiline nose, he looked like he belonged in the Amazon rain forest more than in the Burma border jungle. I introduced myself. In this territory the Kawthoolei pass was worth no more than the paper it was written on, but I had other credentials.

"Mr. Spin's friend! Glad to meet ya! This is your home away from home!" Arnold We exclaimed. I sat on the porch and he went inside to gather up a sheaf of photocopied articles and documents about the Karenni cause for me to read. While I scanned the articles and documents, he explained to me that the land of the Karennis had been a protectorate of the British Raj, but was never actually colonized. How, then, did the British gain the authority to have handed the Karennis over to the Burmese at Independence? I looked at a much-Xeroxed illustration that showed a memorial plaque left by the British to commemorate the Karenni soldiers who'd served in World War II: *At the going down of the sun and in the morning, we will remember them.* When the sun did set on the British Empire, the Karennis were forgotten immediately. Scorned by history, the Karennis still periodically fired off letters to Margaret Thatcher, demanding to know what had gone wrong. Of course the response was an official evasion—Burma's internal affairs were none of Britain's business.

Arnold We's wife, Ohn Khin, emerged from the kitchen at the back of the house carrying a teapot and a stack of moldy *Time* magazines. She had a sulky expression on her beautiful oval face. She didn't dress like a Karenni. She wore a blue Thai blouse and a beige flowered sarong wrapped over her pregnant belly.

"She's not a Karenni, she's a Shan from Loi-kaw, the capital of Karenni State," her husband said. "You know how the Thais call the Shans *Tai Yai,* meaning 'big Thais'? Well, my wife's a reeeally 'big Thai'!" Ohn Khin didn't speak English, but she got enough of Arnold We's joke to grimace at him. He moved out of her way and displayed a large map of the Karenni State he'd drawn, marked with gem mines and ore deposits.

"Here is the Burmese government hydroelectric power plant at Loi-kaw," he said. "They steal our hydro-power to light up their cities."

"Well, why don't you stop them?" On the map it was not very far from the rebel zone.

"For one thing it's hard to blow up a plant like that, so much dynamite would be needed . . ."

"But you don't have to blow it sky high, you just have to dent it a little. If you damage anything it takes forever for the government to fix it. They just don't have the hard currency for spare parts."

"But if we damaged the hydro plant *we* would be stuck having to repair it after the revolution."

"I would think that if the Karenni don't go after targets like that, your grandchildren are going to be doing their homework by candlelight in the jungle while the government enjoys Karenni electricity," I commented. My discussions in Kawthoolei with Daniel had convinced me that the rebels needed to take more drastic action against the Tatmadaw. The older revolutionaries could tell tales of raids on Rangoon and daring sabotage, but much of that fire seemed to have died out some time in the mid-eighties.

Arnold We frowned at his map, then picked up a copy of *Time*. "There is never anything about our revolution in this bloody magazine!" he complained, slapping the page in disgust. "Mr. Spin wrote a very good article on us for his magazine, so what is the matter with the people at *Time?* If they don't come out with a Karenni article soon I will cancel my subscription!"

The Karenni headquarters, like Kawthoolei's utopian communities, was an enclave of university-educated city people marooned in the jungle amongst illiterate but savvy tribal relatives. The rebel leaders tried to make the best of things. Their bamboo houses were beautifully crafted and gardens of corn and tomatoes thrived by the Pai River. Arnold We tuned in to the BBC on his shortwave radio as we ate dinner in the kitchen. We had pumpkin vines and dried fish with our rice.

I noticed a worm-eaten set of the works of Thomas Merton on a kitchen shelf. The Karennis here were Catholics and Baptists. Photos of Pope John Paul II, cut out of *Time*, faded to blue on split-bamboo walls.

After supper, Arnold We's old typewriter clacked away, producing a list of Karenni resources ("Rubies, silver, platinum, wolfram, tin, cobalt, marble, tourmaline"), which would go out in the next Thatcher letter. When Arnold We had finished his work, I went to bed on the porch under a mosquito net. Spin had caught cerebral malaria here so I lit an acrid insecticide coil for good measure.

Morning mixed the fragrance of red hibiscus blossoms with the aroma of Nescafé. Arnold We went off to a meeting. The Karennis had a provisional government, complete with hard-campaigned elections and the occasional political assassination. Late in the afternoon, while Arnold We was still away, a party of Belgians on a trekking tour arrived. Their Thai guide ushered them onto the porch. The tourists had an unenviable collection of sunburns, insect bites, scrapes, and bruises—as if they'd fought their way through the Japanese Army in the battle of Myitkyina. They were on one of the *expensive* tours, which included a boat trip into deepest, darkest Burma. That was where the Karenni rebels came in.

Tourists paid a thoroughly unofficial "departure tax" to some Thai Border Patrol Police stationed on the Pai River, then boats brought them to the Karenni base, where they paid an additional

500 baht each, money ostensibly meant for the rebels. Most of the fee was kicked back to the Thai police. The boats docked at Arnold We's house. If he wasn't there, Ohn Khin sold the tourists T-shirts. If he was there, Arnold We gave a short lecture on the Karennis' political situation. He was usually condescending with tourists, if not outright insulting. His presentations reminded me of Edsel Ford Wong, who had been famous for being the rudest waiter in San Francisco's Chinatown. Customers came to Wong's restaurant from far and wide just to be insulted by him.

The battered Belgians missed the Edsel Ford Wong routine. Clutching T-shirts emblazoned "Karenni Army—Truth Love Unity Peace," they went off to view the Padaung women, who were the latest thing in the tribal tourism trade. The women were from a Karenni-related tribe near Loi-kaw (not to be confused with Prince George's Palaung tribe), who practiced the waning custom of coiling brass spirals around girls' necks from an early age. This would push their shoulders down, creating the illusion of an elongated neck. Since Karenni rebel activity kept Loi-kaw off the list of places the Burmese government deemed safe for tourism, the Padaung women had been hidden from foreign eyes for many years. Sensing their potential as tourist attractions, a sinister Padaung man had recently brought three of the women to the Pai River to draw in boatloads of day-trippers.

Arnold We failed to show up for dinner so Ohn Khin and I ate together, chatting in our equally faulty Thai. After a dinner of rice and weeds and tiny dried fish, we were standing on the porch when the whole house began to vibrate. For a long minute it made a weird humming sound as if some machine was shaking it from the inside. But there were no machines there, no electricity. I had experienced earthquakes in San Francisco and Taiwan, so I knew what was happening. The resilient bamboo held together and the shaking ended. Ohn Khin laughed. "The only thing that can destroy my house is the Tatmadaw," she said.

Later that evening, as Ohn Khin and I sat drinking tea and looking at copies of *Time* by candlelight, I noticed something moving on the porch railing. I shined my flashlight at it: a long, thin serpent with spotted green skin slithered along the bamboo pole. Poisonous. I kept the flashlight on the snake and Ohn Khin held her breath and pitched a bowl of water, which dislodged it. The snake fell under the house. "Tatmadaw spy," I said, and Ohn Khin laughed.

In the morning I went to the training camp in a boat with DONT GIVE UP painted on its side. The soldier crew had written "karenni's army" on their bush hats by way of insignia. Arnold We greeted me at the training camp, where a hundred and fifty recruits in their mid- to late teens practiced marching in formation. The boys wore uniform shirts with checked or striped sarongs. Some had military hats or caps, but others draped flowered towels over their heads to keep the sun off. They were barefoot or at best shod in rubber sandals. Tattoos covered their arms: Buddhist inscriptions or Christian crosses and hearts. One young recruit even wore yellow plastic rosary beads around his neck.

As the day grew hotter, the soldiers gathered and sat in the shade to listen to Arnold We lecture on politics and the need for discipline. But the recruits already looked disciplined to me—they just needed footwear and guns.

Spin had told me that Kachin representatives (from the far north, near Tibet) were stationed at the Pai River base. When Arnold We finished his lecture, I asked if I could meet them.

"They don't really want to see any foreigners," he said. "But you can send a letter to the Kachin colonel by boat and see if he will change his mind for you."

The Kachins, I learned, *did* want to meet foreigners, but the Karennis were possessive with their guests. So the Kachins sat at their camps wondering why no journalists ever came to see them.

That afternoon a boat arrived carrying not a reply to my note to the Kachin but two French photographers, Marc and Remi. They came bearing medical supplies for the Karennis and Padaungs. They had been to the Pai River before and had taken the first published photographs of the Padaung women. French magazines

had featured their photos of *"Les Femmes Girafes"* and something of
a craze among European tourists began. Arnold We was in his
worst Edsel Ford Wong mood. When Marc and Remi presented
him with a bottle of Ballantine Scotch, he let it be known that he
would have preferred French cognac. He was also ungracious about
the medicine, which they had gone to great trouble and expense to
bring. His gripe was that they hadn't cleared the delivery with the
provisional government. To make the situation even more awkward, I had to act as translator. The photographers' English wasn't
all that bad, but Arnold We pretended not to understand them. So I
had to translate their French to English while I tried to persuade
Arnold We to at least thank them for the medicine. Eventually the
thanks came, with phony effusiveness, but only after the Scotch had
been opened.

Marc and Remi were looking forward to a reunion with the
Padaung women. Arnold We said, "I suppose you can go, but
you're not taking those cameras. We have decided that taking
pictures of the Padaung women is exploitive." This had apparently
been decided sometime after that afternoon's boatloads of tourists
had come and gone. "You should go see the Padaung women, too,"
he told me. "Bring your sketching book." I wasn't sure if I was on
Arnold We's good side or just in the middle of something.

As the sun rose, a boat came by with a letter in English from the
Kachin colonel, inviting me to visit his camp. I breakfasted with
Marc and Remi on the bread and strawberry jam they'd brought
and then we waited for a boat to take us upriver to the Padaung
women. By midmorning we heard a boat engine, and up from the
landing marched another Frenchman with a Thai trekking guide.
The Frenchman was large, pale, and nervous, with a freshly shaved
head that made him look less like a Buddhist monk than a Devil's
Island inmate. He said he had visited the Karennis three years
before, but Arnold We professed not to recognize him.

"Oh, I see so many foreigners and you all look alike," Arnold We
said with an airy wave of his hand. "I really can't remember one from
another." This wasn't true. I knew that Arnold We carried on
correspondence with a number of close, foreign friends who had

visited him over the years. I thought he was just trying to retain control of his bamboo homestead, which was being trespassed constantly by contingents of Eurotrash. Foreigners were both his political strength—through them he could guarantee the Karennis outside attention and some income—and the bane of his jungle existence.

The photographers and I took advantage of the trekker's boat. We loaded it up with medical supplies and gift parcels, pretty and useful things from France and Thailand that they'd brought for the Padaung women. After a short trip upriver we disembarked in front of a metal enclosure that formed a perfect square around a fish pond. This was by far the most modern building on the Pai River. We walked through a door in the front wall and out a door on the opposite side. Beyond it was a small dark hut where the women lived with some Padaung soldiers who were in the Karenni Army. The two younger women, in their late twenties, were at home. Both had round faces turned up by their brass neck coils, wide mouths, bangs fringing their eyebrows. Their hair was piled up in bright towel turbans held with silvery pins. They posed, expecting the foreigners to photograph them. They also posed because they couldn't help it. Their movements were so restricted and stylized by gleaming brass—not only the neck spirals, but coils immobilizing their knees as well—that they carried themselves like languid, elegant fashion models.

The trekker snapped photos, glumly. The crassness of the visit was mitigated by the women's delight in seeing Marc and Remi. Here were old friends who even remembered their favorite colors of embroidery yarn. The Padaung women smiled widely. I understood Marc and Remi. They had found a kind of magic here in the middle of a war zone, and they had returned to give it its due, bringing medicine for the Pai River villagers.

Back at Arnold We's house I looked at the black-and-white photographs of the front line he kept in a coffee-stained manila envelope: Karenni soldiers pulling the boots off a dead Burmese soldier; Karennis on patrol in winter's dry brush; wounded Karennis; more corpses—Burmese and Karenni; captured Burmese

soldiers; a spy being interrogated—Karenni soldiers tearing his
shirt off. So far all I knew of the war was talk. I could always find
someone to talk to; so many people up and down the border spoke
English well, or at least some Thai or Chinese. I'd had so many
conversations in the rain, slapping mosquitoes away, drinking
glasses of tea.

Talk and hot tea and warm blankets at night. Now I am moving
vertically along the border, I thought. But when I return I must go
inside, farther west, find out how people live knowing nothing but
this war. I drank my tea, listened to the rain, looked at the death
photographs and into the malarial eyes of a Karenni soldier who sat
with me on the porch. I remembered how on my first trip to Pieng
Luang with Jere and the others I had thought of this as "a cool little
war." Now I knew that was not so. This was a terrible, filthy war.
There was nothing cool or little about it.

There was no rationale, no justification for its having gone on for
so long. Apparently wars didn't have expiration dates like milk
cartons. Sometimes they just didn't end.

The next morning I went to meet with the Kachin colonel. He
spoke excellent English and looked Mongolian. I asked him my
standard question: "What is the goal of your revolution?"

Each group seemed to be fighting for a different reason. The
Shans fought for freedom of expression; the Karens for survival;
the Mons to regain their lost empire; the Karennis for their independence.

"Before, we wanted national sovereignty for our Kachin land,"
the colonel told me. "But we have come to realize that this is
impractical in reality. Now we want a federal union to include all
ethnic groups—like your United States. Equal rights and autonomy: this is the goal of the National Democratic Front, which we
Kachins support. Now it will be backed up by NDF joint military
operations. If we can fight the Tatmadaw together, we can live in
peace when we win."

From the Kachin camp, I went to the Karenni training camp by
boat. Saw Moh Reh, a stocky, gray-haired man who was the Ka-

rennis' president, was giving a speech to some army officers. Since the speech was in Karenni, I went to the administration building to wait for a boat back to Arnold We's house. On the floor, wrapped in a cheap gray blanket, a Karenni government official held a plastic bottle of dextrose solution, waiting for a medic to show up and put the drip in his arm.

"The Devil's own malaria," he groaned to me. When Saw Moh Reh finished his speech he and some senior officers came into the building. They introduced themselves and tuned the radio to the BBC news. The man in the blanket said, "With this fever I cannot make head or tail of the news of the world today."

"Do you know where in Europe Ne Win is?" Saw Moh Reh asked me.

"Maybe Switzerland," I ventured. Switzerland was where he went to get injections of cells extracted from sheep at one of those haute monde rejuvenation clinics. A "Look, no hands" dictator, he was always jetting off to Europe for surgery or dental work with a planeload of gemstones to trade for weapons. He'd always returned, refreshed and undead, fully in power. Burma bled to death, but he lived on: one man, one party, one system.

It was the first sunny afternoon in weeks when I returned to Arnold We's house. Arnold We went hunting. He took his rifle, but his prey turned out to be bamboo shoots. The Karennis loved their guns. They even slaughtered chickens by shooting them. When Arnold We went after wild birds, he left the M-16 home and used a fancy slingshot called a Wrist Rocket that shot steel balls. When not in use, the Wrist Rocket sat on the kitchen shelf next to Merton.

The inevitable rain started as we ate dinner, my last night on the Pai River. Arnold We chewed chili peppers and washed them down with Ballantine and rainwater. Ohn Khin and I crunched the bones of tiny fish and stuffed riverweed in our mouths. We poured banana flower soup over mounds of rice and sliced bamboo shoots into our white enamel dishes. It was a happy dinner. The three of us were in a fine mood. We had newspapers and magazines from the foreigners who had left, and we had batteries in the shortwave. We had hundreds of mosquito bites, but no malaria.

THE LAND
OF THE
TAI

= 1 =

As I was crisscrossing the Burma border, Emma was crisscrossing
Mae Hong Son, riding around town on her Honda, her long dark
hair lifting with the breeze. She knew the location of every safe
house, which dark-windowed trucks were driven by which Thai
intelligence agents, and even which bakery was owned by the
KMT. I wanted to learn more about Shan village life and I wanted

to investigate the situation in Mae Aw. Emma had the perfect contact for me. She brought me to a Shan village not far from Mae Hong Son and dropped me off with her friend Lisa, an American anthropologist.

Lisa lived with a Shan family in their big teak house on stilts, and spent her time collecting folklore and studying Shan traditions in Buddhism, astrology, and magic. We walked around the village, a close-set grid of wooden houses, most on stilts, surrounded by rice paddies. Gardenia bushes bloomed along the narrow, tree-shaded streets. Since this was Thailand, not poverty-stricken Burma, there were more pickup trucks than ox carts, but the ambience was still unmistakably Shan. Everyone knew Lisa, and people greeted her from the houses as we walked. Like me, she was short with light, curly hair and glasses, and we both wore T-shirts and sarongs like the village women.

The usual greeting in a Shan village was "Have you eaten?" followed by "And what did you eat?" So we went around reciting our lunch menu, which was always vegetables and sticky rice, just like everybody else's. "I think I'll call my study of village life 'The Shans—Out to Lunch and What They Ate'," Lisa said.

After our walk, Lisa and I joined her Shan family for tea, which they drank with salt. I was able to go along with cooks putting Aji-no-moto in nearly everything, but I drew the line at briny tea and drank mine plain.

"Here's a story for you," Lisa said. "I heard it from the Shan monks. They swear it's true because they read it in a book in that wonderful temple near the market in Mae Hong Son. This is how it goes: During the Buddha's lifetime, a Karen man, who was very well meaning but not too bright, wanted to give the Buddha an offering. So he brought a nest of ants. Some ants are edible—a real delicacy—but he brought biting ants instead of edible ones. The ants scrambled from the nest and started biting the Buddha all over his legs. The Buddha was not exactly delighted and said, 'Just for that, in your next life you will be a powerful ruler of a great nation.' Pretty good, the Karen man thinks. 'But that's not all,' the Buddha continued. 'You will be eternally tormented by something like these wretched ants, which you'll never get rid of.' So, according to the Shan monks, this Karen man was reincarnated as Ne Win and the red ants are the rebel armies who won't ever go away."

"Speaking of the ants, what's going on over at Mae Aw?" I said.

"We hear shelling from over there, every so often," Lisa answered. "But it's quieted down with the rains. The KMT are having a hard time getting their supplies up the hill to Mae Aw, and that's probably true for Khun Sa as well."

"Do you think it's possible to go there now?" I asked.

Lisa spoke to the family's grandmother in Shan. The old woman put down her tea and spoke agitatedly. "She says 'Don't go!' " Lisa translated.

"Why not?" I asked.

"Because there's Wa up there, and she says the Wa eat people. She doesn't want you to end up as dinner at Mae Aw."

Lisa and I decided to go to Mae Aw without telling the family. I felt it was important to find out what was going on between the KMT and TRC and to see the Wa in action. Lisa's anthropological curiosity was whetted by the grandmother's cautions about cannibalism, even though I told her that the Wa were probably just headhunters. We went to a KMT house in the village where a man told us that the fighting had ceased at Mae Aw, so going there wouldn't be a problem—except that rain had ruined the road. Ordinarily, three Jeep-taxis went there each day, but now none were getting through.

Lisa and I waited at the Jeep-taxi stop, just in case. We flagged down a four-wheel-drive truck that happened to be going to Mae Aw. It belonged to some Thai engineers who were supposed to be working on an irrigation project up there. They admitted that they hadn't been able to get anywhere near the project in weeks, but they were giving it one more try in the brand-new truck.

The area en route to Mae Aw seemed to be receiving considerable attention from the Thai government. We passed agricultural stations designed to introduce alternatives to poppy-growing. The tribespeople were shown how to terrace their land to conserve soil, and to irrigate properly. They had stopped growing opium and cultivated roses, beans, tea, and tomatoes. Opium production had dwindled to a minimum in Thailand (although Burmese and Laotian drugs transited Thai ports rather freely). New roads carried the produce to Thailand's urban markets. Lisa told me that the tomato farms were doing so well that the KMT had gotten into the business. They had taken over a factory and started producing tomato juice that they labeled "El Monte, America's Favorite."

The engineers' truck drove into the mountains and the road got awful: it was as muddy and rutted as any of the other border roads I'd seen, and worse because the grade was extremely steep. Traction was a vain hope, even with the four-wheel drive and chains. The truck got stuck and the engineers got out and pushed. We went a little way and then the truck tipped over. It didn't fall all the way over, just enough to make everyone call it a day. On the way back, we passed the morning's Jeep-taxi from Mae Hong Son. It was going downhill, too. It hadn't reached Mae Aw in days.

In Lisa's village that night, a traveling movie projectionist set up his screen outdoors and showed Thai comedies and romances until midnight. So the next day the village did not wake at dawn as usual. After a late breakfast of sweet sticky rice crusted with black sesame seeds, Lisa and I were off to see the *sayah*. When we arrived at his house he came out onto the porch blinking, running his hands over his short dark hair and wispy gray beard. Lisa apologized in Shan for our barging in, and he dismissed her apology with a high laugh. He greeted me with a *wai* and smiled kindly, displaying a mouth full of bad teeth. Being Shan meant that your village had a *sayah*: a wizard of mystical powers and insight. A *sayah* followed Buddhist precepts of self-denial, peacefulness, sobriety, and honesty. He obtained his powers through his own discipline, and could transfer holiness and protection to others through spells and charms.

We sat on the porch and talked, and the *sayah* agreed to tattoo me. It would be my third tattooing. The first had been accidental: in that province of Hell known as eighth-grade algebra, a sharpened pencil had plunged through my plaid skirt and into my left thigh, leaving a permanent blue dot. Who knew if it had been good luck? I didn't pass algebra, but then I didn't get "lead" poisoning, either. My second was the one professionally etched into my arm with an electric needle and excruciating pain. I felt that any magic it had held was long since used up.

"The Shans do some great tattoos that can turn you into a saint or a monster," Lisa said. "They cover the skin with weird beasties and blocks of mystic letters. But they only do that kind at particular times of the year, definitely not the rainy season."

"That wasn't really what I had in mind anyway," I said. "I've seen Shan men and women with three little circles over their elbows. How about that?"

Lisa consulted the *sayah*. "He says 'Sure.' The circle is the letter *W* in Shan, pronounced 'wa.' It's a little tiny ring of protection that extends its security out over the person tattooed with it. If you get six of them, a set over each elbow, you'll have plenty of protection from evil spirits and all kinds of bad guys."

The *sayah* began mixing the gritty black *yah,* the medicine, in a small dish.

"The *yah* varies from day to day," Lisa explained. "Different recipes have different attributes. They use amazing stuff—bat brains, tiger blood, ashes from Buddhist inscriptions."

The *sayah* closed his eyes and chanted over the potion.

"What's the *yah* du jour?" I asked Lisa.

"Oh, it's a good one. He says it will make people treat you with loving kindness."

We were sitting on the floor, as Shans did. I pushed my shirt-sleeves up and bent my right elbow to the *sayah,* resting my hand on the floor. The *sayah* produced a foot-long stick with a weighted brass point, and dipped the point in the sticky black *yah*. He held it to my skin and hammered it by striking the other end. To my surprise it didn't hurt at all. When he was finished, I looked at the circles just above my elbow. There was little blood. They were rather faint and quite precisely formed:

O

O O

"The main thing is that the *yah* is there," Lisa said. "That's what counts. Sometimes they use red *yah* and sometimes invisible *yah*."

"I'm delighted with them. They're exactly what I wanted. How much do I owe the man?"

"He doesn't want any money. He says it's just something you should have since you go to places like Mae Aw and Pieng Luang."

I gave him Dutch cigars in a tin box. He was particularly pleased with the box and said it would be useful for wizard supplies. Lisa, on impulse, had the circles done on her own elbows. For no known reason, her circles pointed down at her elbows, while mine pointed up. She gave the *sayah* a Ghostbusters sticker, which he affixed to the black shoulder bag he used for house calls. Exorcism was one of his specialties.

Before we left I asked the *sayah* to tie a Brazilian ribbon around my wrist. It was a pink ribbon a friend had brought me from Bahia, a wish ribbon from the African-influenced Condomble religion. You were supposed to tie knots in it, making a wish on each knot, and have someone tie it on your wrist. When it rotted or tore from your wrist, you had to throw it in the ocean or a river, and then your wishes would come true. The Shans performed ceremonies, tying strings around people's wrists, so I was sure the *sayah* would know how to deal with the pink Condomble ribbon. He chanted a Buddhist prayer over it and tied it around my right wrist with a magic Shan knot.

⸗ 2 ⸗

I returned to Mae Hong Son, tattooed and beribboned. Emma told me that a German film crew was in town, gnashing its collective teeth in frustration over not being able to get to Mae Aw and not being able to arrange an interview with Khun Sa. Nobody was interviewing Khun Sa—in fact, Thai newspapers had printed stories that he was dead. Everyone on the border knew it wasn't true;

he was alive and well, but he was not accessible to foreigners. The German film crew was easy to spot: the blond men in camouflage sitting in the corner café by the Mae Tee hotel, looking despondently at the storm clouds.

The night's rain had just stopped when I got on an early-morning *songtaow* bound for Pai. The regular dry-season bus through to Chiang Mai had been replaced by a jumbo *songtaow* on high wheels. The Pai road was in bad shape, but we suffered no mishaps. We only stopped when the driver's boy assistants spotted large white mushrooms growing at the side of the road. The boys jumped out and gathered them up to sell in the Pai market.

My fellow passengers were Lisu tribespeople. The women wore blue dresses with rows of appliquéd trim, and plastic flowers in their earlobes. The Lisus had pigs with them, tied in burlap bags. The pigs squirmed in the aisle. People kicked them when they squirmed onto their feet. The pigs peed in the burlap bags. The pig pee ran down the aisle of the *songtaow* when we went uphill, then back up the aisle when we went downhill. When the *songtaow* made a mushroom stop, the pig bags slammed together and the pigs squealed with great alarm.

I checked into the Pai Hotel, a favorite of mine from previous Mae Hong Son to Chiang Mai trips. In my usual room the gaffer's tape I'd put over holes in the wall the year before was still intact. In the guest book, on a page from earlier that past summer, Spin had signed with one of his aliases, "Rex Archibald." I bathed with rainwater dipped from a huge pottery jar, then sitting on the hotel's front balcony in my black Kachin sarong, I wrote Spin a letter full of revelations about the KMT/El Monte tomato juice connection, signing it "The Management, the Pai Hotel, Pai, Pai-Land."

Pai was a beautiful small town. Mountains surrounded it, looking down on tropical foliage, teak houses with gardens, ox carts, motorcycles, a few shops, and one of the best collections of Shan temples in Thailand. Pai's monasteries had bamboo groves and delicate bridges and brass bells jingling. I discovered tottering wooden towers, white tin spires, gazebos, belfries with bats, miniature houses for ghosts, haunted trees wrapped in yellow cloth. When the Lisus harvested their crops (previously opium, now garlic) they came to Pai on shopping sprees. I called the two main shops "Sears" and "Harrod's." They sold farm implements and earring-sized plastic flowers. A dozen Lisus would rent a room at the fabulous Pai Hotel, get drunk on rice wine, and stumble to the balcony all night to throw up.

Pai's day started before dawn with a Shan market, so it was hard to find a restaurant open for dinner. I managed to find one that stayed open long enough to serve me a fine dish of fried pork with wild mushrooms, then I walked back to my hotel in the quiet evening. Pai was old-fashioned and wild and Shan and tribal. That night, I heard a group of foreign tourists arrive. They were complaining about the Pai Hotel, which was old and dusty and not designed to cater to their needs.

 ⌐ 3 ⌐

After the night's stopover in Pai, I went to Chiang Mai on a bus that had to be pushed out of the mud several times. I slept in Chiang Mai and left for Pieng Luang the next day on the early morning *songtaow*. The road arched into the sky over a ripple of hills. For once the day was sunny, the road was smooth, and we flew. Then the *songtaow* broke down. Whatever the problem was, it could not be repaired easily. While the driver dismantled the engine, his passengers sat on rocks sharing Chiang Mai junk food and chatting in six different languages. A special camaraderie existed since this was, after all, the *songtaow* to Pieng Luang; every passenger probably had something to do with smuggling, drugs, gambling, guns, and/or disreputable politics.

Eventually some trucks came by that picked up the stranded passengers. The truck I boarded was bound for the village just before Pieng Luang. The back was piled high with cargo. I took the best seat possible, on a motorcycle that was strapped to the heap of goods. It was like riding a winged rhinoceros through the air. The truck sailed down the newly surfaced road until the pavement gave out, then took an elaborate detour through a Lisu cornfield, where it got inextricably bogged down. Everyone but the driver abandoned it. Another truck heading for Pieng Luang made it through the cornfield and stopped for us. But on a muddy hill, that truck stalled and nearly overturned. We passengers gave up and began to walk through the darkening forest. We trudged on, and when the trees gave way to a village we boarded yet another truck. It was pitch dark, about ten o'clock, when we finally reached Pieng Luang.

The sleepy soldiers of the Thai Army checkpoint, which had replaced Fort Broken Heart, were not amused by our late arrival. They shined their flashlights in our faces. Here they were, curtailing the smuggling trade, controlling the KMT, keeping Khun Sa's influence out of Thailand. How could they do all that with people in trucks waking them up at all hours? Some small gratuities were offered by the KMT shopkeepers on board to apologize for disturbing the checkpoint staff. One of the Thai soldiers asked me what I was doing there.

"I've come to visit a friend," I said.

"Who's your friend?"

"Prince George at the Sura—TRC—compound." That seemed acceptable. The soldier wrote my passport number in his logbook and waved the truck through.

There were a few changes at the prince's compound. I was surprised to see electric lights illuminating the prince's house (a generator had been installed since my last visit). Some new soldiers were staying there, but my old friends the broth spoilers were still in residence. Prince George showed me to my usual corner bed that was now draped with a mosquito net. The new lights flickered and went off, and we all went to sleep as rain began to pound the tin roof.

The next day I told Prince George and his cohorts about my border trip and what the other groups thought of their Shan army. I had written notes for them on sketchbook pages.

"I suppose your National Democratic Front people on the Pai River despise us over the narcotics trade," K. Sam said defensively.

"No, it's not that," I replied. "Look at all the NDF groups that are involved with drugs, like the Wa. They understand *that*. Their big problem is with Khun Sa, who doesn't fight the Ne Win regime and in fact ran a Ka Kwe Ye militia for the Tatmadaw. They say Khun Sa isn't even Shan, he's Chinese with a Shan stepfather. They believe he's just out to take advantage of you all."

Prince George finished reading my notes. "I appreciate you telling us all this and your assessment of the NDF, but Khun Sa really has changed. He is a Shan leader now. He is powerful and he will help us."

"I guess anything's possible," I said. "Anyway, the Thais still believe he's dead."

"I will tell you a secret," Prince George said, lowering his voice appropriately. "Not long ago I played badminton with Khun Sa. He is healthy." Then K. Sam said, "You will see, we have many plans. For instance, we're working on a Tai constitution with equal rights for minorities in the Shan State, as well as a program to end narcotics production by selling the whole opium crop to the United States government in exchange for foreign aid."

K. Sam's words were only a variation of an old Shan State theme. Beginning with the Carter administration, Shan armies had periodically offered a "preemptory buy-out." The U.S. always rejected these proposals despite their theoretical cost-effectiveness (even a partial buy-out would remove far more opium from the world market than the ongoing, expensive enforcement and eradication programs). But while it lasted, Shan leaders basked for a while in the glow of press attention and congressional hearings. Apparently, Khun Sa and company were gearing up for another round of proposals. "And we have plans for fighting the KMT," K. Sam continued. "And for victory over the Communists."

"What about fighting the Tatmadaw?" I asked. "I'd think that might be a high priority . . ."

"In due time," K. Sam replied. "Of course we will take them on too, but Khun Sa says we must be very strong first. He doesn't want to waste his troops."

"When you visit Mai Sung, you can see some of Khun Sa's men," Prince George said. "They have trained with our soldiers. Now there is no more SUA, no more Sura. Only our alliance army. Politically, there is only the Tailand Revolutionary Council."

"Aren't you worried that it will get confused with the country of Thailand?" I asked.

"Well, when we have our own nation, the Thais can go back to calling themselves 'Siam' like they used to," Prince George answered. "And we can buy up all their old signs and stationery and just take out the H's."

That evening Mo Heing, the old Sura leader who had formed the TRC alliance with Khun Sa, was giving a banquet and I was invited. I walked with Prince George and some Shan officials up the hill to Mo Heing's walled compound within a compound. From the hilltop I could see dark green mountains under silver rain. The high walls and buildings in Mo Heing's stronghold were made of brick and cement, a contrast to the stick-and-bamboo structures below. We entered a reception room, respectfully barefoot on the parquet-patterned linoleum, and sat in armchairs. Mo Heing entered and everyone stood. He nodded and we sat down again. A nom de guerre, *Mo Heing* meant lightning bolt. He was a bristly-haired, compact man in his sixties, not much more than five feet tall. He wore civilian clothes, slacks and a sweater, the left sleeve of which was safety-pinned at the shoulder. His right hand gripped a cigarette.

Mo Heing made the rounds of the armchairs, greeting his guests. He walked over to me and Prince George introduced us. I greeted him in Thai, and asked, "Are you well?" He replied in Thai that he was well indeed. We guests then moved with him into the banquet hall, a drafty cement-floored room. Shan officers filled two long tables. I was seated with Prince George, K. Sam and a few other officials at Mo Heing's round table. While our conversation was subdued, the long tables kept up a mess-hall clatter. A soldier brought a message to Mo Heing, presenting it on bended knee. I had heard the Shans called "feudal" by other ethnic groups, and now I saw what they meant. I found it interesting that protocol would be so rigid when the leader was a born-again Buddhist ex-Communist.

I passed some photographs of my Shan paintings to Mo Heing,

who studied them carefully. He gave me a warm smile. "Your paintings are delightful," Mo Heing told me, with K. Sam translating. "They really show our Shan customs and our revolutionary spirit. I commend your mission to aid communications between the revolutionary groups. I hope you will enjoy this evening's dinner."

We ate first-class Chinese cuisine, undoubtedly catered by the KMT. The dishes revolved on a lazy Susan built into the marbleized Formica tabletop. There was five-spice roast chicken, minced pork with ginger, fried fish, and a clear soup with vegetables. Our plastic chopsticks clicked against small china rice bowls. When everyone had finished eating, the soldier-waiters cleared the dishes away and brought bottles of soda pop and tumblers of black tea. The rainy season was Buddhist Lent, so no alcohol was served. Mo Heing was such a strict Buddhist that he did not like liquor around at any time. It was hard for his officers to match his austerity. Prince George had told everyone he'd given up drinking for Lent, but I had noticed the broth spoilers carrying the usual empties from his room each morning.

The soldier-waiters offered us packets of salted watermelon seeds and packs of Thai cigarettes. Mo Heing rose to leave, and everyone in the hall stood and bowed. He said good night to individual guests. He shook my hand, but to the others he made a rather Zen gesture of a one-handed *wai*. Then he was gone, leaving behind his diffused smile. After he left, the guests smoked their cigarettes and chewed watermelon seeds, and departed, opening umbrellas for the walk down the hill. The rain was hard, and flashes of lightning illuminated mountains full of terrible things.

4

To obtain a permit to cross the border to Mai Sung I had to go to Pieng Luang's new Thai Army post. The Black Shark took me there on a motorbike. He was a Shan soldier who had, until recently, been serving with the Thai Army on the Cambodian border. He had tattoos, but not the Shan kind; his were rough hearts and daggers and a shark labeled in English BLACK SHARK. With little fuss, a Thai officer at the post wrote a pass for me and stamped it. The pass stated that I had to be back in Thailand by ten o'clock that night, and it struck me that things had gotten rather formal since the Rangers had cleaned up Pieng Luang.

The border crossing was now marked with an English sign saying "Thai–Tai Land Border" and a checkpoint manned by Thai and TRC troops. A cement barricade blocked the road to motor traffic and I noticed that trucks waiting on the Shan side had no license plates. I boarded one and sat beside a Mae Hong Son–born Shan who told me of his efforts to make the furniture factory more efficient. The truck bumped through Mai Sung, which seemed to be living up to its name ("grow and prosper"). Many houses and shops had been built since my last visit.

I brought some art books, which Prince George had requested, to the furniture factory. The cabinets under construction looked like the same ones they'd been working on five months before.

"The inlay work seems to be coming along nicely," I said to Acharn Somkit, the Shan from Mae Hong Son.

"We have had so many problems," he said, shaking his head. "I came here because these Shans of Burma are my people. My parents said not to because it's the place of Khun Sa, a bad man. But I wanted to do something for these poor people so they don't have to farm the opium plants. So far we have only made the one thing, a beautiful table that was donated to the temple. The curing process for the wood is not correct. The wood cracks and the pearl pieces fall out."

"Maybe you should think small," I suggested. "Why not use the inlay on small things like boxes and picture frames and mirrors? People would buy those as crafts of the Shan State."

"Thank you for your very good idea. But I think people here want big furniture or forget it. Big ideas or nothing. Big money or nothing. Whole Shan nation or nothing. You know how they are."

In the truck back to Pieng Luang, my attention was drawn to a Palaung woman. I had not seen a woman of Prince George's tribe before. She wore her long black hair tied in a ponytail with loops of multicolored yarn. More yarn, hanks of it in half a dozen hues, twisted into a turban. Strand after strand of fake pearls (shimmering pink and iridescent blue and pale sea green) wound around the yarn and fell in swags across her forehead and over her ears. I stared at her and she stared back at my "exotic" hair and my blue nail polish.

At dinner I told Prince George about seeing the Palaung woman.

"My tribespeople never used to come here," he said, "But now things are so bad in our region that they are moving south and east, scared of the Tatmadaw. Now they are growing opium instead of tea, because that's what people in their new areas grow. Soon they'll end up in Thailand like all the other tribes of Burma." I described the pearl headdress. "Oh yes," Prince George said. "In the old days my mother and sisters wore those. The beads on theirs were made of real gold, though."

Many in the Shan State, not just deposed aristocrats, looked back on the British colonial days with a certain longing. Opium had been worth silver bars to the growers back then. Now the Wa and Palaungs grew the crop just to survive. They could have been growing apples and strawberries, but such things would rot on their way through the roadless Shan hills to market. As far as the Burmese government was concerned, hill-tribe markets were "capitalist decadence" anyway and not to be encouraged. Crop substitution was behavior unbecoming ethnic minorities—Ne Win and his minions liked the hill tribes just the way they were: impoverished, down-trodden opium growers. The women and children planted and weeded the poppy fields and scraped the pods. The men were cannon fodder for warlord armies. The power and profits of the international narcotics trade were utterly unknown to the tribes. For their labor, they got a pittance in trade goods and rations of the rice their rocky soil would not produce.

I returned to Mai Sung to attend the graduation ceremony of some five hundred recruits who had finished their training. (The Thai Army had added the day to my border pass, but maintained the ten o'clock curfew.) A painted tiger crouched on a boulder above the training camp's parade ground. The new soldiers stood silently at attention, uniforms brightened with neckerchiefs of orange monks'-robe cloth to symbolize the holy crusade to save Shan Buddhism from Ne Win's Burmese socialism. They carried good expensive weapons, mostly M-16s, and I wondered if they still borrowed them from the KMT for such occasions.

Mo Heing appeared, and the recruits saluted with precision. He addressed them in a pedantic tone, droning on and on. Mo Heing was followed by a Thai officer who congratulated the combined troops of Mo Heing and Khun Sa, and added, "We Thais support your struggle and hope you will win freedom for the Shan nation very soon." I recalled another gathering at Mai Sung: watching Thai helicopters rout Khun Sa from his stronghold on an outdoor movie screen, while Shan officers drank and tossed back *yah horm* and cursed their enemy, Khun Sa.

When the graduation ceremony ended, I went with Prince George and Acharn Somkit to the furniture factory. There a stage had been set up with a banner above it proclaiming MORALE BUILDING CELE-BRATION FOR THE YOUNG WARRIORS. The new soldiers had preferential seating on the ground in front of the stage, while the other soldiers and civilians crowded behind them inside the big shed. Benches and tables were set up at the back for Mo Heing and his wife, TRC officials, Thai Army guests, and me. Soldiers kept this VIP section well stocked with watermelon seeds, cookies, and tea.

The show commenced at twilight, a vibrant extravaganza of military songs, Shan and Burmese classical dancing, pop tunes, comedy skits, and romantic duets. The highlight was the Yak Dance. No yaks lived in the Shan State, but long ago these people had known the high yak pastures of the Himalayas. Through all the years, as the Tais migrated and settled and fought, the yaks danced alongside. That night at Mai Sung, three yaks appeared, each formed by two men in a brown costume with a white mask. The masks had antlers (instead of proper yak horns) and slanted battery-lit red eyes. The masks sat atop the front men's heads, so the yaks stood tall. They had the bulk of yaks but moved gracefully. The crowd cleared space for them in front of the stage.

Long drums, cymbals, and gongs beat entwined rhythms as the yaks stepped into the light. Two dancing *sayahs* in blue trousers, loose white shirts, and white turbans guided the yaks. The tall beasts shook their antlered heads from side to side, red eyes glowing. They pivoted in unison, pranced lightly one minute, then stomped heavily the next. They approached Mo Heing with offerings of wildflowers in their mouths, which he replaced with envelopes of Thai money. The yaks bowed and swayed, and then they were gone. The music drifted away after them.

The music recommenced, this time more ethereal. Two boys and two little girls moved into the light, dancing the Canary Dance. Circus spangles covered their pink and green costumes and their fanned gauze wings trembled with the vibration of the bronze gongs. The canaries exchanged flowers for money with the warlord then danced into the dark: a Shan fantasy of winged beings, pure and noble and free.

The celebration was still going on when I left. I crossed into Thailand at midnight, Cinderella exceeding her border pass, but nobody bothered me.

The next day a violent thunderstorm broke and I decided it was time to leave Pieng Luang. My visa was running out, and I would re-encounter the Tais on the China side of the Burma border en route back to the U.S. It was the day before my thirty-second birthday, and the broth spoilers prepared a special Burmese/Indian dinner, with canned lychees and chocolate cookies for dessert. Prince George raised his glass in a birthday toast and said, "Next year, if you're still around, I'll see that you meet Khun Sa."

⌐ 5 ⌐

Pieng Luang's regular *songtaow* to Chiang Mai was out of operation for the rest of the rainy season, but I managed to flag down a white pickup truck whose Chinese occupants were going as far as Chieng Dao, a town just north of Chiang Mai. I rode standing in the back with an old man in threadbare clothes and a chubby young man in expensive Thai sportswear. When we passed through villages, other passengers jumped in: local Shan farmers, a young Thai Army soldier, half a dozen unarmed Rangers going on leave, a Lisu family.

We rode through forests into the mountain zone where valleys lay below us, all around us, green. Smoke and dust were gone, cleansed away by the monsoon. The driver was superb. I had seen some great driving during the previous rainy season, but this man was unquestionably the champion. In the muddy parts where all other vehicles became hopelessly stuck, he put chains on the tires and plowed right through. On the smooth parts he handled his truck like an F-16 fighter pilot. He drove like Robert Mitchum with a car full of moonshine in *Thunder Road*, like Yves Montand with a truckload of dynamite in *The Wages of Fear*.

Descending from the mountains between cliffs of red earth exposed by recent road improvements, we reached the main road to Chiang Mai. The chubby young Chinese man from Pieng Luang banged on the roof of the cab to let the driver know he wanted to get off. He pawed through his pockets for change with which to pay the driver. "Why doesn't fat boy get it together and pay the guy so we can go?" a Ranger grumbled. We soon had an answer. A yellow Mazda with blacked-out windows roared out of nowhere and screeched to a halt in front of the truck. Four Thai men in jogging suits jumped out. We were looking at three pistols and a shotgun.

"Oh, great—cops!" a Ranger snarled. "Dope busters! Just what we need."

The chubby informant moved away from the truck to watch from a distance. The four police approached the Chinese passengers in the front seat of the truck.

"Get out of the cab," one of the cops said. They got out immediately.

"Give me your gun," one cop ordered the driver.

"What gun? I don't have a gun," the driver responded. Another cop searched the driver and found a small automatic pistol tucked in the driver's waistband. Oh, you mean *that* gun . . .

The police told the rest of us to get down from the truck. First they searched an elderly Shan farmer, finding a candy wrapper folded around a couple of grams of opium in his shirt pocket. They immediately handcuffed the old man, who looked utterly bewildered, and pitched him into the recesses of the yellow car. Next they searched the old Chinese man from Pieng Luang. A film container in *his* shirt pocket held about a gram of opium. Two for two, I thought. Is everybody in this truck holding dope? The police had the cuffs out for the old Chinese man, but he held out a sheet of paper in his shaking hands. I could see that it was some sort of letter typed in Thai, with official-looking emblems stamped on it. The police read it and put the handcuffs away.

"Must be a note from Khun Sa," a Ranger snickered.

While all this was going on, the passengers had instinctively shifted into three groups. Group One was the Chinese and Shans, who were being searched meticulously. The Rangers and the lone Thai Army soldier formed Group Two. They were being ignored by the police, but they looked edgy anyway. And then there was Group Three, the innocent bystanders: me and the Lisus.

A cop climbed into the back of the truck to inspect the baggage. First he poked uninterestedly at the Lisus' bundles. Then he asked which bags were mine, and I pointed them out.

"Mind if I open them?" he asked.

"Please, go right ahead," I said, and watched closely as he made a quick check of their contents.

"You're a tourist, right?"

"Yes, I'm a tourist . . . sightseeing. Crocodile Farm . . . Elephants at Work in the Jungle . . . ," I agreed, thinking, *Yeah, sure. I'm the tourist who's just come down from Pieng Luang in muddy camouflage speaking Thai and Chinese.*

The cops weren't finding anything really incriminating on the driver's companions, but they didn't seem to want to give up the search.

"We know you're smuggling heroin," the policeman with the shotgun announced, "and we will take this truck apart piece by piece until we find it." They were going to take the driver into custody in Chieng Dao.

"What about all of us passengers?" a Ranger had to ask.

"Oh, we're taking all of you into custody in Chieng Dao, too. Get back in the truck."

We followed the yellow police car. Two cops sat in the back with their guns trained on us. During the search and seizure, I was thinking what a great story I'd have to tell my friends back at Nit's. I was secure in my very American sense of innocence, sure that since I carried no drugs no harm could come to me. But as the truck bounced toward Chieng Dao, I looked down at my knapsack. It was just like the Rangers' bags. What if one of the Lisus got rid of their dope by dropping it into what they thought was a military pack? The police hadn't searched the outside pockets of my bag— yet. *How will I ever explain what I'm doing on the border? "Liaison with the Shans" might not go over well at the Chieng Dao police station. My Thai Army passes won't cut any ice with Thai narcotics police* . . .

I remembered that it was my birthday, and I cast out all anxieties by thinking like a Shan. Nothing bad will happen on your birthday, I told myself. Nobody ever gets arrested on their birthday. It's unheard of.

When we reached the turnoff for Chieng Dao, the police said that they only wanted the driver after all. The rest of us were free to go. The driver insisted on collecting his fares from us. "He won't keep that money for long," sneered a Ranger.

With exquisite timing, a bus bound for Chiang Mai appeared and we all ran for it. As the bus pulled away, I thought of the Thai newspaper accounts of traffic accidents that inevitably ended with "The driver fled the scene." In this case, the passengers fled the scene, leaving the driver to his fate.

⚟ 6 ⚞

With a week remaining before I was to depart for China and the U.S., I returned to Three Pagodas Pass. This time, I brought Spin with me. We took a boat to Sangklaburi and marched on in the mud through the waterlogged Pass. At the Mon village we met an English-speaking Mon rebel who invited us to the headquarters of his faction. There, young women recruits in rain-darkened uniforms shouted "Boom, boom, boom" for effect as they charged a bridge with bamboo practice guns. Men, young and old, mostly barefoot, rehearsed ambushes with Chinese rifles. The women soldiers laughed in the rain. The boys wore scarlet ribbons on their guns. We watched them drill, counting their ancient numbers in their Mon language.

The next day the Mons sent us off to walk unescorted through their territory to Three Pagodas Pass. We followed the old Death Railway line. Every so often we noticed signboards at the side of the narrow trail, which bore skull-and-crossbones symbols and lots of writing in the curlicued Mon script.

Spin veered off the trail to take pictures of the signs. He was lucky that day. Later we found out that the signs said: "This area is heavily land mined. Do not under any circumstances leave the trail. Unless you're Tatmadaw."

The Parcheesi *chedis* and the bazaar delighted Spin. I introduced him to Joshua and Iris, who were still handing out advice and medicine. I'd left my camera in Bangkok because the auto-rewind was malfunctioning, but I had brought the photos from my previous trip.

The villagers greeted me as if I was a long-lost daughter. They gave me presents as I gave them their portraits. My favorite Bengali tea shop owner, whom I'd photographed standing at the *roti* pan wearing a purple T-shirt that said "Bowling," gave me a small iron weight shaped like a duck. A Yunnanese grandmother pressed a wad of kyat into my hand when I gave her a photo I'd taken of her in front of her smugglers' shop. Spin started keeping a list in his notebook called "Blade's Tribute." We also listed the different ethnic groups at Three Pagodas' bazaar, and came up with a dozen—a microcosm of Burma living in commercial harmony. We also went from shop to shop making a scavenger-hunt list of "Things for Sale with Animal Names." Much of the merchandise was Chinese-made, since China manufactured cheap, sturdy goods just right for the Burmese market. The Chinese concept of brand identity was to stick any old animal name on a product's label, so we found Tiger Head flashlights, Flying Horse blankets, Seagull batteries, Zebra toothpaste. Spin squashed an anopheles mosquito in his notebook and I labeled the bloodstained page "Hunting Trophies." At last I met some Wa people, two boys working in a shop. Spin took my picture with them. A Dracula mask was nailed to the front of their shop, symbolic of headhunting, I was sure. One of the boys wore a Culture Club T-shirt with Boy George's disembodied face on it, and I had on Spin's enormous sweater. I made my own list, this one without a title: the sound of bamboo, wearing men's sweaters, deep kisses, marzipan.

"Miss Edith, there is a Shan man in the bazaar who was human rights abused. You can interview him," Joshua said to me one morning.

"OK," I said. "Spin can tape him for his magazine story."

"I mean you, not your boy," Joshua said with his famous gap-toothed smile. "This is *your* job. Human rights."

"Well, Spin can take his picture, anyway." We went to the house where the Shan was staying. He didn't speak Karen and Joshua didn't speak Shan. Burmese was the shared language and Joshua translated for us.

"My name is Pota," the man said with one of those giggly Shan laughs that seemed to teeter on the edge of hysteria. Pota was a strong-looking man with light skin overlaid by blue-black tattoos. "I was working at the tin mine, a day north of here. Just a few weeks ago, the Tatmadaw came to the mine. They told us, 'Come here, we won't hurt you.' They caught all of us and tied our hands with rope. They said, 'You work for the Karens in this mine, so you are our enemy.' Five men they took away to be their porters, to carry their things. They left then, but we were still tied up and one Tatmadaw man stayed behind to kill us. Six of us were there with our hands tied. The soldier looked at us and raised his machine gun." Pota paused in his story, spat betel juice, and laughed. "This soldier shot us. We all fell to the ground, and then he was gone away. I am dead, I thought. But I was only wounded, and not even badly. The other miners, all five were dead. Now I come here to stay with my relatives. I am a man who comes back from the dead, they say. I was saved by the Lord Buddha, and also by my Shan tattoos, which are of a very powerful *yah* that prevents death by penetration of knives or bullets."

Joshua, Spin, and I went for a hike in the jungle after the interview with Pota. I thought about the Cameron Highlands and how I'd gotten so distracted by the beauty of the jungle there that I'd lost my way and climbed the same mountain twice. I had made my second climb to Three Pagodas, and now, with Joshua guiding me, I had found my way. He had assigned me to the human rights detail. How wise he was. It was perfect for me. With my market research background, I knew how to interview people and process the information into clear, useful reports. People trusted me and wanted to tell me their stories without even being asked. I had exceptional access to the border and had set up a network of rebel contacts that few others had. Through the rebels, I could reach the civilians and gather information on the war's effects. I would record Pota's story and others like it to send to the United Nations, to human rights groups, and to my government, to try and force them to pay attention to Burma's war zone.

Our hike took us to a riverside outpost, the front line. Spin was besieged by soldiers wanting him to photograph them. This was the only time I'd seen Karen and Mon soldiers together. In the bazaar, they usually ignored each other. Now they posed arm in arm for group shots, begging Spin to take more pictures until he convinced them he'd run out of film. Joshua found a bamboo shack open for lunch. "Burmese refugee lady, not a very good cook," he cautioned. Aluminum curry pots sat in a row on the table. Joshua lifted the lids in turn and announced the contents in each: "Pork. Chicken. Beef. Chicken. Pork. Monkey." Spin's face lit up. "I haven't had monkey since I was in India!" he exclaimed.

So we ordered the chicken in red sauce and the monkey. We spooned the curries over rice and sampled them. The chicken wasn't too bad. I spooned up a tough morsel of monkey meat in its greenish gravy. I recalled a song we'd sung in primary school out of earshot of the teachers that went, "Great green globs of greasy grimy gopher guts, mentholated monkey meat . . ." I fought my gag reflex and won, but barely. "This is *horrible*," I whispered to Spin. The monkey was not the most disgusting thing I'd ever sunk my teeth into (that honor belonged to a nightmarish boiled pork kidney at a sukiyaki dinner with an ex-governor of Chiang Mai), but it ran a close second.

Spin had taken his usual huge mouthful and was looking distinctly poleaxed. "Jesus wept!" he gasped. "This monkey's gone off!"

The problem with the monkey wasn't what you'd think. No little primate hands or anything at all recognizable. The curry was simply rancid beyond imagination.

"I told you this Burmese woman is not a good cook," Joshua said, eating his chicken curry.

"You're not kidding. She's Ne Win's secret weapon," Spin said.

I recalled that jungle Karens liked their meat extra gamy and were even known to enjoy a paté of the half-digested leaves found in monkey intestines.

I beckoned to an eight-year-old Karen commando, saying, "We're just so full of this excellent food that we can't possibly eat another bite. Won't you do us a favor and please finish this dish of *delicious* monkey curry?" The child was glad to oblige. He even enjoyed it. But then, he looked like he ate bullets for breakfast.

*   *   *

After a couple of days at Three Pagodas, I had to return to Bang-kok. Spin would visit Uncle Benny and the Karen mission family without me. We left Three Pagodas in a typical downpour, Joshua waving to us under his umbrella, and headed down the main trail. Spin's poncho draped over his backpack to form a monstrous hunchback, so he scuttled along imitating Quasimodo. His height proved advantageous when we reached the logging road quagmire—he only sunk in up to his knees, while I got mud-coated to crotch level. A human derrick, he hoisted me out of the mud several times before we got to the Songklia River. After we made an undignified crossing on the pontoon bridge (Spin fell off, but managed to keep his camera bag out of the water), we stopped at a tea shop to dry off and wait for a *songtaow* to Sangklaburi.

Two young Thai men were sitting inside the shop drinking coffee. One casually walked up to our table, asked if we were having a nice day, and if he could have a look at our passports. "We don't have any passports," Spin said, presuming him just some local nuisance. I noticed that the man was wearing tan trousers, police uniform trousers. "Spin, he's a *cop,*" I said under my breath. We showed him our passports. He wasn't all that interested, and we went on our way when the *songtaow* showed up.

I said good-bye to the Thailand/Burma border and Spin in Sang-klaburi, and a few days later I was in Yunnan, China. On the map I was very close to the Shan State, but borders being barriers, I had to fly there from Bangkok via Hong Kong. From Kunming, Yunnan Province's capital, I went south to Sipsongbanna. This was the home of the Dai people, close relatives of Burma's Shans. The Dais lived in thatched houses on stilts amid palm groves and rice paddies. Tribes like the Akha and Lahu, down from the hills to market, joined the familiar scene. The main town, Jinghong, hugged the banks of the Mekong River.

Yunnan's "Wa Autonomous Region" was east of Jinghong. I had

been intrigued by the Wa since Prince George's stories, but the Chinese government kept their Wa homeland off-limits to foreigners. The Wa were the most impoverished of China's ethnic minorities. China kept them hidden away, like mad relatives in gothic novels. I decided to try reaching Xiemeng, a town in the Wa region, anyway. I talked my way onto buses, traveling for a couple of days into the adjacent "Lahu Autonomous Region." But halfway to Xiemeng, I was taken to a Public Security police station. The police handwrote a notice to me, which read: "We are very sorry, but you are not supposed to be in this town. You were also not supposed to be in the town where you stayed last night, and you are absolutely not supposed to be in Xiemeng." They bought me a ticket for the bus back to Jinghong, which would depart the next morning.

On my way to the Xiemeng hotel, I walked through a marketplace full of Lahus selling mushrooms, pinewood, and animal skins. A ragged boy, with swarthier skin than the other tribespeople's, stood in the middle of the street staring at me. He was a Wa. I took a picture of him grinning wildly.

Back in Jinghong, I walked down to the Mekong, the great river that flowed south between Burma and Laos, then between Laos and Thailand, and through Cambodia and Vietnam to its delta on the South China Sea. My pink Brazilian ribbon had broken during the bus trip, so I threw it into the Mekong, the *sayah*'s magic knot intact. The current carried the ribbon off through the lands of the Tai and the homes of the brave to the sea.

DOWN THE
RABBIT
HOLE

⚊ 1 ⚊

In the courtyard, a young dancer swayed to the taped tones of a bamboo xylophone. Her hips switched the long train of her turquoise brocade sarong. She bent swiftly to the ground, turned her shoulders, and rose slowly. She bent, turned, and rose; bent, turned, and rose, her hands extended in the formal gestures of Burmese classical dance. The jewels on her blue gauze jacket glittered with

145

her movements and flowers quivered in her black hair. The audience, in business suits or sarongs of rich fabric, applauded. "She's
half Russian, half Burmese—interesting combination," an American in a dark suit remarked.

I searched the crowd for familiar faces. Knots of Burmese from
the embassy stood chatting with American academics under the
Oriental arches of the Freer Gallery in Washington, D.C. The
academics' June 1986 Burma Studies conference had just ended,
without controversy or political commitment as usual. I had not
been included in the conference, but I'd managed to get an invitation to the closing cocktail party.

Wearing a black and red dress from Jim Thompson's Bangkok
silk shop, I sipped a glass of Coca-Cola and eavesdropped carefully
until an American professor I'd met in Thailand appeared. This no-
nonsense, gray-haired man was a Burma expert of impeccable
credentials and a rebel sympathizer, so he was someone I could talk
to (quietly) in the midst of Burmese government apologists and
informers.

"There's someone here you should meet," the professor said. "He
works for the U.S. government in various capacities and he knows
Burma's frontiers." He introduced me to the stocky man in the
dark suit who'd known that the dancer was Russo-Burmese.

"Edith has just started an information project about Burma," the
professor said.

"It's to get the word out about what's going on over there," I
added.

"And what is the word these days?" The man in the dark suit
smiled.

"Right now I'm particularly concerned about the 2,4-D spraying program that the State Department is sending to Burma," I
said.

The man's smile faded. "When did you find out about that?" he
asked.

"Only two months ago. I got a letter from the Shan State Army
and one from the Tailand Revolutionary Council. I might have
discounted the whole thing as a weird rumor, except that it came
from two different Shan groups who hate each other."

"And in the Shan State, weird rumors do have a way of being facts, don't they?" the professor noted.

The letters I had received from the SSA and TRC had claimed that the Tatmadaw was spraying some kind of chemical from aircraft in the Shan State, and that people were getting sick from it, and cattle were dying. The SSA letter was an emotional appeal to call international attention to the abuse of civilians, while the TRC letter included charts showing how many people and animals had died in each sprayed area. I investigated and found that the chemical had been donated by the United States government to Burma for narcotics suppression. It was supposed to kill opium poppies, but I suspected that Ne Win wouldn't mind if it killed more than poppies in the hills of the Shan State.

"You're on to something with this," the man in the dark suit said. "I told them at State that this is Ranch Hand all over again, but they didn't listen."

"Ranch Hand" was the code name for Vietnam War herbicide spraying, and the comparison was appropriate. In Burma, the herbicide being used was 2,4-D (2,4-Dichlorophenoxyacetic acid). The Vietnam War formula called Agent Orange was 50 percent 2,4-D and 50 percent 2,4,5-T. The 2,4,5-T herbicide had been banned in the U.S. when it was discovered to be contaminated with TCDD, the most toxic dioxin substance known.

I had spoken with officials at the U.S. Environmental Protection Agency, who told me 2,4-D was contaminated with "moderately toxic dioxins." Both of Agent Orange's ingredients had been extremely hazardous. 2,4-D was under Environmental Protection Agency review, a process that could take years. Meanwhile, the State Department was giving it to Ne Win's Tatmadaw to rain on the hill tribes.

"The effects of aerial spraying on the tribespeople must be devastating," the professor speculated. "They're terrified of strange phenomena, and here is a cloud of chemicals killing their crops. They aren't healthy to begin with, so the herbicide could really do them in."

The Reagan administration's international anti-narcotics programs were headed by Ann Wroblesky, whose previous governmental experience had been assisting First Lady Nancy Reagan with her "Just Say No" campaign against drug use. Ms. Wroblesky, as Assistant Secretary of State for International Narcotics Matters, promoted aerial chemical spraying as the most efficient way to eradicate drug crops overseas.

The legal guidelines for herbicide spraying in the United States were ignored when the chemicals were enlisted in the international war on drugs. The State Department's Burma officer told me that 2,4-D was "only a harmless weed killer." Indeed one could buy 2,4-D anywhere in the U.S. and sprinkle it on the front lawn to kill dandelions. But one certainly could not take it up in a helicopter and spray the whole neighborhood with it, which was what the Burmese government seemed to be doing. Its agricultural use in the United States was restricted, and it was banned in national parks.

"You'll find that an Environmental Impact Assessment was done before the program started," the man in the dark suit said softly. "It made clear that spraying in Burma would be environmentally risky and of dubious effectiveness. State buried the report and went ahead with the program anyway. Spraying began last winter."

"The program was never tested adequately," I said. "And it's not monitored at all. The Burmese government doesn't let anyone from the U.S. check on the conduct of the spraying or its effects."

"The U.S. ambassador to Burma, O'Donohue, told our conference that the spraying program was the greatest success in recent U.S.-Burma relations," the professor said, shaking his head.

"Sure—it's perfect for Ne Win," I said. "Military aid with no strings, no oversight. But it's not a success in any other terms—the opium crop is still huge. I think Congress will want to know how the five million dollars a year for this program is wasted."

"Now that the program is in place, it's highly unlikely that anyone can do anything to stop it," the professor said pessimistically. "Congress won't care. This is part of the 'war on drugs' and nobody wants to speak against that."

I had found congressional staff members sympathetic about the alleged spraying effects but unwilling to attack an anti-narcotics program. An anthropologist, David Feingold, had brought word of the 2,4-D damage to United Nations narcotics meetings, but no one seemed very concerned there, either. I could see that exposing the chemical spraying of the Shan State was going to be difficult.

"Keep at it," the man in the dark suit said encouragingly. "I'm glad to see that you've taken this up. Good luck with your project."

I gave him my card. It read: "Project Maje: to encourage American awareness of the political situation in Burma." I had started Project Maje only a month before. I did not want to organize people, so it was not a group. I organized and distributed information. My project would be to disseminate information from groups opposed to Ne Win's regime without joining or endorsing any of them. I looked for an obscure name for the project because I didn't want to favor one frontier ethnic group over the others with a Shan, Karen, or Mon name. In *Hidden Land*, Ursula Graham Bower's 1953 book about the Apa Tani tribe of remote northeast India, I found the word *maje,* the Apa Tani term for Tibetan bells venerated by the tribe. A perfect symbol: a bell-ringing for enlightenment in the Eastern sense, and as an alarm going off in the Western context.

I prepared a background report called *Burma Frontier Insurgency* (which included a map showing where the war was and where the Wa were) to give to congressional staffers and human rights workers. I mailed a questionnaire to every English-speaking person I knew on the Burma border asking for specific data on human rights abuses that had occurred during the previous three years. I compiled the responses into a report to show the big, international human rights organizations that Burma documentation was available, despite its being a "closed country."

My research revealed a consistent pattern of abuse by the Tatmadaw in the frontiers. The horrors were not the spontaneous acts of soldiers lost in alien jungles, or of isolated warlords—they were counterinsurgency strategies carried to the nth degree by well-disciplined troops. The Tatmadaw was aiming to deprive the rebels of civilian support by terrifying, dehumanizing, and eliminating the civilians themselves. The same operations to destroy villages and press-gang porters were carried out in every area from north to south. The same methods were used to extract information: with electricity where available; otherwise with bamboo stakes, molten plastic, boiling oil.

Soon the word was out that I had Burma information. I got calls and letters from academics, journalists, and other researchers. I provided copies of documents and news articles, human rights data, reprints of scientific literature on 2,4-D, and border contacts for researchers who wanted to conduct firsthand investigations. New information arrived daily by mail from my network of insurgents and observers.

While Project Maje was gaining ground, my art career was losing it. My paintings were rejected by thirty-six New York art galleries. They liked my style but objected to the subject matter. Political art was okay, but "exotic" political art was not. The gallery directors insisted that their patrons just wanted "New York paintings." I was doing some of my best paintings ever, but I gave up on the art business.

Project Maje received no funding. It was one thing to study remote tribes—one might get grants for that—but to take up their cause, particularly when the tribes bore arms and raised opium poppies, was more than faintly disreputable. I paid the postage and Xerox bills that kept the information flowing with a series of dismal temp jobs I took while staying in New Jersey at my mother's house. The most memorable job entailed wearing a cardboard sign advertising running shoes while handing out coupons to lunch-hour passersby near Wall Street. I was cold and my feet (shod in the damned running shoes) ached. The only positive part of the job was making friends with the three-card monte dealers, shoe-shine men, and African umbrella peddlers who shared the pavement. And it paid for the human rights survey report. Eventually I got an indoor job taking phone orders for college textbooks, which lasted long enough to pay my way back to Bangkok.

I had been stranded in the U.S.—in New Jersey, which I detested—for a year. My normal recreation, horseback riding, was too expensive, and, needing exercise, I found my way to a karate school. I loved it from the start. Karate was so graceful and deadly. I became one of those tattooed people who hang out at karate studios, getting bruised and strong.

At the beginning of December, just as I was about to go back to Asia, one of the tougher black belts said to me, "You wouldn't catch *me* going to the middle of no war zone!"

"Oh, I'm not going to the middle," I demurred. "Just around the edges."

But this time I knew I had to go further than the border. I had to try to reach the hidden valleys of the Shan State where American chemicals were being sprayed. I had to reveal the lives of the people who lived trapped behind Burma's lacquered screen of isolation.

− 2 −

The Thai government had declared 1987 "Visit Thailand Year," and when I arrived in Chiang Mai at the end of 1986 tourism was already rampant. I decided to take advantage of it. The trekkers sat in the grungy cafés scrawling postcards to wherever they came from about the great time they'd had trekking among the hill tribes. I typed up an appeal:

> The Burmese Government is using 2,4-D herbicide (an Agent Orange ingredient), supplied by the U.S. government, in aerial spraying that endangers the hill tribe people of Keng Tung Province (northern Burma). The herbicide spraying is supposed to be anti-narcotics, but it is in fact a form of chemical warfare. If this matter is of concern to you, please send postcards (picturing Akha, Lisu or Lahu tribespeople) to the following U.S. officials, urging them to stop the supply of 2,4-D to Burma.

I included the addresses of two State Department officials and two congressmen, plus a *New York Times* article about the spraying that had appeared in November. I Xeroxed a couple hundred copies, and using techniques taught me by the running shoe company, I whisked through the tourist hangouts, passing them out. I had already started a letter-writing campaign in the U.S. but I figured some exotic postcards from Thailand might draw a little extra attention in Washington.

My main purpose in Chiang Mai wasn't to launch a postcard campaign, however; it was to get into the sprayed area of the Shan State. If I could go there and obtain evidence of the spraying's effects, then maybe reporters and camera crews would follow. The sprayed areas closest to the Thai border were in southern Keng Tung Province, and Khun Sa's bases lay between that zone and Thailand. A few days before Christmas, I met with Prince George and K. Sam to discuss the possibility of travel in Keng Tung. Christmas in Chiang Mai brought gusts of frosty mountain air and skies that wanted to snow but just couldn't. Patrons of the charming tropical outdoor restaurants shivered while hill-tribe urchins in dirty sweaters pestered them to buy roses and strawberries. We went to Nit's Sandwich Bar.

I had never been in Nit's at night. Ropes of Christmas tinsel decked the halls, and Nit himself manned the cash register, diplomatically out of earshot of all the interesting conversations in his booths. Prince George drank Singha beer instead of eating dinner. K. Sam ordered chicken soup and a glass of milk, and I had the "beef stroganoff" (which was actually buffalo). I drank Coca-Cola with my buffalo. Since I'd taken up karate, I disdained alcohol, for the same reason I eschewed high-heeled shoes: it slowed you down.

The dinner conversation was typically Sura. They always talked in spirals around some covert subject—hint, hint, hint. But eventually K. Sam mentioned an upcoming festival.

"What kind of festival?" I inquired.

"Oh, just another graduation ceremony for new troops."

"I see. At Pieng Luang?"

"No, a different location," Prince George said. "Someone very important might be there."

"Such as?"

"Someone everyone wants to see. They thought he was dead."

"Khun Sa? He'll really be there?"

"The general will be there," K. Sam said firmly, wiping off his milk mustache with a paper napkin. "And you can meet the general there."

"You may ask the general for permission to travel in Keng Tung for your investigations," Prince George added.

What a Christmas present, I thought. A Shan festival where I can get a laissez-passer from the big man himself, General Khun Sa.

"But you should be aware of one thing," K. Sam said with the little poker face he wore for all his jokes. "The general is a womanizer."

Prince George shot him a pained look and said, "Excuse K. Sam. He is awfully silly sometimes. An attempt at humor."

"Well, in that case I'd better bring Spin as my bodyguard," I said, "although now that I know karate, maybe I should act as his bodyguard." They laughed. "Seriously, can Spin come? You know he is dying to meet the general."

"This is not for journalists," K. Sam said. "It's just a Shan festival, and we're not sure that Khun Sa wants to talk to any reporters. Maybe it's better for people to keep thinking he's dead."

I knew how much Spin wanted to interview Khun Sa. He thought of the warlord as Conrad's or Coppola's mad Kurtz. Only one journalist had interviewed Khun Sa in the past few years: the Malaysian who'd done time in a Burmese prison. Sometimes I felt sorry for Spin. He was gregarious, yet one of life's loners. He wanted to be Hemingway-in-Spain. He wanted exclusives, and he got rat bites, malaria, and the odd bit of shrapnel.

While I had been in America, Spin had been in New Zealand. Now that we were both back in Thailand, our paths had crossed (as they always did) in Chiang Mai, but only for an hour. Spin had been rushing off, down to Three Pagodas Pass, to cover some Tatmadaw shelling as if it was the siege of Madrid. I turned my gaze on Prince George. The prince's wife had suddenly and mysteriously returned from her captivity but she had taken up with another man. Prince George was deeper into the sauce than ever, ordering up another liter of Singha.

"Oh, come on, *please* let Spin come, too," I said.

Prince George nodded to K. Sam, who took out a memo book and commenced writing in Shan. "This is your invitation," K. Sam explained. "You must appear at this address in Mae Hong Son, ready to leave, on January seventeenth. Show this to the people there and they will bring you to the festival." He wrote my name on the page and, barely hesitating, added Spin's.

Triumphantly, I Xeroxed a copy of the invitation and sent it, with instructions, to Spin's Bangkok post-office box, in a pink envelope marked "You May Already Be a Winner!"

⸗ 3 ⸗

Before the Shan festival was to begin, I had a couple of weeks to spend on the Pai River, where the Karennis and other ethnic rebels camped and trained. To my relief, when I showed up in a rented boat Arnold We not only recognized me, he greeted me as a friend. Ohn Khin showed off their baby girl, who was walking and talking in baby Karenni. They were living in a new bamboo house in a slightly different location above the river. The Tatmadaw had burned down the old one. Arnold We filled me in on what had happened.

"Last winter, some Thai bigshots from Mae Hong Son wanted our Padaung women to be brought to town for the Winter Fair. The one that has sections for different hill tribes."

"I know that fair," I said. "It has that Miss Hilltribe beauty contest where the teenage contestants get auctioned off to be mistresses of Mae Hong Son police and officials."

"The bigshots wanted the Padaungs for showing at the fair. We said, 'No. They are not animals to show like a zoo.' But the bigshots said, 'Well, we can close you down. We can shut your border.' So we sent the Padaungs to the fair. They were very afraid. Sick stomachs. They sat in the fenced place three nights, and people paid the Thais to come in and look at them. Then they came back here. A few months later, Chiang Mai bigshots came, wanting the Padaung women for a fair in their city. We refused to let them go that time. So the Chiang Mai men were very angry at us and they told Burmese spies all about this camp. Right after that, Tatmadaw invades here. Tatmadaw knew exactly where to go and what to burn. Easy for them, because the Thais had been here and told them. Everyone from here ran over to Thailand for safety, and the Thai police stole some of our guns, but the Kachins helped us fight back at the Tatmadaw. We drove them out. But it is not secure like before."

This is the story of Helen of Troy, I thought. Back in Karenni hands, the Padaung women were still attracting tourists. Now it was my job to give the orientation lecture to the tour groups who visited the base. I put them to work writing protest postcards, and made them all promise to join Amnesty International. I gave them copies of *The Karenni Journal*, an eccentric English-language political quarterly published by an elderly Karen gentleman, Uncle Mika, who lived in a Karenni village. I'd first met him when he walked up to me on a muddy riverside path and inquired, "Are you a Peace Person?"

"Absolutely," I replied.

"Good, we need all we can get, for the peace movement of Burma." Uncle Mika subsequently admitted that there was no such movement, but we agreed to try and start one.

Arnold We's porch was my bedroom. I slept in a sweater and sweatpants; it could get remarkably cold in the tropics. One night, gunfire crackled, waking me. Arnold We moved swiftly onto the porch, rifle in hand. The gunfire was coming from the mountains around the perimeter of the camp, right where the Tatmadaw had broken through Karenni defenses a few months before. But the guns went *pop . . . pop . . . pop,* not the rapid staccato burst of full-auto night combat. I heard Arnold We talking at the house next door, first in urgent tones, then angrily, then laughing. He came back and said, "This gunfire . . . I forgot, it's 1987, New Year's Eve!

Our soldiers waste their ammunition firing at the moon to welcome a new year. This year regulation forbids them to fire full-auto. At the moon, at least. I was asleep, I thought maybe we had a Tatmadaw breakthrough again."

"Well, Happy New Year, Arnold We," I said. The gunfire died down, and I went back to my warm nest of sleep.

During my stay, the Pai River training camp held a graduation ceremony for a National Democratic Front joint-command force. The troops were young tribesmen (Karenni, Wa, Lahu, and Pa-O), integrated, wearing NDF insignia, and taking commands in a mixture of English and Burmese. They marched clumsily but spiritedly to a bamboo flute and drum corps on a misty parade ground. As the soldiers drilled, Karenni civilian supporters stood in formation beside them. Some Thai intelligence types from Mae Hong Son and a boatload of tourists watched from the sidelines. Saw Moh Reh asked me to stand with his Karenni constituents, which I did, feeling honored.

Rice and curry were served to everyone after the parade. The soldiers mixed with each other instead of separating into their different ethnic groups. They looked as if they'd be a strong guerilla force, used to hardship at home in the jungle, well combat-trained. Before, I had thought of the National Democratic Front as an alliance on paper, to be manipulated by one of the bigger components, the Karens or Kachins, who had armies of about eight thousand each. Now I believed that the NDF was the best hope of the smaller armies such as those of the Karennis and Pa-Os, who were caught between the Tatmadaw and Khun Sa. If they could band together like this they might be able to capture and hold some territory.

I was taking photos with my Minolta and a bulky old Pentax when some NDF officers invited me to stay at the camp for a bonfire.

"We want to talk to you and steal you from Arnold We, who keeps all foreigners to himself," said Major Otto, a Pa-O former law student.

"Yes, please do stay. You can see our tribal troops in their element," added a Kachin I'd met on my previous trip.

I gladly accepted the invitation, and I had dinner at the officers' mess where I met and interviewed a Wa major. Fighting had ceased at Mae Aw but still flared between drug factions to the north, and the Wa were still everybody's low-rent Gurkhas. The Wa didn't fight for the Wa. They fought for Burmese Communist Party cadres, and old KMT kingpins like General Lee Wen-huan, and for Khun Sa. The young Wa major blinked his dark eyes nervously and fidgeted with a cassette case as I taped him.

"Sorry my English is not at all good," he stammered. "My people, the Wa, are not so politically informed. We need leadership to develop our politics."

I began our interview by asking him my standard question: "Generally speaking, what are the goals of your revolution?"

He only caught the first word. *"General Lee?"* he gulped, panic-stricken, thinking I had led off with a direct question about his army's KMT warlord patron. I repeated my question. The major apologized and said the goal was to follow National Democratic Front policy, which meant fighting for a federal democracy. "You can learn more about Wa people when my troops set fire to the big logs tonight," he offered.

When night fell the tribal soldiers circled the bonfire and danced, wailing their war songs. They lifted their arms like the wings of hornbills, and stomped the ground to the beat of long drums. The Pa-Os sang; the Lahus sang; and then the Wa sang their song, twisting and turning away from the flames and then back to face the fire.

"I know this song!" Major Otto exclaimed, laughing.

"What are they singing?" I asked the Wa officer.

"The song is like this," he said:

> We want
> To cut off
> Ne Win's head
> And put it up high
> In front of
> Our village.

Now this is atavism at its finest, I thought. This is the Wa being the Wa. Enough of the cultural inferiority complexes, wanting leaders to follow. They should just be let loose on the Tatmadaw.

The soldiers howled their song at the moon, "Aroooooo . . ."

"This is Ne Win's worst nightmare," I remarked to the officers. "I bet the old man is tossing in his bed right now, seeing this in his dreams." I watched the soldiers dance in firelight.

A Pa-O soldier swooped in front of the bonfire with a sword in each hand and gave a demonstration of martial arts prowess with a set form, combating invisible opponents. In karate we called this a *kata*. The Pa-O's swords sliced the air to ribbons. Then Major Otto said, "Now it is your turn. The soldiers would like to see some karate, please." I handed him my jacket. I stood and bowed, then lunged into the most complicated *kata* I knew, kicking, blocking, punching; pivoting to the points of an inner compass. The soldiers applauded, and the Wa major followed with a kung fu *kata*. I caught my breath, my skin hot, my eyes watering from wood smoke and joy. What a great year 1987 is! I thought.

◦ 4 ◦

The National Democratic Front was based at Manerplaw, the Karens' general headquarters. Major Otto gave me instructions for getting there. I returned from the Pai River to Mae Hong Son, took a bus to Mae Sariang, and spent another night in its dreary hotel. In the morning I caught a *songtaow* to a village on the Thai side of the Salween River, which formed the border with Burma. I went to a smugglers' shop, gave the proprietor a note from Major Otto, and was shown to one of the NDF's fleet of longboats. The Salween, one of the great wild rivers of the world, flowed tumultuously down from Tibet to lower Burma. My boat cruised one of its calmer stretches, to the confluence with the Moei River. On the Burma side of the river border, elephants rolled teak logs with their trunks, bringing them to Karen sawmills. The boards would then be floated to the Thai side for sale.

Many longboats were moored at Manerplaw, and a wooden archway proclaimed it the headquarters of the Karen National Union (the rebel political organization). The Karens shared their base with the NDF, whose guest I was, having arrived on their boat. I was given my own little mosquito-netted room in the NDF information office where soldiers were busy pasting together a new edition of *The NDF Journal*. The NDF had ten member groups: Karen, Karenni, Mon, Arakanese, Shan, Palaung, Pa-O, Lahu, Kachin, and Wa. I met with representatives of each, except for the Palaungs, whose man was away.

Aged revolutionaries from the Karen cabinet invited me for dinners and discussions. They brought me to meet Bo Mya. With the possible exception of Khun Sa, Bo Mya was the most famous person in the war zone. The Karen rebels' military and political leader, Bo Mya had been in the Karen rebellion from the start, and in World War II before that. He differed from most of his cabinet ministers in that he was a Seventh Day Adventist rather than a Baptist, and in his relative lack of education. Unlike the other Karen leaders, Bo Mya did not speak English. His Foreign Secretary, a physician named Dr. Marta, translated our conversation.

Bo Mya sat at a large teak table, and a half dozen of his cabinet ministers sat on benches along the veranda of the house Bo Mya used for meetings. I sat near him and accepted a glass of tea. Bo Mya was not grossly fat by Western standards, but among the slender Karens he cut quite a portly figure. His full face ruminated over a quid of betel nut. His curly hair was disheveled and his plain green fatigues were wrinkled. Jackie Gleason, I thought. Spitting image. Ralph Kramden at the wheel on the road to Mandalay. His pistol belt lay on the bench beside him.

Eyes half closed, Bo Mya began speaking, and Dr. Marta translated in large chunks. It was a set piece that he must have recited for hundreds of journalists over the years. Manerplaw was where they came to hear about the Karens and their resistance to Ne Win. I listened and took notes, but I had already learned the same from refugees and soldiers of Kawthoolei. When his monologue was over, Bo Mya glanced at me as if to check that I was still there.

"You may now ask your questions," Dr. Marta said.

"Maybe I should explain why I'm here," I said, as a soldier brought a plate of cookies and a bowl of fruit to the table. "I have started an information project to tell people about the Karens' struggle." I took an orange from the bowl and held it up. "To the outside world, Burma is like this orange. It looks beautiful. But on the inside, maybe it is rotten. Not just rotten, but with a big worm in it—and the worm is Ne Win." I dug a fingernail into the rind and pulled it down. "So my job is to tear open that orange and show the world what's really inside." I set the orange on the table thinking, Oh, I am such an idiot. I just told them the fruit at Bo Mya's house is rotten! But then I realized that the cabinet ministers who had been following my statement in English were all smiling and nodding. Dr. Marta was translating it into Karen. Bo Mya cocked his head and grinned at me. He let out a hearty guffaw. The cabinet ministers joined in the laughter, repeating, "An orange, rotten on the inside, yes! Ne Win, a big worm in it, yes!"

The interview was dispensed with. Bo Mya pushed the plate of cookies to me and I took two. He asked Dr. Marta something. "Miss Edith, he would like to know why you are dressed in camouflage uniform. Are you a soldier?"

"I'm not," I answered. "But I dress like this to show solidarity with the revolution."

"You can be in our Karen Army anytime," Bo Mya said.

"Thank you, I'm honored," I replied. "But you already have a courageous army of thousands. I can offer something else to the revolution, another army of thousands—those in the outside world who will write letters and protest their governments' Burma policies. They can change the Burmese regime's standing in the world. In this way we can hit Ne Win on many fronts."

The Wa representative at Manerplaw told me I could go to Mae Aw to see the Wa and Shan State Army troops stationed there. I returned to Mae Hong Son and arranged passage on a pickup truck from there to Mae Aw. Even though it was the rainless winter season, the steep road to Mae Aw was still a difficult climb for the truck. Mae Aw, a gentle green valley, cradled a village of low thatched houses and blossoming Chinese plum trees. The driver dropped me off at a house where a few soldiers with triangular SSA insignia on their caps were waiting for me. A Karen ordnance expert whom I'd met at the Pai River told me they'd been radioed from Manerplaw to expect me. The Karen was on loan to help them with their defense against Khun Sa. The Shan soldiers served tea, and soon a Wa lieutenant arrived. He spoke the Yunnanese dialect of Chinese, which was close enough to the Mandarin I spoke for communication. We walked along a cow path, uphill to the border.

There, an old Thai Border Patrol Police post was now manned by Wa and SSA troops, doing the BPP's job for free. "Look over there, the next ridge," the Wa lieutenant said, handing me his binoculars. "There you can see the camp of Khun Sa's men." It was less than a mile away. "For some months, there has been no fighting between us, but unfortunately neither is there trade on this route. Before, this was one of the best routes. But the Pa-Os got pushed out by Khun Sa and he wants to fight us for what's left. If the Thais allow us, we can stay here and fight him back." The ordnance man was setting up a Karen-manufactured mortar. "We had better point this away from the Khun Sa camp for now," the Wa said. "If they see it aimed at them they might break the cease-fire."

I gazed over at Khun Sa's green-bunkered hilltop. In a few days I would be in his territory. I had spent the first weeks of the new year with the real revolutionaries of Burma. The ones who trained and fought and died to drive Ne Win's Tatmadaw from their land. I wondered if Khun Sa would ever join their cause, or if he would remain an interloper in rebel territory.

I stayed in the village of Mae Aw that night, and met Maha Seng, the Wa prince, when he arrived at dinnertime. Like Khun Sa, Maha Seng had been in the government's Ka Kwe Ye militia, and a shifting series of alliances since. Currently he was leader of the National Democratic Front's Wa force. He was in charge of Wa troops at Mae Aw and other KMT-controlled border villages. The

Wa soldiers seemed devoted to him, although he was rumored to be an opium addict. He was a slim man, elegant in subdued civilian clothes, with heavy-lidded, glassy eyes. I could believe there was more to those saurian eyes than the green cashew liqueur we were served before dinner in a village house. I ate with Wa officers in a circle on the floor, dipping sticky rice into red hot sauce. I slept with lots of blankets and three Wa children in a chilly storeroom stacked with ammunition boxes and hung with slabs of dried meat.

⹀ 5 ⹀

I had managed not to say anything to the National Democratic Front people about the upcoming Tailand Revolutionary Council (TRC) festival, which was to feature Khun Sa. Nobody brought it up, so I figured it was a secret and let it remain one. Only Emma knew, because she knew everything that went on in Mae Hong Son. When I got back from Mae Aw, however, Emma showed me a copy of the previous day's *Bangkok Post.* It announced that Khun Sa would be holding a press conference at his new Shan State head- quarters due west of Pai. "A *press conference!*" I groaned. "I told Spin it was his exclusive interview!"

I presented myself with invitation, as instructed by K. Sam, at the new TRC safe house. An English-speaking Shan teenager recog- nized me from Pieng Luang. "You can go up tomorrow, in our truck," he said. "Two other foreigners will go as well, the writer Mr. Kevin Corry and his wife, Mrs. Hannah Corry, who come from England." I visited the couple, who were staying at one of Mae Hong Son's other hotels. Kevin was writing an exhaustively re- searched history of Burma's ethnic minority politics. Walking back to the Mae Tee, I passed a restaurant where the Shan teenager was drinking with friends. He called me in to introduce me, announc- ing, "She's going to see Khun Sa tomorrow," so the whole place could hear. So much for discretion.

I expected Spin to arrive that evening with Kulok, my American friend who was supposed to bring a month's worth of my mail. When they did not appear, I waited in my room at the Mae Tee with Emma, eating cookies and looking at the *Bangkok Post*.

"They're not coming," I said at nine o'clock.

"Well, they could just be late," Emma said. "Maybe they'll show up tomorrow."

"No, I'm sure Spin saw the thing about it being a press conference and decided to skip it. I don't know which I'm more upset about, no Spin or no mail." Emma went home but I stayed up past midnight watching for trucks coming in on the Chiang Mai road.

When I left in the morning I gave the Shan kids at the Mae Tee desk a note for Spin, informing him that I'd gone on to the festival and he could arrange a ride at the safe house. An hour up the road from Mae Hong Son, Kevin became feverish and thought it might be malaria coming on, so he and Hannah got out of the truck to catch a *songtaow* back to town. The TRC truck drove on, packed with Shans, many of whom had come from Pieng Luang for the festival. We left the Pai road and veered off onto a newly bulldozed dirt logging track. Thai logging camps were hacking away at the forest in a feeding frenzy on the last stands of precious hardwood left on the Thai side of the border.

No Thai checkpoints existed to disrupt our trip, and no welcome sign indicated our crossing. I knew we were on the other side when I saw Shan soldiers lurking in a shady bamboo grove, with a field of poppies in heavy bloom just around the bend. We drove down into a valley, entering a Shan village, and the village gave way to Tiger Camp. Khun Sa had conquered the valley and was making it into his own Utopia. Well-irrigated rice paddies spread out from the village and camp, and vegetable terraces were being built up the hills. Ornamental gardens and pristine pathways connected Tiger Camp's neat bamboo huts. All sorts of festival structures were being raised: triumphant bamboo archways with painted Shan slogans, reviewing stands, and snack bars. The truck pulled into a festival parking lot and I climbed out, brushing off dust. A TRC video unit taped my arrival, presumably expecting a grander contingent of foreign guests. K. Sam and Prince George were there, and they introduced me to a Shan education official and Khun Sa's English-speaking aide-de-camp.

A row of *bashas* (temporary huts) had been built for the expected guests. One was a dormitory and the others were duplex *bashas* with two bamboo bunks in each room. Mine was provisioned with new wool blankets, a pillow, candles, matches, boiled water in an ornate bottle labeled "Regency Brandy, Made in Thailand," and bug spray. "All of the amenities, none of the conveniences," K. Sam commented dryly. I shared the *basha* with the only other guests—three Thai citizens. One was Dr. Pongsri, a Mon academic who knew both of Burma's Mon rebel factions well, and the others were a Shan couple who lived in Bangkok and for some unfathomable reason were posing as brother and sister.

In the evening we visited Mo Heing for tea, and I gave the old man a photo of a painting I had done of a Dai woman in Sipsongbanna. The parade of newly trained recruits had been rescheduled—pushed back two days—because the parade ground wasn't finished. The TRC had hired three Thai bulldozers, with drivers, from a road crew that was supposed to be working on improving the highway between Mae Hong Son and Pai. They worked around the clock to flatten out Khun Sa's parade ground. Their grinding gears resounded all night and a generator that lit the whole area hummed accompaniment. Cold mountain wind whipped through the loose *basha* walls.

Soldiers, jogging and chanting cadence at dawn, woke us. After breakfast K. Sam announced, "You will now meet our general." On cue, Khun Sa walked up from his *basha,* which was somewhat larger than the others and distinguished by a fence with an arch painted with a Shan phrase, "Brave Blood," which K. Sam helpfully translated as "Old Blood and Guts."

The first thing I noticed was Khun Sa's military bearing. He had superb posture, which made him seem taller than he was. He strode with his head thrown back, hands clasped behind him, in pressed green fatigues (no insignia of any kind) and a bulky olive drab jacket. His straight black hair was combed neatly from a left part. I noticed something familiar about his face, but I wasn't sure what.

Eventually one of the guests identified it: "Mao at Yenan. The young Mao Tse-tung before he got bloated. In the old filmstrips." Khun Sa had that same oval Chinese face, the same bearing. "Our general has charisma!" Khun Sa's aide-de-camp beamed, pronouncing the "ch" as in "charm." *Ch*arisma.

Prince George introduced me, and the man known as the opium king of Southeast Asia shook my hand in a strong, two-handed clasp. His skin was remarkably smooth, except for crow's-feet that emerged when he smiled. His eyes had a strange, amused look, like those of a child with a big secret or an old, old man who doesn't give a damn about anything anymore. He was a few weeks away from his fifty-fourth birthday.

"Nin hao ma?" I greeted him in reasonably respectful Mandarin. *"Hen hao, hen hao."* Very good. Deep crow's-feet. He liked my Mandarin. "Please excuse these very poor accommodations," he continued. "We are only a poor, lousy old army camp. We've lost so much face."

"Please, never mind," I said, Chinese style. "This camp is beautiful, better than I deserve. It is I who have lost face, because my country is giving the Tatmadaw a chemical to spray on the Shan State."

Our conversation continued, nattering old-fashionedly about the weather, as if we were a pair of senile Mandarins in a Suzhou garden. He punctuated his Chinese with a typically Shan, hysterical laugh. Khun Sa may have been Shan only by adoption, but he did have the laugh down pat. He posed for a few photographs, arms crossed as if straitjacketed, looking deadly serious like the young Mao. After he chatted with the Mon and the Bangkok Shans, he walked off toward the training area.

I spent most of the afternoon seated at a picnic table in the warm sun, using K. Sam's typewriter. The Shan education official had given me handwritten lists of villages affected by 2,4-D spraying, with statistics on acreage sprayed, ethnic identity of villagers, and persons and animals killed. I retyped them with carbons, to distribute to the journalists who were still supposed to arrive. I had brought along my own press releases about the spraying program and I hoped I could use the press conference to interest reporters in the 2,4-D issue. The statistics claimed that crops were destroyed by spraying in twenty-three Lahu, twenty Akha, three Chinese, and two Shan villages. The hill tribes certainly seemed to be bearing the brunt of it. I was skeptical about the casualty claims. Certainly if planes flew low over a village spewing noxious fumes on the crops subsequent deaths would be blamed on the spraying, no matter what the actual cause was. 2,4-D was a dangerous chemical, but the only way to determine for sure if it was causing fatalities in the Shan State would be to send in pathologists to perform autopsies. And that wasn't going to happen—I would be lucky to get myself in.

The Shan official gave me a few sets of photos taken in sprayed fields. They showed Shan farmers standing among whitened, distorted plants. Thin people in drab clothing, they stared bleakly. These people should be on the cover of American magazines, I thought. Americans should know what we're doing in Southeast Asia in 1987.

I had written a flyer that was translated and distributed by rebel groups called "How to Survive a 2,4-D Attack." It put American safety measures in simple terms, and one of its main directions was to avoid touching anything that had been sprayed. Labels on the 2,4-D weed killer sold in American hardware stores said to wear protective clothing and wash exposed skin with plenty of soap and water because the chemical could seep right through your skin to your nervous system. But the farmers in the photographs didn't own shoes, and if they had water to wash with, it was near the sprayed fields. Were they supposed to wash their 2,4-D exposed feet in 2,4-D contaminated water?

A truck brought Dr. Pongsri, the Bangkok Shans, and myself to a dinner party in the village. On the way, a truckload of press people (none of whom I recognized) passed us on its way to Tiger Camp. They looked at me (in camouflage, amongst Shans) oddly, it seemed. Khun Sa and Mo Heing were at the village party, along with all the Shan officials, a renowned Shan poet, old KMT cronies,

a crooked ultra–right wing Thai general, a bevy of Thai intelligence agents, and some photogenic tribespeople. Khun Sa, attired
in baggy Shan trousers, white shirt, and straw peasant hat, bolted
his dinner and got up to work the crowd. He table-hopped, shaking
hands, cracking jokes, posing for pictures with guests. A crew of
Shan soldiers armed with camcorders and Nikons followed his
every move. Gathering the tribespeople to his side, he staged photo
opportunities with Reaganesque aplomb.

Mo Heing was eclipsed. His warm, diffuse smile was no match
for Khun Sa's professional eye contact and theatrical gestures. Mo
Heing might spend time contemplating the consequences of his
actions—if only to justify them—but Khun Sa (glad-handing,
backslapping) lived for the moment. Mo Heing meditated while
Khun Sa finessed the art of the deal. Khun Sa in his peasant hat
was a man of the people. The people at his dinner table. Just let
this man loose on the international press, I thought shuddering, as
the warlord posed with his arm around the shoulders of a Lahu
chieftain.

My *basha*-mates and I walked back to Tiger Camp after dinner,
and met up with Kulok. He handed me two manila envelopes full
of mail and told me he'd driven his truck up with Kevin, Hannah,
and Spin. The boys at the Mae Tee had given them my note.

"Where's Spin?" I asked.

"Oh, the big asshole's up at the dining hall. He's *still* eating."

I ran over to the guests' dining hall, and Spin was there—
shoveling in the rice—at a table with Kevin (who had turned out to
be malaria free) and Hannah. I *wai*'d Spin and said, "Welcome to
my island." He swallowed his rice and leaned over and kissed me. I
sat down and a soldier brought us border coffee.

"We have got to go to the Salween River from here," I said,
taking out my map (a *National Geographic* map showing "The
Peoples of Mainland Southeast Asia"). "In the old days this was the
SSA trade route, right along the trail that goes behind the village.
Prince George let it slip that it's only a couple of days' walk from
here to the river." Spin had a detailed map of Mae Hong Son
province that covered the Shan State to just past the Salween, and
we examined the route on it.

"Yes, Blade, well done!" Spin said. "Have they told you we can do the trip?"

"Oh, you know how those guys are. They never come out and say you can do anything until the very last minute when it just happens," I replied. "I'm sure we can go."

"Don't tell those other bloody journalists. It'll be just us—Kevin, Hannah, you, me, just don't tell *anyone,*" Spin said. "Especially not Zuber."

"Oh, he's here? Which one is he?"

"Over there. Looks like a Thai Bob Dylan. Definitely not to be trusted." Zuber was the Golden Triangle correspondent for a Thai newspaper, notorious for making news of the Shans, Wa, and KMT even more incoherent than it already was.

"What other journalists are here?"

"All the riffraff. A Japanese TV crew, French TV crew, Hong Kong film types, an Indian from Singapore, an Indonesian woman. The rest are Thai stringers for the wires and magazines and a few local papers. They're only here for the bloody press conference. They'll leave afterward. They won't even stay for the troop graduation since it's been postponed." Spin was a happy camper. His dark brown hair, which had stood in a brush cut when I first met him two years before, had grown long enough to pony-tail. He was winter pale, bundled up in layers of sweater and down vest. When we had met up in Chiang Mai after a year of separate continents, I was irritated by his running off to Three Pagodas and I'd thought, what did I ever see in this long-haired goof? But now I knew the long-haired goof was who I'd loved all along. I was a happy camper too.

⌐ 6 ⌐

The assembled journalists waited for the warlord in the morning fog, stamping their feet and rubbing their hands to warm up. I stood with Kulok and Spin. Khun Sa came up the hill with K. Sam, who introduced Kulok first with, "This is an old friend of ours from Pieng Luang."

"And Kulok speaks Chinese very well, too," I added in Chinese. Kulok denied any such linguistic ability in the formulaic self-deprecation of proper Mandarin. Khun Sa, delighted, nodded and gripped Kulok's hand in his tight clasp.

Moving past me with a familiar Chinese greeting, Khun Sa then reached for Spin's hand.

"This is my illustrious journalist friend from New Zealand," I told him and Spin, as I had coached him, greeted the warlord in Shan: *"Mai sung!"*

Khun Sa glowered comically at Spin and said to me in mock disgust, "He's too tall." Then he said something in Shan, which K. Sam translated as, "The general says it is obvious you have been in places like this before. You have the look of the jungle about you."

After Khun Sa shook hands with all the journalists, everyone moved to picnic tables that had been arranged in a square. The journalists sat at three tables, with camera crews standing behind them. Khun Sa lorded over the fourth, flanked by Kulok on his right, Dr. Pongsri and me on his left. We were the only *guests* present aside from various Thai intelligence types (some of whom had donned TRC uniforms) who skulked in the background.

K. Sam acted as press secretary and translator. "To begin with," he said, "you may ask questions of an ordinary conversation nature. Then will come an opportunity to ask your 'hard news' questions." For a moment, nobody spoke. Then a Thai reporter asked Khun Sa his age, and another asked about his family. Spin joined in with, "I see you're smoking imported 555 cigarettes—why don't you smoke Shan cigars?" (Same reason he's not tattooed, I thought, because he's not Shan.)

"Oh, I don't like Shan cigars because little sparks blow off and burn holes in your clothes," Khun Sa said. He lit another 555 with his camouflage Zippo, held the cigarette vertically between his fingers as he drew on it, and blew smoke, looking so amused. Cameras devoured each gesture, each shift of expression.

"What countries would you like to visit?" a Japanese reporter asked.

"Oh, Japan, of course. And Singapore, and Thailand, too. But I am unable to travel, I could be arrested." Khun Sa was widely known to spend time in Chiang Mai and even occasionally visit his wife in Bangkok, but he was coyly going along with the Thai fiction that he was a wanted man with a price on his head.

"Do you feel safe here?" someone asked.

"I never leave my own area, so I am safe among my own people." Security indeed was lax around one of the most notorious criminal kingpins in the world. None of the visitors had been searched and the place was overrun with shady Thais. Khun Sa's hundreds of trainee soldiers were armed only with carved wooden replicas of M-16s. And he had only a solitary Wa bodyguard, who wore a long black raincoat. Spin was spreading a rumor among the journalists that the Wa packed an Uzi under his coat, but more likely Khun Sa's only real protection was his own pistol and that obnoxious combination of hail-fellow-well-met munificence and unpredictable violence. I had heard stories of his killing high-ranking officers who displeased him—murdering on impulse, drunk, apologizing afterward. Any threat to him would probably not come from foreign agents, it would come from his own men. Khun Sa certainly didn't seem worried about security. The Shans told me he went for long pony rides by himself, showed up at farmers' huts alone, and wandered the camp at night, a lonely, insomniac drunk.

The press conference shifted gears when K. Sam announced, "Now you may ask the general any questions you wish."

"How many heroin refineries do you have?"

"How much opium do you control?"

"How much money do you make from drugs?"

Khun Sa answered: "We will have nine hundred tons of opium this year. We tax the opium traders and refiners in our area, to finance our army. It is very expensive to maintain this army, so that is what we do." The journalists were beside themselves; this was better than they'd expected. The warlord wasn't bothering to deny his drug business—as narcotraffickers were supposed to—but boasted of it, bragging that production had been stepped-up a couple of hundred tons over the previous year. Then Khun Sa got on to the topic of America's Drug Enforcement Administration. DEA agents operated in Chiang Mai, although not in Burma, and they were the warlord's *bête noir*. He was off and running about how the DEA used his existence to justify their jobs, to get money for lavish life-styles. "If the DEA can kill me, do they think opium will go away from the Shan State?" he demanded.

As he ranted on, I sensed the press conference derailing. What about the Shans? Their story certainly wasn't being told. The 2,4-D program didn't have anything to do with the DEA—it was all from the U.S. State Department (the DEA weren't policymakers, they were just cops). The spraying hadn't even been mentioned yet. I leaned over Dr. Pongsri and interrupted Khun Sa. I placed my hand in front of my mouth and whispered, "Please tell them about the airplanes spraying chemicals . . ." He nodded, mentioned that poor farmers' land was being sprayed, and proceeded to blame it on his nemesis, the DEA. As he went back into his DEA harangue, I realized that my whispered cue had been picked up by all the journalists' tape recorders, which K. Sam had lined up neatly in front of Khun Sa. Oh well, at least they can't accuse me of taking directions from him, I thought.

"Who is that woman?" a French cameraman, squinting at me, asked Spin.

"Oh, she's just one of us," Spin said.

"No, she's not," the cameraman said. "She's one of *them*."

The Thai reporters suddenly figured out that Khun Sa could understand simple Thai, so they began asking their questions directly, getting answers in Thai, which left the other journalists in the lurch. Zuber crouched in front of Khun Sa, firing off questions in an old fashioned Chiang Mai dialect that was extremely close to Shan, thus undercutting even his compatriots. Being a warlord means you can walk out on anything that bores you, and Khun Sa, bored at last, stubbed out one last cigarette, rose, and left. I handed out press packets on the 2,4-D spraying, including sets of photos.

Khun Sa returned, this time trotting briskly up the hill on a fine black pony, to pose for equestrian pictures. Their appetites for combat whetted by the verbal competition, the journalists jousted

strenuously for the most advantageous spot from which to photograph the mounted warlord.

After dark a big open-air party was held in the village. I stood by
a fire with some Shans as the troupe I'd seen in Pieng Luang danced
the Yak and Canary dances for the cameras. Much of the magic had
gone for me. At Pieng Luang, they wouldn't consider doing those
dances unless a *sayah* and several monks had deemed it auspicious.
Here it was just another show, part of the warlord meets the press
cavalcade.

Khun Sa sat with his officers and KMT and Thai guests, grilling
buffalo kabobs on charcoal braziers. He was deep into his custom-
ary Regency brandy, which the foreign reporters (except the
French) assumed was some kind of expensive imported cognac.
Khun Sa was doing his Royal Drunk. In civilian clothes and his
heavy jacket, he danced with Akha women, a tribal dance. He
brought a Thai lady intelligence type who wore TRC fatigues and
me in my camouflage into the Akha group with him. We did an
Akha dance where we had to lock legs in a circle and jump around.
Flashbulbs bleached the night. The Regency flowed ruthlessly.

A Shan band—drums and gongs and an instrument that looked
like a violin with a gramophone horn attached—began a *ramwong*
tune, the first of many, and dancers formed a line, in pairs. The
ramwong was a popular dance in Thailand, Laos, Cambodia, and
the Shan State. Couples paraded forward around the perimeter of
the dance floor with a simple step and graceful arm motions. The
Shan education officer took my arm and showed me the routine:
two steps forward, one step back. Like Shan politics, I thought. The
arm motions were easy enough and I twisted my wrists and fingers
the way the Shan girls did. The song lasted for three leisurely
circumambulations of the dance floor.

Khun Sa's aide-de-camp propelled the warlord onto the dance
floor and steered me over to dance with him. Khun Sa did the walk,
the stroll. He was unsteady on his feet by then. He looked at his
watch. Amazing, I thought, who gets that drunk, practically legless,
and looks at his watch? Does he have an appointment? The
drunker he became, the more self-conscious he seemed. The

amused look had left his eyes and they'd become guarded, preoccupied. The more he cavorted, joked, and shouted, the more inhibited he seemed. He was *ramwong*ing the tightrope between his out-of-control ritual drunk and his need to be totally in control of every situation. When the song ended, he shook my hand and thanked me as if I'd just given him directions home, and staggered back to the barbecue with his aide-de-camp holding him up.

Spin quit photographing and asked me to dance. He was adept at the *ramwong,* something he'd picked up in Indochina. Shan officers wanted to dance with me, and Shan theater troupe girls wanted to dance with Spin, so we only started each dance together for the first few steps before we got cut in on. The *ramwong* tunes were hypnotic, the dance was flirtatious (unless your partner was looking at his watch), and the band played all night. It was fiercely cold in the Shan mountains that winter, and we turned to the *ramwong* and cheap brandy to keep us warm.

The next day the Tailand Revolutionary Council held a civilians' meeting, a chance for people who'd traveled from other parts of the Shan State to air their grievances. First Mo Heing (soothing tones) and Khun Sa (exhortations) delivered speeches. They shared a reviewing stand with Shan monks, and the journalists sat on benches under thatched roofs, overlooking the parade ground where the civilians occupied picnic tables in the hot morning sun.

During the speeches, the aide-de-camp, Si Paw, a tattooed, cigar-smoking university graduate, informed Spin and me that Khun Sa was illiterate. The warlord spoke Chinese, Shan, Burmese, some Thai, and could toast "Cheers up!" and count in English—but he supposedly couldn't read or write any of it. I wondered how any Shan speaker couldn't learn modern written Shan, which was utterly efficient: only seventeen consonants. I supposed it was like the old joke about the rich boy in the wheelchair: Of course he can walk, he just doesn't have to.

"The general's staff reads his correspondence to him," Si Paw said. "He has aides-de-camp for English, Chinese, and Burmese.

And he likes very much to listen to his favorite book, *The Three Kingdoms*." That was a classic Chinese tale of warlord chicanery written in the Ming dynasty. "The general has a most wonderful memory and can recall everything in a letter that was read to him days before. And he knows the name of every one of his soldiers."

Shans and tribespeople stood at a microphone and complained of abuse by the Tatmadaw, BCP, and KMT ("Black Burmese, Red Burmese, and White Chinese," K. Sam translated it). One woman told of her husband's disappearance after he was seized by the Tatmadaw. Others told of fleeing their villages as refugees, and of daughters and sisters who had become prostitutes in Thailand. A Palaung and two young Shans referred to herbicide spraying in their areas. I went to find Prince George. "I want to interview these three men," I said, and showed him their names.

When the meeting dispersed, the Palaung tribesman came to sit at a picnic table near the guest *bashas*. I had informed the journalists that eyewitnesses to the spraying would be available for interviews, but only Spin, Kulok, Kevin and Hannah, and the Hong Kong film crew were interested—the rest were off tagging after Khun Sa somewhere. Kevin and I did the interviewing, with Prince George interpreting. The middle-aged Palaung smoked a curved tobacco pipe, appearing relaxed. I asked him about the spray.

"If you breathe it, you get dizzy," he said. "If you eat the plant that has been affected, you get stomach trouble, stomach swelling." I was well versed in the routes of toxicity of 2,4-D. Inhalation was not the worst of it, unless you were allergic or already had respiratory problems (as many in the Shan hills did). Subcutaneous absorption caused nerve damage, dizziness, headaches. Ingestion had the strongest effect—severe gastric illness. High levels of 2,4-D could cause birth defects when received by pregnant women, and studies had shown it to be cancer-causing in large doses.

The second witness was a Shan in his twenties who looked down at a glass of tea as Kevin and I questioned him. He described the chemical as "Smoke or gray color, like dew," and swore he'd seen the bodies of seven Lahu tribespeople who had died from its effects. He had watched the Lahus' hill fields get sprayed from the safe vantage point of his valley village. I asked him if the area was insurgent territory and he said that it was actually government-controlled, even having a new government school. I wondered why the Tatmadaw would spray in an area they already controlled, and then I realized that it was probably because they'd get shot down in insurgent-controlled zones, like the BCP domain. Considering all hill tribes a security risk, the Tatmadaw went after the easiest ones, regardless of political affiliation.

K. Sam took over as interpreter when we interviewed the second Shan, who toyed with an unlit Thai cigarette. He had seen the spraying of a hill-tribe village. I asked him about the tribespeople: "Will they try to plant the same fields that were sprayed?"

"They have to use fertilizers, and if fertilizers aren't available, then animal manure. And most of the animals are dead now, and they haven't the money to buy fertilizers."

"Have any of the people gone to another place?"

"There were many. Mostly they moved nearer to towns. And some, those who were bitter enough, became soldiers in the *Ba Ca Pa*." K. Sam translated that as "became soldiers in our Shan army."

"Excuse me," I said, "but I really thought I heard him say '*Ba Ca Pa*'—the abbreviation for Burmese Communist Party."

"Oh, well, I guess he did," K. Sam admitted. Of course tribespeople angry about the spraying would join the BCP, which at least fought the Tatmadaw, instead of the TRC, which didn't. The extraordinary thing was that before the spraying the BCP had to shanghai their recruits, and now—thanks to the U.S. State Department—people were actually *volunteering*.

After the interviews, we were sitting in the sun drinking tea when Zuber came up in a lather and waved the previous day's *Bangkok Post*, which had just arrived at Tiger Camp, in our faces. MEDIA WARNED ON KHUN SA said the headline over an article reporting that the Thai government had issued orders prohibiting journalists from crossing into Burma for Khun Sa's press conference. A police intelligence general warned that for foreigners to do so would be "violating departure and re-entry regulations" and for Thais it would be "crossing into another country without permission." He further stated that the Thai government "would not like reports published that would disrupt the good relations with the Burmese government."

"What can we do?" Zuber moaned. "We're already all here. They'll arrest us all!"

"Forget about it," Spin said firmly. "Half the Mae Hong Son police department is up here at Tiger Camp for the festival. They're on the bloody payroll. Nobody's going to arrest anybody. Since when has Thailand treated Burma border-hopping as a crime, anyway? We come and go as we please. Don't sweat it, man."

"And what's this nonsense about Thailand's good relations with the Burmese government?" I added. "Thailand has better relations with Khun Sa than with official Burma."

"I don't know," Zuber said. "To me this looks serious. This kind of noise usually doesn't come from so high up. Usually a regional commander would talk big like that, and it would all stay regional, with the usual payoffs and all that. But this is coming from Bangkok! It puts pressure on the local police to really go after us!" We laughed at Zuber's pinched, worried face because we knew the system better than he did.

That night the party resumed at Tiger Camp, with more Yaks and Canaries and a monumental *ramwong* on the parade ground. Khun Sa invited Spin and some of the other journalists to one of the *bashas* for beer and an informal chat. When he returned to the dance party, Spin told me that Zuber and the others had expressed high anxiety about their imminent return to Thailand, as if hoping for reassurance from Khun Sa. "I told them, 'Hey—*Mai pen rai!*'" Spin said, using the Thai expression for "It doesn't matter." "Those buggers are really paranoid. The road up didn't even have a checkpoint—how are the Thais supposed to arrest anyone?"

"Right. There are boatloads of tourists going down the Pai River every day," I said. "Nobody arrests them. The border is open!"

As a special festival treat, Chinese strongmen put on a show. They reminded me of similarly dreadful buskers I'd seen in the dusty town squares of Datong, Lanzhou, Kaifeng. After my long-haul trips through China, I found many Chinese things depressing. T'ang poetry and Song porcelain would always thrill me—but much of the rest seemed, like the strongman act, unbearably tawdry. The star strongman bent spears with the point at his chest and walked on his hands on a bed of broken glass. The Shans were rapt, but Khun Sa was bored. He yawned ostentatiously and walked out during some dramatic swordplay. "Just as well," I said to Spin. "You know how he always likes to participate in the dances—I can just see him demonstrating a sword trick and in an unfortunate incident sending a Chinese strongman's head flying into the audience."

In the morning Khun Sa responded to the journalists' arrest anxiety with a thoroughly Oriental gesture: money envelopes. Si Paw and the Shan education officer went from *basha* to *basha* handing out envelopes, each containing five thousand baht, to the guests. I assumed that it was for bribing our way out of any unpleasantness that might develop at the Thai border. Spin, Kulok, Kevin, Hannah, a Thai from Reuters, and a couple of others immediately gave the money back, as did I. "Please donate it to the monks and schoolchildren," we said. The other visitors apparently kept their envelopes of purple notes.

Most of the press left that morning. Si Paw saw them off with paper-wrapped parcels containing Shan flags, and Shan jackets for the men, cotton sarongs and blouses for the women. They would all miss the graduation parade in the afternoon.

"Why don't you at least stay one more day and see the parade and tonight's banquet and dance performances?" I asked the Indonesian reporter.

"I'd like to, but I only brought enough clothes for two days," she replied.

"You could wear your Shan outfit. You'd look great in it. Khun Sa was only the beginning of the story. Stay and see more of the real Shan people."

"Love to, but I gotta file." So that was it. They were satisfied with what they'd gotten: pictures of the warlord on his horse, the warlord dancing. Enough words and pictures to prove that Khun Sa was alive, nothing more.

The Hong Kong film crew stayed, as did Kevin, Hannah, Spin, and the non-journalist guests, but the press festivities were over. I was in my *basha* struggling to load my Pentax to take parade pictures when the Shan official appeared at the door with two packages.

"The general wants you to wear this," he said. "Also, you have been granted permission to travel in the TRC territory to the sprayed part of Keng Tung."

He left and I unwrapped a package to find a pink-and-silver lurex sarong and high-collared blouse. Milt Caniff's idea of Shan State evening wear. As I slithered into them, I thought, this is just like a movie: they have to get the female lead into an evening dress instead of her jungle/desert clothes, so the warlord presents her with one. I smiled and brushed my hair out of its ponytail.

It must be my Shan tattoos, I thought. People on the border were always giving me things—flowers, tea, old books—their generosity was endless. I fought for their cause in my own way and was rewarded with infinite kindness every step of the way. Even a "womanizing" drug despot had treated me with respect and had given me shimmering Dragon Lady lurex to replace my worn old camouflage.

The other package contained a black cotton aviator's jacket for when it got cold later on. The sun was still strong, so I carried it and put on my pitch-black Ray-Bans to go outside. Fortunately, I happened to have silver plastic sandals to wear because my hiking boots would have ruined the effect. I walked down to Khun Sa's front garden for a photo session with him and Mo Heing, then I went to watch the parade. Spin caught me in the sunlight and I posed for his camera. "Blade is dazzling," he said. He loped off to the *basha* he shared with Kulok and returned with a little brown paper packet. "Here, Blade, I've been waiting for the right moment," he said. I unwrapped a pair of tiger earrings made of thin lacquered wood. He had bought them for me in Bali, on his way back from New Zealand, and had managed to bring them all the way to the Shan State without breaking them.

"This is some year," I said to Spin. "January isn't even over and I've met Bo Mya and Khun Sa and Maha Seng, been to a Wa bonfire and almost too many Yak dances. And I'm going to Keng Tung to blast the 2,4-D program wide open. And now I have tiger earrings. What else could happen?"

"Perhaps a trip to the Salween River . . ." Spin said.

Three flags flew over the parade ground: the Shan national flag with its red, green, and yellow stripes; a training camp flag with a fountain pen and an M-16 (the same size) crossed over an open book; and a flag showing three yellow mountains—which Si Paw told me was "the SUA flag, Golden Triangle." The new troops, hundreds of them, marched by in precise formation, goose-stepping.

"They goose-step because they were trained by KMT drill instructors," Kulok explained to me, puffing on a Shan cigar. "And the KMT was trained in the 1930s by Germans." A girls' drum corps, crisply uniformed, beat time. Many of the new soldiers were little boys of nine or ten, and none had guns. At least seven times as many troops paraded at Tiger Camp as I'd seen in the Pai River National Democratic Front training graduation ceremony, but there was no question in my mind who the real soldiers were: the NDF boys—the ones with the guns, who bumped into each other in close-order drill, who had ragged uniforms, flute music, and a battle with the Tatmadaw staring them in the face—those were the young warriors. Tiger Camp, in contrast, was a Chinese opera or a page from *The Three Kingdoms*: beat the drums, fly the flags, and hope your enemy will run away or, better yet, strike a deal.

Kevin and Hannah left before dinner because Kevin didn't feel well enough for the Salween trip that Spin and I were planning. Kulok planned to drive the Mon and the Bangkok Shans to Chiang Mai the next day. The Hong Kong film crew would stay on to film Tiger Camp for a few days. Paul Tsang, their director, had spent some time at Pieng Luang while making a long-term documentary about Shan culture (which reminded me of Brando P. Bryant's ongoing video epic on the Karens, *War in Flowerland*). Paul was a tough, sharp artist, who wore blue jeans and a denim shirt and a

TRC cap. He had a cameraman and a soundman with him. Spin called them "the triad."

Paul directed his cameraman to film the new graduates as they filed on to the parade ground for their celebration banquet. A hundred big banana leaves were spread out as picnic cloths for the troops, with smaller leaves for their mounds of rice and curry. Bamboo cups held fruit wine, a special gift from the general. In the center of the field, the remaining guests joined Khun Sa and his officers on colorful mats. Theater troupe girls sat beside Khun Sa at the head of the mats. Plastic bowls and chopsticks were laid out, and soldiers brought Chinese chicken, pork, and vegetable dishes, all artfully prepared. They set out glasses and bottles of peach wine, beer, and Thai whiskey. Khun Sa was doing the honors with a bottle of Regency.

After dinner, Khun Sa rose and began shouting toasts to his officers, who had to match him by draining their glasses. He collared the men, raised his glass, and threw back a Regency with each. Then he swooped into the midst of the trainees and bellowed, "Your general has an announcement to make! Brave young warriors: Drink up! Tomorrow is your holiday! No work! No drill! No practice! Drink up! *Mai sung!*" He held his glass high over his head, and then he drained it, and pandemonium ensued. The theater girls and guests stood, clapping hands in rhythm. The soldier boys leapt in the air and flung their caps aloft, yelling tribal war cries. Officers poured beer and whiskey into the boys' bamboo cups and threw packs of Thai cigarettes for them to catch. Chanting, the boys lifted Kuhn Sa to their shoulders, bearing him through the tumult. Spin rushed into the thick of it, crouching and stooping, with tape recorder in one hand, camera in the other, at one with the chaos. Soldiers hauled him up on their shoulders, too, and carried him away on the tide.

Paul Tsang wrenched the camera away from his cameraman and moved into the pandemonium. As chaos reigned, he gave the camera back and set to work provoking Khun Sa's royal ritual drunk to even more frenzied heights. Paul seized an empty rice bowl and filled it with beer, raising it to Khun Sa. The warlord raised his brandy glass, *Mai sung!,* and drank. He turned his brandy glass upside down. Empty. Paul turned his rice bowl upside down, too. Not a drop. Then he filled the bowl to the brim again.

Khun Sa poured another Regency. They raised the bowl, the glass, above their heads, *Mai sung! Mai sung!* A charisma contest, and Paul Tsang was gaining on the kingpin. They roared toasts, they emptied their bottles, and as Paul was reaching for another liter of beer the tribal soldiers went into their tribal dances. Khun Sa reeled off into the dance with the boys from the cold mountains, doing the Wa bird-walk. The Wa and Lahu troops stomped like thunder and howled their ghost-tiger yells, delirious at the Thai cigarettes in their pockets, ecstatic over a cup of beer, wild in the dust.

At nightfall the Shan band took over and played all night. Yaks did the Yak Dance, canaries did the Canary Dance, and everybody and their sister danced the *ramwong.* Prince George, turned out in an immaculate white trench coat and plaid ascot, sat with me and Spin, whiskey-swilling his way through a head cold and a malaria attack. His wife had left him, his revolution had been eaten alive by Khun Sa, but he refused to concede defeat. Looking up at the stars, he said, "My people, the Palaungs, are loyal to me. If I ever wanted anything, they would do it. They would come out of the hills to do anything for me. Anything at all." I danced with him. The dance went on endlessly, the dancers' breath forming steam clouds in the cool night air. A little bazaar with eating stalls had sprung up around the festival. "This is a little bizarre," I said. We ate noodle soup there at midnight.

⹀ 7 ⹀

While Spin and I were eating breakfast the next morning, Si Paw walked up and said, "They are readying your horses. Will you be able to set off in one hour? I shall accompany you on your trip to the

Salween River." Six well-armed young soldiers and their sergeant would also make the trip, on foot.

At the edge of the village, poppy fields were bright with ivory petals. I wondered why Khun Sa hadn't gotten rid of them, since he was trying to present himself as the man with the solution to the Shan State's opium problems. Situated on the trade route to Thailand, only a few hours away from Mae Hong Son market by truck, the farmers should have been given something else to grow. The poppies presented a nasty image for the invited foreign press. Then I understood that Khun Sa really didn't care what the foreign press thought. Mo Heing and his Sura people who now found themselves cemented into the TRC cared about the outside world. But to the main man, Khun Sa, the outside world was only an amusement, a diversion, like the Chinese strongman show.

The Salween trade route was a slim track that curved into the mountains. Spin, no rider, decided to walk, which put us at eye level, quite a novelty. My Shan pony was Khun Sa's favorite, black and lithe with a bridle trimmed with red tassels. Si Paw didn't know his name so I dubbed him Road Warrior.

"Isn't this the Dragon Lady and her Wa army?" Spin said.

"You know that's what I always wanted. The Wa are like the Ronin, the lordless samurai of feudal Japan. Everyone has Wa troops, why not me? You may interview me. Our economy is based on tax and trade. We trade in thumbtacks. What we want from the outside world is a transport plane full of M-16s."

"Generally speaking, what is the goal of your revolution?"

"Our goal is to build a skull avenue from here to Ne Win's front door."

The route was busy. Men, boys, slender women, all humping black market cargo over the mountains. The smugglers traveled in small groups. When Spin and I passed them, they managed not to look terribly surprised, although we were the first foreigners on the route since Khun Sa's takeover. It was simply Shan courtesy not to make outsiders feel ill at ease by gawking at them. I greeted them with a Shan phrase Lisa had taught me: *"Gwa lul?"* (Where are you off to?) They replied that they were off to Thailand, or Taunggyi, "to sell things," and smiled courteously. This was Burma: refined and noble people reduced to beasts of burden.

We traveled all day, and at dusk we stole quietly through a darkening grove of silvery bamboo and birdcalls. Spin walked at my side and whispered, "This is the enchanted forest." The pale dust of the trail glowed and twisted under vaults of bamboo. When light vanished completely, I dismounted and led my pony, shining a flashlight ahead. Spin and I had met watching an old sepia film of the Shan State, and now we were walking in the film. Smugglers camped around small fires in the clearings, like picture-book gypsies.

We reached a Shan village, where our hostess was an old lady who lived in a big bamboo house with her children and grandchildren. The grandmother welcomed us graciously and brewed tea for us over a fire that smoldered on a bed of sand in the middle of the front room. She had an incessant hacking cough, and gently asked Si Paw if we might possibly have medicine to cure it. We didn't. It was probably tuberculosis, aggravated by the smoky fire and the rough cheroots she puffed. Everyone was coughing.

Sunrise flooded the village with a golden light. The shaggy rooftops glittered with it and the sky above was the most intense blue possible. The villagers, in indigo homespun and sun-bleached calico, warmed themselves at small bonfires. The women and girls wore towel turbans and glass earrings. Some of them had goiter-bloated necks. Far from the sea, the lack of iodine in their diets enlarged thyroid glands, and Si Paw told me that not far away a whole village was populated by victims of goiter-induced cretinism. UNICEF's injectable iodized oil was all it took to prevent the disease, but Burma's war zone was off-limits to such measures. With Ne Win keeping inoculation programs out of the frontier, this was the last place on earth such health care would reach.

Early that afternoon we reached a hill overlooking the Salween River at a crossing point where the TRC provided a ferry service to the smugglers (for a fee). After stopping at the ferry master's house for tea, fried peanuts, and chunks of palm sugar, we walked down to the wide, slate-blue river. Mountains rose steeply from the Salween's banks like fins, in graduated shades of blue and gray. At the ferry landing, Spin questioned the smugglers about how much their goods cost in Thailand and how much they sold for in Burma. The profit margins seemed low, until one took into account Burma's per capita income of less than two hundred dollars a year. Smugglers could earn that much in just a few trips—provided they evaded bandits, land mines, rebel shakedowns, and the Tatmadaw.

The smugglers sat hunched on the sand with their rolls of polyester fabric and nylon netting, truck tires, BMX bicycles mounted on bamboo carrying poles, and ponies laden with Aji-no-moto tins. It reminded me of a familiar image. The people on the Salween beach were positioned in exactly the same composition as the people in Seurat's painting *Sunday Afternoon on the Island of La Grand Jatte.* A woman in a bamboo hat sat upright in the fore-ground, a man reclined, others approached. It was the painting exactly, down to the pointillist light of late afternoon.

When the ferry showed up, the smugglers hitched their ponies to its sides, loaded their bundles, and boarded the narrow boat. A Shan soldier started the motor and the ponies panicked, kicking and struggling, but they had no choice but to swim along for the swift crossing. We followed on another boat, took some photos on the west bank, then returned to the ferry master's house for a dinner of bony Salween fish and a cold night's sleep on the porch.

We headed back to Tiger Camp the next day and stopped again at the Shan village for another smoky night, another golden morn-ing. We traveled on along a different route until poppy fields filled forest clearings and the festival flags, arches, and peaked rooftops of the warlord camp came into view.

Spin and I sat in the dining hall telling Prince George and K. Sam about our trip. A soldier brought us fruit from Khun Sa: a papaya, a pomelo, and a luscious honeydew melon. The Shan education officer presented me with a laissez-passer for my Keng Tung trip, and K. Sam told me how to arrange it from Chiang Mai. Spin was still hoping for a private interview with Khun Sa, but Prince George and K. Sam were being typically vague about it. We gorged ourselves on the fruit, the rinds of which bore Chinese writing. Since all the other guests had gone, we had our own *basha* and all the blankets and bug spray and candles they'd left.

It was the last night of the festival. The wind was fiercely cold and I wore the jacket Khun Sa had given me over my camouflage jacket. The Chinese strongmen gave an encore performance. This time the star had trouble with his chopstick-throwing trick. He lobbed chopstick after chopstick at the plywood board, but they just would not penetrate as they had a few days before. Some shattered on contact. I was sitting next to Khun Sa's uncle, who was rumored to be the real mastermind in charge of his operations and who had kept an extremely low profile when the press had been at the camp. The uncle picked up some of the chopstick pieces and we examined them to see if they had steel shafts inside, but they were just plain plastic. The performer kept trying and the chopsticks kept bouncing and breaking. I found this excruciating to watch. Perhaps he feared getting dragged off and beaten to death by the uncle's goons. At last, one of the chopsticks stuck in the board, and then two more. The strongman bowed triumphantly with a horrible show biz smile, as if he had missed before on purpose, just to build suspense.

"This is what killed vaudeville," I remarked to Prince George and Si Paw.

"Indeed? You know someone who was killed by chopstick throwing?" Si Paw asked.

A new troupe of dancers entered the arena for the festival finale. Prince George was full of misinformation as they began a series of various ethnic dances. Whenever Spin asked him about the origins of a dance, he would prevaricate.

"This is a traditional Shan dance," he said authoritatively.

"It is not, it's Kachin," I whispered to Spin, because I knew the costume.

At the end they announced what it was, and the Prince admitted, "Oh, of course, that was actually a traditional Kachin dance." This happened with a succession of performances: Lahu, Akha, Burmese. Prince George was drinking very steadily, and when the time came for the Yak Dance he said to us with a rakish grin, "You've

heard of the Yak Dance? Well, this is a *herd* of the dancing yaks!"
And it was: ten colorful yaks, moving in time, followed by a flock of
canaries, winged-child dancers. And at last there arose a stomping,
howling Wa dance from the far north. A great crowd of atavists
joined in and naturally Khun Sa, who so loved to dance, was right
in the thick of it, stomping with the wildest of them.

⌐ 8 ⌐

Just after dawn, as the mist was pierced by spears of light and the
ramwong orchestra began to pack up its drums and gongs, K. Sam
summoned Spin for his exclusive interview with Khun Sa. When
he returned, Spin told me that Khun Sa had ranted about the U.S.
Drug Enforcement Administration again and had admitted to
taxing heroin refineries that were set up in his territory on a
franchise basis. At the end of the interview, Spin (a master of Asian
small talk) had asked Khun Sa if he took any vitality tonics like
ginseng or rhino horn. Khun Sa said that he didn't, but that he did
like to eat honey gathered from forest hives.

As our truck was leaving Tiger Camp for Mae Hong Son that
morning, a soldier came running up with two Regency bottles full
of honey, Khun Sa's parting gifts for Spin and me.

The truck was white, and I should have seen that as an omen
since the Thai police episode en route to Chieng Dao had involved a
white truck. Prince George had shown us Zuber's newspaper article, already published. It pictured Khun Sa dancing, and recounted
his boast of the opium crop increase. It seemed calculated to pro-
voke a Thai government reaction, but there had been no reports of
any problems on the road for the journalists who'd left before us.
Spin and I weren't nervous. We knew no police would be waiting at
the border a week after the other foreigners had gone.

Spin and I sat in the front seat with the middle-aged driver, who was inscrutable behind aviator shades. He stopped so a Shan villager, his little boy, and a few monks who'd attended the festival could jump in the back. I put a Los Lobos cassette in the tape deck. The driver, who presumably had never heard Tex-Mex music before, seemed to like it.

The monks wanted lunch, and since monks weren't supposed to eat after noon, we stopped at the first little village in Thailand. Spin and I only knew it was Thailand because he asked a shopkeeper what country we were in. My nose was running and I was sneezing. "You must have caught a cold at the old lady's house, with all the smoke and coughing," Spin said, and bought me some orange juice. The driver handed Spin a sprig of forest wildflower, which I put in the band of my Gurkha hat, and we drove off again. I inserted another cassette.

"What's that?" Spin asked as the music started. "More Tex Mex?"

"No, this is Warren Zevon, from L.A. You'll like him." Just as the next village came into view, a song called "Lawyers, Guns and Money" came on. We smiled. Zevon was singing:

> I was gambling in Havana,
> I took a little risk.
> Send lawyers, guns, and money,
> Dad, get me out of this . . .

The driver clicked the tape deck off and stopped the truck. A Border Patrol Police roadblock stood in our way. It was one of those temporary bed-headboard type barricades. Six police in tan uniforms approached the truck, assault rifles pointing at the cab. "Get out, please," one of them said, polite but edgy. This was directed at Spin, the driver, and me; the monks and the villager with the little boy sat in the back and watched. Innocent bystanders.

"May we search your bags?" a young police officer asked me.

"Yes, please, go ahead," I replied.

They took Spin's backpack and camera bag and my two shoulder bags out of the truck and opened them. They reached in at random

and turned up several items of interest. The main attraction was
Spin's plastic bag full of exposed film. They also made a fuss over
his detailed map of the border area. It hadn't occurred to us to
conceal anything.

"Are you with the *Bangkok Post?*" the police asked.

"No, we're not even reporters," I said. Spin's sketchy command
of Thai wasn't up to the bullshit level the situation called for, so I
handled all the questions.

"If you're not reporters, what were you doing at Tiger Camp?"

It was pointless to deny being there. "We are in this area for
cultural purposes," I said. "I'm an artist and I'm studying the tribal
cultures in the hills. He's photographing the festival dances." The
police didn't notice my maps as they searched, or the few rolls of
film I'd managed to get my uncooperative cameras to shoot at Tiger
Camp, or the reams of Burma-related printed matter I carried. But
they did find my photos from the Pai River and Manerplaw. Most
of them were artistically double exposed because I'd changed the
batteries in my Minolta and accidentally rewound the film, but two
shots from the end of the roll, of Manerplaw, were clear as day. The
police showed them to each other. "Bo Mya," they said, recognizing
the big man in olive drab.

"Are you sure you're not from the *Bangkok Post?*"

"I'm not. I'm quite sure I'm not."

"What about him? Photographs for the *Bangkok Post?*"

"Absolutely not. Anyone from the *Post* would be back in Bangkok by now."

It was not a routine border check. The BPP were there to catch
journalists coming from Khun Sa's camp. Orders must have come
from high up in the government to find some reporters and make
an example of them. Since the BPP around Mae Hong Son were
said to be on Khun Sa's payroll, I supposed they must have dragged
their feet in setting up the roadblock, in hopes that all Khun Sa's
guests would be gone by the time they were in place. So Spin and I
were the lucky winners of the BPP reception.

A couple of police walked around to the front of the truck and
conferred quietly with the driver. Good, I thought, this is where the

purple bank notes discreetly change hands, so we can go on our way. The police walked back and the driver shot Spin and me a grim look, raising his eyebrows above his dark glasses.

"We're in for it," I whispered to Spin. "One of you-know-who's checks to the BPP must have bounced."

The officer in charge looked all of twenty years old. I noticed that he wore a gold watch, a gold bracelet, and a large gold ring. "Excuse me," he said. "We have to come with you to Mae Hong Son." He and two other cops with rifles jumped into the back of the truck. The monks made room for them and we headed for Mae Hong Son.

"Maybe they just need a ride into town," I said to Spin. But I knew what this felt like. We both did. It felt like being taken into custody.

The driver gripped the wheel hard. "Trouble," he said. "Maybe small trouble. Maybe big trouble."

THE
OPERA

⚊ 1 ⚊

Spin held the heavy pistol in both hands and aimed it, but he did not
fire. The young police officer who had given it to him to play with
had emptied out the bullets first. We were killing time in police
custody on the road to Mae Hong Son. Our white truck had gone
off on a dirt track to a monastery, with the monks. After fifteen
minutes, they returned, and we continued to the Border Patrol
Police headquarters just outside of Mae Hong Son. There, Khun
Sa's driver and the other passengers were allowed to go on their
way, unsearched. The police only wanted Spin and me. A BPP
officer drove us to the Immigration office in town.

The Pai River boat trips had transformed sleepy Mae Hong Son into a tourist town, and outside the Immigration office backpackers strolled by. The local police had posted signs saying "Welcome Tourists. May we solve your problem block?" Spin and I sat on a bench in the office, and our "problem block" was a magnet for agents of Thai Army Intelligence, Border Patrol Police, Special Branch (an antisubversion unit), and the Ministry of the Interior. They crowded the room, discussing us with the Immigration officers. A BPP man brought us bottles of orange soda. My cold was rapidly sinking into bronchitis.

Some of the intelligence types asked us to give them the names of the foreigners who had been at Tiger Camp and we politely refused. Others already knew exactly who had been there. None of the reporters had been taken into custody, except Zuber, who'd been briefly questioned in Chiang Mai. "Looks like Zuber did the 'Canary Dance,' " Spin muttered.

An effeminate English-speaking plainclothes officer interviewed us separately. He tape-recorded us, first asking us casual questions about where we'd gone to college and what we studied, and then getting very specific.

"Did you see Khun Sa?" he asked.

"I have nothing to say about that," I responded. "There have been enough newspaper reports from people who were there, and Thai intelligence agents were there. You don't need to ask *me* about it."

The man had not identified himself, but I guessed that he had come up from Bangkok to oversee the journalist-catching operation. He was at least kind enough to reveal that we actually *were* under arrest, for illegal border-crossing. He told us that if we signed a confession saying that we had crossed at an illegal point, we would be tried the next day and fined a small amount. We would have to leave Thailand, but we'd be allowed right back in. Thai justice liked quick confessions and speedy trials. Spin and I conferred and signed the confession, and the BPP took us to the Immigration jail.

The jail was a small facility in the district police station. We were told to sit in the station lobby while the police fetched dinner for us from a nearby restaurant. When we had finished our pork-fried rice, guards took us behind an elaborate altar of glittering Buddha statues and through the lock-up door. They gave Spin a cursory fully clothed body search and didn't touch me at all. The lock-up corridor had three small cells. Two were crowded with prisoners, some of whom had probably just been evicted from the empty center cell, which was to be ours. It had been cleaned, and a bottle of boiled drinking water and a cake of soap were provided. The floor, upon which we were to sleep, was teak. A wall hid the toilet and washbasin at the back. Sliding bars closed us in. Spin and I had to admit that we'd paid money to stay in worse hotel rooms.

We settled in, opening the novels we had with us. "No wonder we're in jail," I remarked. "Look at what we're reading." Spin was reading Kerouac, I was reading Mishima.

A quavering voice reached us from another cell: "Hello, mister and missus, do you have any cigarettes?"

"No, brother, I'm sorry," Spin answered. "We don't smoke."

"Well, if you want cigarettes, we have them," the voice offered. "We are all foreigners in this jail, sir. We came from Burma."

"So did we," I said. Appreciative laughter burst from the other cells. I tried the few phrases in Burmese that I knew, and said that if we were to stay long, I would like the voice to be my Burmese professor.

A bit later, the voice said, "Would you like to read the Bible while you are troubled, sir?" and a little English-language Bible was passed through our bars from his cell. Spin thumbed through it and returned it, then resumed *Desolation Angels*. Running a slight fever, I set aside Mishima and slept.

⌐ 2 ⌐

I awoke, and it was no dream; I really was on the teak floor of a jail cell. My brain somewhat overheated, I visualized a great chute, down which Spin and I had slid from the Salween River, to land behind pale green bars. Spin lay beside me, arms folded on his chest, looking like a medieval tomb sculpture.

"Spin, wake up," I rasped in my bronchitis voice. "It's Wednesday and we're in jail."

His chiseled features scrunched and stretched in a yawn. "Right then, we'll have to get to work on a tunnel, won't we?"

My laugh turned into coughing that came from deep inside, bringing up gray-green phlegm.

The other prisoners, all men, began shuffling into the corridor for their breakfast, which was served with much clanking of pails and tin dishes. Our restaurant meal, chicken curry and rice, arrived in a china bowl. The bars were left open to the corridor, so Spin and I went out to meet the owner of the voice from the night before. His name was William, and he was young and slender. His big Karen eyes widened as he told us how he'd wound up in the jail:

"My brother-in-law and I had the idea to bring some Buddha statues to Thailand, but the Thai police, they caught us and charged us for smuggling antiques. We had to pay policemen the customs duty, but they put us in jail anyway. So now they keep us and we must have sixty thousand baht for our freedom. An impossible sum. Now we are here a few months, and we have one year left, unless God provides the money. Sometimes our relations come here when they are in Mae Hong Son for smuggling business. They come many times. But for me, when I was caught, it was my first trip."

The police brought Spin and me into the front offices for processing. I was interrogated in Thai, as none of the police there spoke English. The office had no copy machines or carbon paper, so dozens of forms had to be filled out one at a time, the police tapping our answers out on old manual typewriters. Our fingers were mashed on inkpads for page after page of fingerprint forms. The tedium was broken up with phone calls from the *Bangkok Post* and United Press International, who interviewed us about our arrest. A fat Thai newspaper reporter came by to get copies of our mug shots for his front page.

The processing took all morning, and the police were unfailingly courteous and good natured. One of them even brought me a package of bronchitis pills without being asked.

In the afternoon, the police drove us to the nearby district government office. We were left waiting in a hallway for about an hour. A young man who spoke English walked up and started telling us that we should behave contritely at our trial.

"Are you our lawyer?" I asked him.

"No, no," he replied. "I am not a lawyer, I am a veterinarian. I work in the district livestock office."

"Do we look like we have hoof-and-mouth disease or something?" I groaned. "Actually, you can help us," I said. "Have you got a phone in your office?"

He let me telephone the United States consulate in Chiang Mai. The consulate was closed for Chinese New Year, a major holiday of several days' duration in Thailand, but I reached a consular official on duty.

"We heard of your arrest last night, and we were trying to reach you, but we couldn't get through," the official said. "Are you being treated decently?"

"Yes, they're being nice enough," I said. "And now we seem to be on our way to the trial."

"Please call me back afterward and let me know how that goes," he said, adding, "and if there's anything we can do to help. . . "

The courthouse was an unimposing one-story stucco building. A young official from the district offices showed up to present our defense, which was that the border was unmarked. A court reporter interpreted for us. No one else was present when the judge, an Indian-looking woman in her thirties, marched to the bench. She arranged her robes, sat, and sneered down at us. We did look shabby in our slept-in sweaters, Spin's face unshaven, my trousers ripped at the knees. We *wai*'d humbly to the judge. Within minutes we were found guilty of illegally entering Thailand. "You will each pay a fine of one thousand baht," the judge said. That was around forty dollars. "If you make another mistake against the law in Thailand during the next two years, you will have to serve one month in jail, which is your suspended sentence."

We *wai*'d again, and went outside to pay our fine. We were getting low on cash, and no banks were open because of the holiday. We thought we might make the evening flight to Chiang Mai,

using my credit card to buy tickets, if the flight wasn't booked by
New Year's celebrants. Spin's Thai visa was close to expiration, so I
told him, "If there's only one ticket left, you take it and I'll stay in
town. My visa's got plenty of time left on it."

"No," Spin said. "If you stay here alone the cops will be knocking
on your hotel room door all night. I'm staying with you."

Then the police brought us to the Immigration office, and informed us that we would have to remain in custody until we left the
country. Transport out of Mae Hong Son was sold out, so we might
have to remain in jail for several days. We cursed the new Year of
the Rabbit. I called the consulate again from the long-distance
bureau in town. Alone in the phone booth with the caring, American voice of the consular official, I began to cry.

"Oh dear, it's not that bad, is it?" he said.

"I'm sorry, it's just that I've got bronchitis."

"Is there anything I can do? Anything at all?"

It seemed strange that he was trying to be helpful when I was in-
country for the express purpose of sabotaging an American State
Department foreign-aid program, but I knew there were many
within the State Department who knew the 2,4-D program for the
travesty it was, including Chiang Mai staff who were close enough to
the scene to understand that the spraying was not good drug policy.

That night our jailers were extremely solicitous. They asked me
if I wanted to see a doctor; I declined. They told us we could sleep in
the corridor instead of the cell, which we also declined because the
cell was darker and quieter.

⌐ 3 ⌐

Our cell door was left open, and the next day William stopped in
for a visit. "Most of the men in my cell are Mo Heing's soldiers," he said. We had noticed that our walls were etched with
Tailand Revolutionary Council graffiti. "Mo Heing is the only true

revolutionary in the Shan State," William commented. "Khun Sa, he is just a businessman." I spread out my *National Geographic* map of Asian ethnic groups for William to look at. Spin was finishing *Desolation Angels*. I took a dose of the bronchitis pills and felt dizzy. I curled up on the floor and Spin stroked my hair as he read. A prisoner was singing a Chinese song.

Late in the afternoon the police told us we were going to Bangkok, so we left William and the other prisoners, with wishes that the Year of the Rabbit would bring their release. We were brought to the Immigration office again. Emma found us there, bringing sodas and the latest *Thai Rath* newspaper. She translated the story headlined TWO FOREIGNERS WHO VISITED KHUN SA ARRESTED. It said that we had been "found wandering in the forest near the border," and although we "insisted that we were just admiring the natural beauty," our behavior "was suspicious," so the Border Patrol Police arrested us. Apparently the BPP didn't want to admit to the press that people drove in and out of Khun Sa's Tiger Camp by truck.

A toadlike Immigration officer from Mae Sariang would drive us to Bangkok that night in a truck with two of his Immigration cronies. Spin and I were just an excuse for Mr. Toad, Mr. Mole, and Mr. Weasel's junket to the bright lights of the big city. Immigration needed a few more sets of fingerprints before we left, and Mr. Toad managed to both caress and hurt my hands in the printing process. Glancing at Spin, he asked me, "Is that your husband?"

"No," I said. "That is my *cellmate*."

Mr. Toad took the wheel of his truck and Mr. Mole and his wife occupied the rest of the front seat. Mr. Toad asked me to squeeze in between him and Mrs. Mole. Instead, I climbed in the roofed-over back with Spin. Mr. Weasel joined us there. All three Immigration officers were drunk, but Mr. Weasel was by far the drunkest. The forest road from Mae Hong Son was crinkled with hairpin turns, and Mr. Weasel kept banging his fist on the side of the truck so Mr. Toad would pull over for him to clamber out and pee or throw up. He had more and more difficulty getting back in the truck. Spin and I hoped the Toad would drive off and leave him.

Mr. Toad drove abominably, jabbing the brakes. I took a Dramamine and played *Turandot* at maximum volume in my headphones. Then I put the headphones on Spin and played him the brilliant, triumphant finale of the opera. I told him the story of Turandot, the wicked Chinese princess, and Calaf, her Tartar captive. We stopped for dinner at a forlorn café where pots of unappetizing curry had been sitting out all day. The Immigration men selected their curries and a bottle of whiskey. I ate nothing. Spin wolfed down a heaping plate of desiccated beef and rice.

We stopped at the Mole residence in Mae Sariang to drop off Mrs. Mole. Then it was a jolly drunken night's drive down to the plains of central Thailand for the Toad and Mole, while the Weasel snored in the back like a sprung accordion. Spin was pinioned diagonally in cramped discomfort, and I clutched at sleep in the corner space that remained.

When morning glared angrily at us, we stopped for gasoline and breakfast at a dingy truck stop. Spin and I sat across the room from the Immigration men. Spin was haggard and his jaw twitched. My skin was paper white. Our fatigues were rank. I soothed my cough with Coca-Cola. The waitresses stared at us from the kitchen. Spin worked himself into a hoarse rant about the degeneracy of Thailand, culminating with a hissed, "The Vietnamese Communists will *make mincemeat* of this country!" When we left, Mr. Weasel climbed in the back with a new bottle of whiskey to welcome another glorious day.

= 4 =

It was noon by the time we reached Bangkok's Immigration center. A detention facility for illegal aliens was hidden in a three-story building in back of the offices where tourists and business travelers went to renew their visas. We passed Vietnamese families crouched amid their possessions on the detention center's ground floor. They were about to be sent off to new lives overseas, or back to camps on the Thailand/Cambodia border. Our escorts from Mae Sariang deposited us in an office, where we sat at a long table by ourselves. The Bangkok officers refused our requests to call the American or New Zealand embassies. One officer asked me if I had the embassy phone numbers, and when I admitted that I didn't, he showed me the phone directory. It was in Thai, and I was in no condition to try to decipher it.

The afternoon wore on. Spin requested food but was ignored. I went to the bathroom, and looking at the Vietnamese graffiti I started to cry. I went back to the office, passing by a picnic table where Mr. Toad and his friends were consuming whiskey and Danish butter cookies. Finally, an Immigration officer entered the room and asked us, "Have you got airplane tickets out of the country?"

"No, we haven't," I said.

"Have you got money to buy tickets with?"

"No, but I can use my credit card."

They allowed me to go out and buy the plane tickets. If I got a flight out that day, we could leave immediately. It sounded good, but as I left I said to Spin, "The opera ain't over 'til the fat lady sings."

Accompanied by an English-speaking officer, I took a taxi to my usual Bangkok travel agent. She looked dismayed to see me in winter army clothes, ill, with a policeman. She told us that all flights to Penang that day had already left, so I booked seats for the next day.

"Better make them round-trip tickets," the Immigration policeman said.

"Excuse me, why?" I asked.

"Because we don't want people to think that you think that we don't want you to come back," he replied.

"Curiouser and curiouser." I sighed. "Okay, please make those return tickets."

The travel agent typed Spin and me into her computer, and said, "Which hotel are you staying at, please?"

"In *jail,*" I answered.

The officer took the tickets and, as we left, I surreptitiously dropped a note on the agent's desk, asking her to call the U.S. and New Zealand embassies and tell them that we were being detained in Bangkok.

Back at the Immigration jail, Spin and I were photographed and fingerprinted a few times by Cambodian "trusty" prisoners who did such work for the police. Then we were separated to be confined in the men's and women's wards for the night.

The detention wards were on the upper floors, two for men and one for women and children. Each was a large room with a smaller room walled off within it, and shower and toilet stalls at one end. The walls were grimy concrete, and barred windows faced corridors. Fluorescent lights stayed lit twenty-four hours a day and ceiling fans feebly stirred the stale air.

Each ward was occupied by a hundred or more foreigners, mostly refugees. They had escaped, fled, bought, and fought their ways out of a dozen different dictatorships, only to get caught in Bangkok. Many had broken out of the big refugee camps on the Cambodian border, where they had lived in squalor, subject to the depredations of gangsters and the Khmer Rouge. A few were Western travelers who had overstayed visas or work permits, and some had been released after serving prison sentences (usually drug crimes) and were waiting to be deported. Locked in the wards, the detainees were hardly ever let out. There was no exercise, no sunlight, no fresh air. Some were held a few days, many a few months, and others up to two years. For the refugees, the wait was either for asylum in a new country or for return to a Thailand/Cambodia border camp.

About forty women and fifty children were crowded into my ward. Most of them were from Indochina: Cambodia, Laos, Vietnam, the former French colonies that the United States had fought over and then abandoned to communism. Many of them were ethnic Chinese, from Indochina's cities, who had made their way to Thailand through jungles or on the perilous sea, and who had hoped to go undetected in Bangkok. Several Bengalis from Burma were detained there as well. The Bengalis, an Indian-related,

Moslem ethnic minority, were subjected to intense racial discrimination in Ne Win's Burma. The dictatorship considered them aliens, brought in by the British colonists, despite the fact that the Rohingya Moslem culture had existed for centuries in western Burma. Even if their grandparents had been born in Burma, the Bengalis were not citizens.

Each woman had set up a little home floored with sleeping mats and walled with cardboard boxes of family possessions. Mosquito nets gave some of the sections a pretense of seclusion. The floor space was tightly occupied, with narrow lanes between the mats and boxes. Buddhist shrines perched over the steel door, adorned with plastic flowers. Cambodian children ran around the room laughing, their long hair flying.

Some of the women acted as shopkeepers, selling noodle soup or coffee from electric pots wired up to the lighting system. Thai vendors came to the corridor windows, and the detainees bargained with them for provisions. The women passed the time by visiting each other's "houses" for coffee and hand-rolled cigarettes and spent hours putting on makeup and nail polish.

I dropped my sleeping bag near the door. The children came over to make friends with me. A little girl brought me a cup of sugared orange juice sent over by her mother. I sat with a young French traveler and a Filipina, and I listened to their stories of expired visas, false job offers, lost passports.

At night, the guards brought me downstairs. An Immigration officer named Captain Chun interrogated me in English. He wanted information about Khun Sa. I replied that I had already paid my fine for illegal border-crossing and I would not answer any more questions—my case was closed. He brought me to the main Immigration office. Spin was inside talking to the head of Immigration, who Captain Chun called "the Commander." We went to another room where Captain Chun and a fellow officer sat behind a desk, and I was told to sit down.

"I haven't been allowed to call my embassy yet," I said. "You should let us use the telephone."

"We have been so nice to you already," Captain Chun said. "We let you buy air tickets. So you should be nice to us and give us the film of Khun Sa."

I realized they were after Spin's bag of film from Tiger Camp, and the few rolls I had shot there. I was sure that if they had any right to the film, it would have been confiscated. I figured they wanted it to show to their friends, or to sell to the Thai newspapers.

"I'm not talking about this," I said. "We are supposed to call our embassies."

"You are stupid, stubborn, and pig-headed!" the other officer shouted. It was apparently the old "good cop, bad cop" routine. I felt sure they couldn't physically abuse me because the story of our arrest had been publicized in the newspapers and on the radio. The Thai government was image conscious, always trying to attract tourism and investment from Western countries. Thai police would certainly draw the line at slapping around an American human rights activist, I thought.

"Spin has already given us his film," Captain Chun ventured. "Why don't you give us yours?"

"I don't think he has. Why don't you bring him in to tell me so?" I countered. "I'll have nothing else to say until you bring Spin here or let me call my embassy." I walked away from them, ignoring a command not to move. I sat down across the room and did not respond to Captain Chun when he called out questions like "What is your name?" to get me speaking again.

About fifteen minutes later, Spin appeared and sat down with me. He whispered that some Cambodians in his ward had hidden his film for him.

"I think we've held them off," Spin said. "The Commander was really trying to get his hands on the film. They told me we could be charged with sedition by Special Branch if I didn't give it up. But I don't think they'll really do anything of the kind. We've already caused them enough trouble, enough negative press. They have to let us go." But as I held his hand, sweat was dripping down his wrist, and wet blotches spread on his olive drab T-shirt. He was silent for a moment, and then he groaned, "It never ceases to end!"

"Do you realize what you just said?" I laughed.

An Immigration officer came over and said, "I do not understand you. First you are crying, now you are laughing. It is time for you two to return to the detention wards."

When I returned to my ward, my sleeping bag had been unrolled next to the mat and boxes of a beautiful young Cambodian named Vanne and her little boy. Vanne's husband had been killed and her family decimated in the days of Khmer Rouge power. She had walked out of Cambodia with her son, and was robbed by bandits in the Thailand/Cambodia border mountains. She escaped a refugee camp, but in Bangkok a policeman had heard her speak Khmer to her son. She didn't have enough money to pay off the police, so she was taken to the Immigration jail.

"Sister, I have now two chances to get out before they send me to a border camp," Vanne said. "A Christian husband and wife in the state of Montana have sent a letter saying they will sponsor me and my boy to go there. And a missionary who visits this jail, he might marry me. But while I wait, sister, I cry every night." She lit a bundle of incense sticks and placed it on a small Chinese Buddhist shrine.

Others came to talk with me: two Cambodian Chinese girls whose relatives had reached the United States, and a Bengali lady who had come from Rangoon on the Karen rebels' smuggling route. They spoke with tears in their curving eyes. Southeast Asia was full of open wounds, inflamed, corrupt. The refugees were the real prisoners of politics, innocent, displaced, condemned.

Vanne manicured my nails, removing my cracked green polish. She filed them to points and applied two coats of lacquer that made them shine like precious jade. She painted and repainted each nail painstakingly, until they were all perfect. It was an act of kindness, but also of compulsion. The detention ward was driving Vanne insane.

The women had a "mail service," paying a trusty to deliver messages between the men's and women's wards. I copied three T'ang poems from my paperback anthology and sent them over to Spin:

On Meeting Li Kuei-Nien Down the River (Tu Fu)

I met you often when you were visiting princes
And when you were playing in noblemen's halls.
. . . Spring passes . . . Far down the river now,
I find you alone under falling petals.

A Song of the Spring Palace (Wang Ch'ang-Ling)

Last night, while a gust blew peach-petals open
And the moon shone high on the Palace Beyond Time,
The Emperor gave P'ing-Yang, for her dancing,
Brocades against the cold spring wind.

Over the Border (Wang Ch'ang-Ling)

The moon goes back to the time of Ch'in, the wall to the
    time of Han,
And the road our troops are travelling goes back three
    hundred miles . . .
Oh, for the Winged General at the Dragon City—
That never a Tartar horseman might cross the Yin
    Mountains!

⸗ 5 ⸗

Our flight to Penang would leave at 1:00 in the afternoon. In the
morning, anticipating a thorough search of my bags, I took out all
political material except for the human rights interviews and 2,4-D
effects photos, which I hid with my film in the linings. I took the
rest of the Burma material into a toilet stall and burned it. At the
same time, in his ward, Spin was chewing and swallowing his own
incriminating papers, including the invitation to the Tiger Camp
festival. He kept only the envelope that said "You May Already Be a
Winner!"

Vanne gave me a white handkerchief that she had trimmed with crochet, a skill she had learned as a girl in a Phnom Penh convent school.

At 11:30, the guards brought Spin and me downstairs and gave us back our passports, which now had paragraphs handwritten in Thai stating that we had been arrested for illegal border-crossing and fined one thousand baht each. Two Immigration officers whom we hadn't seen before took us to the airport in a police truck. We were sent to the head of the check-in line, and then, unsearched, to an empty office in the transit lounge. A reporter from Associated Press called me on the office phone. Immigration officials had assured him that we were "not blacklisted and therefore could return to Thailand." Spin and I drank ice water as we waited. My cough was gone.

Our flight to Penang was called. The Immigration officers *wai*'d and waved good-bye to us at the boarding gate, and said, "Please come back to Thailand soon!" We joined the throng of passengers walking down the passageway to the plane, our steps buoyant. "I can hear the fat lady bursting into song," Spin said. "A whole goddamn aria, in fact."

THROUGH
THE
LOOKING
GLASS

⹀ 1 ⹀

"Are you happy to be back?" Emma asked me as we sat on her porch, afternoon sun taking the chill out of a January day. She had moved to Chiang Mai from Mae Hong Son. It was 1988, and I had returned after six months in the United States.

"I'm glad to be here, and I think I have a good chance of getting into the sprayed area this time," I replied. "But as far as Thailand, I think I have a piece of the Snow Queen's mirror in my eye."

"The Snow Queen?"

"In the Hans Christian Andersen story, it was a mirror that magnified and emphasized all the bad things in the world. Demons owned it, and when they dropped it tiny pieces flew into people's eyes, giving them a negative outlook on everything. Since the arrest, I don't see the charm of Thailand anymore, only the bad side."

Spin had been unenthusiastic about Thailand even before the arrest. The new mirror shard in his eye seemed to affect the way he saw me. We had been inseparable amid Penang's Chinese New Year bonfires and fireworks, but as soon as we returned to Thailand, a mere week after our expulsion, he iced a distance between us. I spelled trouble to Spin, and trouble was something he'd had enough of, at least until he could scrape together the airfare for another trip to Afghanistan's war zone. I, on the other hand, had not had enough of trouble, and my mission to the sprayed fields of the Shan State's Keng Tung Province never left my mind.

I had tried to follow through on Khun Sa's permission as soon as I returned from the expulsion, but by that time the situation on the northern border was in flux. As the Year of the Rabbit began, Thailand had announced a campaign against Khun Sa, and had moved troops north along the Burma border. Nothing came of it— the war was fought only in the Thai newspapers—but the troop presence blocked my access north to Keng Tung. I waited for months in a northern town for the situation to change, undercover with the alias "Alice Ryder." I hiked to a border village and interviewed tribal and Yunnanese refugees from Keng Tung under the nose of the Border Patrol Police, but did not cross over. When the monsoon came, I paid a quick visit to Kawthoolei, then left for the U.S. I made lobbying trips to Washington, roaming the corridors of power in my scuffed pumps. Lugging a dented Halliburton attaché case full of reports on human rights abuses, I argued that Burma's narcotics production could only be ended if the war was ended.

The level of apathy I was up against in Washington was exemplified by a State Department report on the use of herbicides for narcotics eradication that blandly stated: "U.S. citizens visiting or residing in foreign countries involved in the eradication program should not be adversely affected. Spraying programs will be employed in remote areas where the public is not likely to be exposed." The fact that people actually lived and worked in those remote areas was of no importance, for they weren't Americans. They were just what a State Department official called "the criminal hill tribes."

I kept Project Maje going, cultivating interest in Burma wherever I could find it. When people asked why Burma, why me, I told them it was like a cave-in in a mine. If a miner was trapped underground and you walked on the earth above, not knowing, then you didn't have to do anything. But if you heard his cries for help, you were morally obligated to try and rescue him. Knowledge bred responsibility, and I lived with it. The spraying season, winter, arrived. I got a Thai visa, borrowed money, and headed for northern Thailand.

I was careful this time. I did not cross the border to see Khun Sa or any of the rebel leaders. I met quietly with National Democratic Front representatives at their safe houses and in shady hotels in Chiang Mai and Bangkok. I would only cross the border for the people, not the warlords. I hoped to go into Keng Tung with permission from NDF groups—the Shan State Army or the Wa, because they were somewhat more respectable than Khun Sa's Tailand Revolutionary Council. My attempts to arrange a trip with them fell through, however. Opium transport and heroin refining were going on in the SSA and Wa border zones, and they were apparently ashamed of this. Khun Sa had less face to lose by letting me see his territory, and although I hadn't seen Prince George or K. Sam, I received a written message informing me that my laissez-passer from the year before was still valid and that I should proceed to Ban Kong, a KMT village on the northern border, as soon as possible.

Chinese New Year was approaching, the Year of the Rabbit scurrying like hell to get out of the way of the Year of the Dragon. The KMT village was decorated with gold foil dragons to herald the cycle's imminent change. When I arrived at my contact's house, hopes high, the scholarly Shan agent was surprised to see me. I told him why I'd come to Ban Kong and he said, "But we have no such information here. I have heard nothing from the general; I would have no idea how you are to proceed across the border. I am so sorry, they haven't set anything up here for you."

I was furious. The Shans must be the most disorganized people on earth, I thought. I held my temper in check in front of the agent. I gritted my teeth and muttered, "I can't spend months waiting around this time, like last year. It looks like the TRC is not really sincere about wanting outside awareness of the human rights situation in Keng Tung. *Never mind.*"

"Miss Edith, I will send a message to the general's headquarters about it. I, for one, want your mission to succeed—this chemical war in Keng Tung is a very terrible thing. Stay here tonight, and then spend three days or so in town, and come back at the week's end. I will have got a reply by radiogram by then."

Three days later I returned, sure that Khun Sa's permission would not come through and prepared to settle for interviews with smugglers and refugees in Ban Kong.

"I have good news for you," the agent said. "You'll go into Keng Tung Province tonight. A boy has arrived to bring you over the border to the TRC base." Khun Sa had issued orders to his TRC to get me into the sprayed area and then get me out of Keng Tung before the Burmese, the rebels, or the Thais heard of a foreigner's presence. It was to be a surgical strike, and Khun Sa risked antagonizing his sponsors and trading partners. I thought he was going through with it to humor Prince George and K. Sam, and (most importantly) because he wanted to honor the permission he'd granted me the year before.

I set off in moonlight with a Palaung soldier boy who'd been sent for me, a Yunnanese to act as interpreter (translating everyone else's Shan to Chinese for me), and another man to carry the provisions that my contact and I had selected in Ban Kong. I had walked the road to the refugee village the year before in hot sunlight. Now there was a cool breeze. I tucked my hair up underneath my felt

"Gurkha" hat, and pulled the brim low over my face whenever we passed other night travelers. No one came close enough to get a good look at me. It was the smuggling route, so they avoided contact with other moonlight walkers.

My party climbed into the hills. To avoid the refugee village, we scrambled up a field and pushed our way through thick scrub. When we found the path that led high into the hills over the border, we sat beside it to rest. Then, just as we got going again, the Palaung boy whispered that some people were coming. Maybe our crashing about in the thicket had alerted Border Patrol Police from the refugee village. The Yunnanese interpreter stayed back to investigate, and the rest of us quickened our pace. Voices drifted up. Our pursuers were catching up to us. I realized the language spoken was Yunnanese. They were not Thai police, but smugglers. They passed us without a look or a question.

We walked on, single file, along a ridge, in and out of patches of moonlight. A human form emerged suddenly from a shadow, a Shan sentry with his M-16. The Palaung gave him the password. I was out of range of the BPP. I was back in the Shan State. We had crossed into Keng Tung Province. We continued on, in dense forest, the path rippling with deeply eroded ruts. The TRC camp lay all around us, but the moonlight had ebbed and I saw nothing of it. At a cluster of *bashas* my companions asked for water, and an officer came out and talked to me in Chinese. He told me that we had another two hours to reach the local commander's campsite, where I was expected. Tired, I walked slowly, stumbling from rut to rut. A couple of hours later, we came to a low bamboo building where Shan girls appeared with glasses of cold water for us. A lieutenant, Sai Neng, introduced himself. This must be the place, I thought, but another half hour of plodding over ruts remained.

Everyone was waiting up for us at division headquarters, even though it was two in the morning. The commander was away, but his next in command, a thin major in his fifties, welcomed me in Thai and shook my hand. They showed me to a bamboo *basha* with two rooms, one for me and one for my Yunnanese bodyguard/ interpreter. But since this was the Shan State, I couldn't just crawl inside to sleep. Soldiers lit a charcoal fire and cooked up noodle soup and began serving tea. The major told me my expedition to the sprayed area, with a military escort, would get underway in a day or so. I could rest up at the camp while we waited for mules to arrive the next day. Officers sat around the fire smoking Shan cigars and discussing the upcoming expedition. I tried to follow their conversation, but I finally gave up. I excused myself and retired to the *basha,* where border blankets of soft gray recycled wool had been provided. I put two over my sleeping bag and was perfectly warm. A few hours later, I awoke to hear the Yunnanese next door murmuring in his sleep. I drifted back to sleep, feeling safe, and feeling happy to be back in the forest.

◄ 2 ◄

When morning came, the headquarters, a huddle of *bashas,* was a picture of tranquility. Tall trees shaded and camouflaged the hilltop. A soldier climbed a bamboo ladder propped against a tree to send coded radiograms. Soft music came from a cassette player. Breezes wafted through. The day began with Chinese tea, then milky coffee. A late breakfast was served at a table behind the major's flimsy little *basha.* He chided me about my appetite: I only managed one bowl of rice, while the officers kept refilling theirs. After the meal, the major brought out salted watermelon seeds and lemon candies to go with more Chinese tea. Young soldiers asked if I was the lady in the *Freedom's Way* book, and I admitted that I was. The TRC had printed up a colorful Shan propaganda paperback with that title after the Tiger Camp festival. It contained a photo of me, the Dragon Lady in pink lurex, posed between Khun Sa and Mo Heing. I rarely looked that glamorous, but the soldiers seemed impressed. The day passed in peace and quiet.

My Yunnanese interpreter headed back to Ban Kong, since

Lieutenant Sai Neng would head the expedition force and he spoke enough Thai to communicate with me. At the major's table, I was urged to eat at least two bowls of rice to gain strength for the trip. "Please eat more rice," Sai Neng said. "I don't want you to starve from our poor food." Sai Neng was well briefed on my mission to get evidence of the 2,4-D spraying, and he was totally committed to it. In his thirties, he had deep brown eyes and a devastating white-toothed smile. He wore a pistol slung gunfighter-style on one hip and a walkie-talkie in a knitted case with a Shan emblem on the other.

A buff-colored mule and a smaller white mule would make the trip. Soldiers hoisted a pack frame onto the white one, and the buff one was saddled for me with a green steel military saddle padded with my sleeping bag and blankets. I called the riding mule See-nuan, the Thai word for her color. A Shan teenager, Ai Lo, with an AK-47 was assigned to me, mainly to look after my mule. As we left, descending the hill on the northbound path, Seenuan's every step was balky. I kept up steady kicks and rattled the bit in her mouth, and whenever she stopped completely, Ai Lo yanked her forward.

The major had sent about a dozen soldiers off with Sai Neng and me. They were all rather young and seemed a bit Boy Scoutish, lacking the hard aura worn by seasoned NDF jungle fighters. The TRC cat-and-moused it around the Thai border, avoiding conflict with the Tatmadaw. Its troops were Shan, Palaung, Akha, Kachin, and Wa kids who were taught to read and write Shan and were paid one hundred baht a month (a salary no rebel dared dream of) to fight for the TRC. Or at least to march around and guard opium convoys for the TRC. Khun Sa's troops in the region of Keng Tung that bordered Thailand were overseen by a reputedly brilliant Manchurian general, but they were rarely put to the test of battle. If nothing else, my escorts were well armed, in contrast to the Tiger Camp trainees with their toy rifles. Most carried M-16s or AK-47s, and a young Akha trooper carried an M-79 and its weight of gold-snouted grenades.

When we reached the bottom of the hill, we entered a bamboo

forest. The bamboo grew in panpipes and blades and thin feathers. I
loved its cool darkness and hollow sounds, but on Seenuan I had to
be alert for low spears and whiplash fronds that could knock me off
or impale me. I pushed them out of the way with gloved hands, or
leaned back in the saddle like a limbo dancer. I thought of the
previous year's trip to the Salween River, when Spin had walked
beside me at dusk in a silvery, spidery bamboo grove, which he
pronounced the Enchanted Forest. Now he was off with the Afghan rebels in the Hindu Kush. I rode through the bamboo forest,
my own forest with my own little army, Alice through the glass at
last.

Tunnels and vistas took turns as the day proceeded. For a time we
would be in dark forest or caverns of bamboo, and then we'd burst
out onto a ridge top, with blue mountains visible for a hundred
miles. We did not see people or signs of them until midafternoon
when we stopped in a small, derelict Lahu village. The headman,
the village chief, reclined at his hearth, drawing gurgles from his
opium pipe, while his wife brought me a gourd of cool water. The
Lahus did not wear their tribe's traditional embroidered black
tunics, which I'd often seen in northern Thailand. Instead they
dressed in extremely shabby Shan or Thai clothing. It was too much
trouble for them to weave cloth, to embroider. Southern Keng
Tung Province was agriculturally depressed, and the tribes were
under pressure from the Burmese government to fade away, to just
disappear across the Thai border.

  We traveled on along ridges amid grassy fields where tribal
cultivators had abandoned the exhausted soil. At another Lahu
village, Sai Neng asked if any of the men would volunteer as
porters. They would be paid to carry our supplies only as far as the
village where we'd spend the night. It was a better deal than the
Tatmadaw—who enslaved porters until they dropped—would
offer, but there were no takers. The Lahus didn't want to leave
their crops, their opium, their families, even for a day. Perhaps they
were afraid of battles or did not believe Sai Neng about the wages.

Sai Neng increased the payment, then resorted to threats. I was a participant in human rights abuse, I realized; now tribesmen were being coerced to work in the name of my expedition. Finally, two porters shouldered their loads—baskets of food and ammunition—grumbling and over paid.

On a hilltop we met up with a Palaung woman returning from a day's work in the fields with her little daughter, and she invited us to stay in her village. It was just getting dark when we reached it, and Sai Neng and I were directed to the headman's house. We sat at the hearth, where the headman's family crouched peering at us through the smoke. They asked Sai Neng if I was "a princess from China." Farther than China was impossible to imagine for all but the oldest, who remembered the British days.

The Palaung women wore huge silver earrings, concave circles stuck on stems in their pierced earlobes. The earrings gleamed like headlights in the firelight. We sat looking at each other until an old man entered the house carrying a live white chicken. The headman made a speech: "To come all the way from your faraway land to meet us, Lady Visitor, you must have exceptional luck. Therefore we believe your visit will bring luck to us, as well." He spoke in Shan and Sai Neng translated it into Thai for me. The headman gave me the chicken to hold. I smoothed its white feathers and thanked my host. Then the chicken was taken off to be killed and roasted for our dinner.

Among the provisions carried by our pack donkey and reluctant porters were several bottles of beer, cans of Coca-Cola, and a couple of kilos of oranges from Thailand. I gave a bowl full of oranges to the headman for his family and the children were thrilled. Citrus fruit was a rare treat in the barren hills of Keng Tung. The headman told Sai Neng and me that he had fathered eight children, but only three had survived. His sister told us that her husband had joined Khun Sa's army, but she had not heard from him since, three years. The Tatmadaw came to the village once or twice every year and confiscated whatever it could. The Palaungs there didn't have much worth taking (the women would run into the forest to hide, with their silver earrings) so it was the pigs and chickens that soldiers stole. The Tatmadaw operations showed the Palaungs that they had a government, and that government was the Tatmadaw. To fight back meant disappearing into the forest for years at a time, and it was apparently useless anyway. So there was nothing to do but try to raise rice and opium. "Please pray for us that the Tatmadaw doesn't come here again," the headman requested.

⌐ 3 ⌐

It was cold when we left the Palaung village in the early morning, and I wore my leather jacket over my fatigues. I was reminded of World War II aviators in their leather jackets. Many pilots had bailed out over Burma during that war, and many had been saved by tribespeople. We passed an elaborate water-powered machine the Palaungs had devised for husking rice. Our path took us high in the mountains, so high that pine trees grew and wind blew fiercely through their long boughs. The soldiers had left the Palaung village without eating breakfast, and they began to complain of hunger and about their Chinese canvas sneakers, which gave them blisters.

We continued along mountain ridges overlooking a vast valley without any sign of human inhabitants. The valley narrowed, and I saw a large building on a high bluff. As we neared it, I realized it was a Palaung Buddhist temple, with a double-cupolaed thatched roof. When we rounded a bend in the trail, the village adjoining the temple became visible. Two boy novices in crimson robes ran across the temple yard. I called the village Shangri-la.

Sai Neng told me we would stop for lunch there before continuing. The village had several multifamily longhouses. When we entered one, I saw that each family had its own hearth. Sleeping platforms were partitioned, but most of the long teak floor space was undivided. When I gave a pair of oranges to two little girls, they immediately called other children over to share them. The girls wore red sarongs, black jackets, and bamboo hoops around their waists, just like their mothers. The little boys dressed in odd bits and pieces of cast-off Thai clothing: torn T-shirts, ragged shorts. Aside from the Thai rags, some plastic shoes and boots, and old plastic kerosene cans that were used to fetch and store water, I saw nothing post–Industrial Revolution. The Palaungs made their necessities with great skill: baskets, ironware, silver ornaments, water power, bamboo buildings. The villagers had owned radio-cassette players, they said, but the Tatmadaw had stolen them on the last raid, along with the standard pigs and chickens.

Shangri-la's headman presented me with a shallow basket of rice topped with a few hard-boiled eggs, candles, and Shan cigars, and he made a welcoming speech in Shan. Sai Neng translated it, and I replied: "I have come a long way to see how beautiful your people are, especially the children. I will tell the outside world about you, so you will not be alone in the world."

"We are peaceful people," the headman told me. "We do not really need anything except peace."

Flavorful red rice was cooked for our lunch, and Sai Neng used Thai money to purchase some more for the soldiers. A few months before, Ne Win had arbitrarily demonetized Burmese currency, declaring all but the smallest bills valueless. Nobody trusted the kyat anymore, so the border trade was relying on Thai or Chinese currency, or old silver coins from the Raj. The soldiers loaded their rice rations in sausage-rolls of blue cloth, to be worn like bandoliers. We hired more porters. The Palaungs, desperate for the income, were much more eager to work for us than the Lahus had been.

In the midday heat we were sequestered for siestas in various longhouses. I was on the longhouse veranda, amusing the children with the Velcro straps on my high-top Reeboks, when a buzzing sound came from the air. Sai Neng told me to get inside, a plane was coming. It was a small black plane, one of the Turbo Thrushes donated by the United States for spraying. Now it was being used for reconnaissance, something forbidden by the terms of the foreign aid agreement. The Tatmadaw had apparently heard of troop movements in the area and sent the Thrush over to check us out.

Perhaps they already knew about my presence. Sai Neng cast his radio net about for local intelligence: were there any Tatmadaw troops on their way? We had met another dozen TRC soldiers at Shangri-la, and all stayed hidden for an hour after the plane buzzed away, waiting to see if it would return.

When it didn't, I walked over to the temple. Inside, paper cutouts hung in streamers, and magic diagrams and inscriptions were penciled on colorful scraps of paper. Small, gilt Buddha statues were grouped on a high altar. Light sprinkled through the thatched roof. The temple had only one elderly monk, and the two novices. They conducted a school for the village boys.

A Shan family was passing through the village, a father, mother, and three teenage daughters. Traders from the Shan town of Mong Hsat, they brought goods like salt and candles, and bartered them for forest herbs and opium. Opium poppies grew sparsely in a field right beside the village, and the Shan girls picked the mustard greens called *pakkard* from among them for their dinner. In pristine pastel sarongs and blouses, the girls delighted the soldier boys, who, even if tribal, had acquired Shan ideals of beauty. The bolder ones found some pretext to introduce themselves to the girls, who were closely watched by their parents, but most hung back, too shy. When we set off again, the Boy Scouts seemed more cheered by the encounter with the Shan girls than worried by the Thrush over-flight.

The afternoon was a long push through elephant grass and tall weeds that overgrew our trail. The grass hit me in the face con-stantly, the trail was narrow and bumpy, and I had to keep jerking Seenuan's mouth out of the weeds so she'd watch where she was going. Ai Lo looked very tired. I offered him my canteen of tea, but instead of drinking from it, he carried it, a burden added to his rice-roll and AK-47.

It began to get dark. I could see no villages, but opium fields lay alongside the trail. The poppies were mostly a deep, seductive shade of mauve, with some white ones interspersed. Although the harvest had been underway for a month, many were still at the stage where the petals had just fallen and the pods were slit to release the narcotic resin overnight. The smell of the raw opium seeping out awakened a strange craving in me. The fumes from the tribal smokers' pipes had only turned my stomach, but this raw, pure smell made me long for a taste.

I dismounted when Seenuan began stumbling in the dark, and led her. I walked into a Palaung village, dogs barking at us. That night I stayed in a longhouse, at the hearth of a headman who presented me with a chicken and a basket of rice and told his *dokka* (his troubles) to Sai Neng and me.

═ 4 ═

At dawn, Ai Lo brought me a glass of milky tea and a few crackers, and then we set off. I rode the white mule and Seenuan was given the supply panniers. We moved through an arid zone where new fields were being burnt, and plunged along paths overgrown with fire-toasted weeds. Southern Keng Tung's villages were so hidden from our route that any buildings came as a surprise, and it was particularly startling to ride into a thatch-roofed bridge in an area where most streams were forded, not bridged at all. Inside, it was graffitied with charcoal words of Shan, and the new Akha script's Roman letters. Akha had been unwritten until some Western missionaries in Thailand had devised a script, using the alphabet of their own language.

When the troops and I crossed the bridge, an Akha woman crouched in the tall weeds as if to hide, although her silver-studded headdress reflected the sun. As we filed past, she stood and watched us, silently. We began a long, hot ascent of a hill. One of the Palaung porters pulled himself upward by clutching my mule's tail. An Akha village of many houses spiraled around two adjacent hilltops. When I rode in, a guard dog ran up, barking and growling, its teeth bared. A look of annoyance crossed Ai Lo's face, and he swung his

AK around and aimed it at the dog. Ragged children ran up,
throwing pebbles at the dog to drive it away before Ai Lo could fire.
I was in the Shan State's Keng Tung Province and guns were
power. If a dog barked at us, we could shoot the dog. If a villager
disobeyed us, we could shoot the villager. Or his whole family. Or
the whole village. Interaction between the TRC soldiers and local
tribespeople had seemed easy and courteous on both sides. Men,
women, and children were coming out of their houses and smiling
at us. The Akha boy with the M-79 was chatting happily with the
Akha villagers. But still, we had the guns—we had the power.

The hilltop village I dubbed "Camelot" was tidy and well laid-
out, with large houses in various styles, some on stilts, some not.
Some houses were two or three stories high. Bamboo aqueducts ran
through the village, and children bathed under splashing taps. It
was a throwback to the old, peaceful days of Keng Tung, when
tribespeople lived in villages and towns of their own, before ceaseless war made them nomads; and it was a hold-out village of Akhas
who would make a last stand after so many had fled to Thailand.

When I dismounted, I noticed a mirror hung on a house post. I
hadn't seen my reflection since leaving Thailand. I looked incredibly pale. My eyes were an absurd green. My hair was a bizarre color
like toasted weeds. The Akha mirror showed me as the Akha must
have seen me.

A woman asked me in Shan to wait and meet her mother, who
was in her eighties and had never seen an American before. The
octogenarian, bent but handsome, was helped out of her low bamboo house into the sunlight. Her gray hair was long and thick under
her Akha helmet of silver buttons and coins. Her earrings were Raj
relics, George V in imperial profile. Grinning and exclaiming to her
daughter, she examined the silver lacquer on my fingernails. She
gestured that she wished to touch my hair. I pushed my hat back
and bent my head down so she could stroke the strange mane. After
a while, we smiled to each other, and I walked on to a house with a
sunny elevated porch.

The "sheriff" of Camelot, a thin man in well-mended Thai
clothes, beckoned me up to the porch. He pulled out a rough

wooden chair for me, placing a folded red blanket on it as a cushion. From my lofty vantage point I watched little boys chase a white chicken all over the village until they captured it. Then it was presented to me, and went to its fate on the grill. I drank Chinese tea with an old man in grimy homespun who climbed up to the porch to sit in the sun with me. It would have been fine with the troops to spend the afternoon in Camelot, but the sheriff told Sai Neng and me that a field that had been sprayed with 2,4-D a little over a month before was not far. He said it was "about an hour-and-a-half walk away," so we left for it after our lunch of chicken, *pakkard*, and red rice. Spirit gates decorated with carved wooden figures stood sentry at Camelot's exit, and we were careful not to touch them as we passed through.

As we hit the third hour of walking since Camelot, Sai Neng and I realized that the "hour and a half" was an Akha estimate. They sped through the mountains like Inca runners in the Andes, but our footsore soldiers trudged at a slower pace. We halted at a charred hilltop with a view of the next valley. We could see three small Akha villages, one of which had been deserted because of the spraying. It was the Akha custom to abandon a village if evil events had transpired there, leaving it to the ghosts.

"The planes came to the valley from over that hill, and sprayed the whole day long," the sheriff told us. "And at the end of the day, they flew over the ridge and sprayed the field just above those three villages."

"Like dumping the last drops of water out of a canteen before you fill it," Sai Neng commented, looking through a battered pair of field glasses.

"It is not far to this hillside field," the sheriff said.

"We can't go to the next valley," Sai Neng told me. "The Tatmadaw is definitely there, and we had better not run into them. But I think we can reach this field that we see. Is that good for your purpose?"

"Yes, it's good, but we ought to get moving," I replied. "I have to photograph the spraying effects, and I need daylight to do so. We have to get there before the light fades."

An hour later, we were on the hillside, but the small, thinly planted fields we passed were unsprayed. The sheriff sent a boy to run ahead and fetch the headman of the nearest village. I steeled myself for failure. Sai Neng, sensing it, said, "Don't worry. We will proceed with your mission to find a sprayed field, no matter what our risks, until we reach one, even if it means going all over the province."

The headman trotted up, a gaunt gentleman in a too-large blue suit jacket and homespun trousers. He wore a World War II–vintage Gurkha hat (the sheriff sported an even more antiquated British pith helmet). He led us off the main path, into an extremely steep field of poppies and vegetables. The sprayed field was just above it, at the ridge top. I suggested that the soldiers take a rest, and Sai Neng and I continued to climb with the Akha guides. I walked, as the steepness might endanger the mules. The dark, dry soil was loose and soft. I found it difficult to hike uphill after riding with my legs locked in one position all day, and I was out of breath. I forced myself to keep going. Near the top, the sheriff reached out his hand for mine and pulled me along, and we crossed into the sprayed field.

The plants were an unnatural bleached-out white, with purplish tinges in the leaves. Poppies and *pakkard* had grown tall and spindly, in baroque deformation. The herbicide worked by attacking growth hormones through the plants' leaves, causing them to grow themselves to death over a week or two, then dry up and decay. The mutants included cilantro, ferns, and long white hanks of dead bean vine. Undersized pods topped elongated poppy plants, and some had been slit in the villagers' desperate attempt to salvage opium from them. The headman said they'd been unsuccessful in getting resin from the pinheaded plants. Since the spraying, a few green weeds had poked through the dry soil among the ruined crops. It was ironic that the State Department's "weed killer" had managed to kill everything *but* the weeds. *Pakkard,* the staple winter vegetable in Keng Tung, which I'd had at every meal, was here collapsed in a rubbery phase of decay.

I walked through the steep, rocky field shooting hundreds of pictures of the destroyed foliage, working fast before the light would fade. Sai Neng reloaded my Pentax for me, to save time. I was at once elated to be at last at the scene of the spraying, getting the evidence; and depressed by the repulsive science-fiction scene of crop eradication. I was overjoyed and broken-hearted. No chemical smell remained, but I felt dizzy there. A strong wind blew down over the hillside as the sun began to set in gold. I thought how spray drift would have been unavoidable on the windy slope, perhaps wafting down to the villages. The next field over lay fallow. The villagers had meant to plant rice there.

I used my knife to gouge a soil sample from underneath one of the poppy plants. We returned to the field below, where the soldiers waited. One of them had been dispatched to gather a water sample from a stream that flowed down from the sprayed field to the village. It was presented to me in a small bottle that had contained Lipovitan, one of the sweetened vitality tonics popular in Thailand. "When I have this tested, they'll think the Tamadaw is spraying the field with Lipo," I remarked to Sai Neng. "At least we'll find out what's really in Lipovitan."

The soldiers had been eating Thai peanut cookies while they waited. Each packet contained a set of stickers, so the Boy Scouts entertained themselves by plastering their assault rifles with monsters, super heroes, and robots. I recalled the safety guidelines for minimizing 2,4-D exposure. We had been incapable of following them ourselves, and I realized how impossible it would be for the tribespeople. I had handled the sprayed plants, collecting samples, and now if I was to wash my hands, it would be in water that had flowed through the same contaminated soil.

As darkness fell completely, Sai Neng made the decision to stop for the night at the Akha village just below the fields rather than march back to Camelot. Both options were risky. By staying, we would be on low ground, which Sai Neng hated, with the Tatmadaw only about five hours away. In the headman's dark, dirt-floored house, I drank a Coke with a bowl of instant noodles prepared with the probably contaminated water, had a small shot of searing rice whiskey, and washed at the bamboo aqueduct that brought water from the hillside. I slept deeply and woke before dawn. When light came, a crying baby woke the others.

We returned to Camelot, to spend another day in its lofty security. Sai Neng and I had just finished our red rice and *pakkard* lunch when a crusty old man, with sharp eyes and a long nose, stopped to speak with us.

"Back during World War II," he announced in Shan, "when the Japanese came, they killed a lot of people. And then when the Kuomintang came, they killed people and they also killed animals. But these Burmese come and they kill people, they kill animals, and now they're even killing the vegetables!" He spat betel juice as he told of forced labor, of the Tatmadaw's systematic pillaging, of torture and murder and the new chemical spraying. He said that the Akha knew perfectly well how to live without armies or governments. They just wanted to be left alone.

tribespeople climbed up to the porch and I taped interviews with them. Most were old men who were used to having their observations and opinions valued, but I drew out women and youths as well. I'd had my interview questions written out in Shan, and I told Sai Neng which ones I wanted him to read; when I wanted to ask other questions, he translated my Thai to Shan. Most of the interviewees knew Shan, but for some I needed an additional interpreter to translate from Shan to Akha.

The stories related that afternoon described repeated 2,4-D spraying of Akhas' fields, and made clear that they felt trapped by the Tatmadaw. They no longer had enough currency or trade goods to follow the well-worn escape route to Thailand. Their food and trade crops had been devastated. "What the government did is not good," a sixty-three-year-old man said, "and the things that I have told you now, I want them to reach the authorities. Will it reach them? Whatever we do, they don't see us as human beings. We are looked down on like dogs and pigs. The government is useless. There is trouble all over the country. I'm very sad, but come rain or sun, we must stay here. We must bear it all."

I interviewed a woman who owned the sprayed field I'd visited. Before the spraying, she could get about a viss of opium (three and a half pounds) from the two fields she tilled, which would earn her the equivalent of forty dollars, enough for some clothing, medicine, and tools for her and her three children. Now it was all gone, along with the vegetables they needed for everyday nutrition. The woman sat primly at the edge of a bench, her knees pressed together below the hem of a short homespun skirt.

"It is not good," she said. "I'm very sad. You want to eat decent food, wear decent clothes, but you cannot. I am very downhearted. There is nothing to feel good about. Even if we wanted to move to another place, we wouldn't have anything to eat. An opium smoker doesn't die from smoking it, and I myself only harvest opium. I eat only rice. I want to die, but I don't really want to die. I feel like I want to die, but I cannot die yet. I just feel sick at heart. This government is very foolish. I think it is extremely stupid. I am very, very angry."

The tribespeople told of children who, having been exposed to 2,4-D, had hard coughs and bloated faces, lingering illnesses. Villagers had drunk the water from the mountain streams. When vegetables rotted after the spraying, they dug them up and fed them to their pigs, because that's what they always did with rotten vegetables, and the pigs began dying off.

Sai Neng translated my questions patiently, and his kind manner and gentle voice put even the stiffest interviewees at ease. I did not record the tribespeople's names, or even the names of their villages. I was sure that the punishment for talking to me would be severe if the Tatmadaw found out about the interviews. Camelot was not in an insurgent-controlled area. Before I entered southern Keng Tung, I had pictured it as something like Kawthoolei's rebel territory, only run by Khun Sa. But Khun Sa's army came and went, escorting the occasional opium convoy, and the rest of the time the villagers were completely vulnerable to the Tatmadaw. It was a gray area. I asked the villagers questions about armed groups charging tax in the area, and if any fighting was going on. Their replies indicated that the rebels and Khun Sa were not in control, and the Tatmadaw did as it pleased. Southern Keng Tung Province was not an insurgent zone, it was a victim zone. The people I interviewed had no idea who or what the Burmese government was. They only knew about the soldiers. They had seen the airplanes, but they didn't know that what they sprayed came from my country.

Camelot's people believed they had some strength in numbers. The high hilltop afforded advance warning of Tatmadaw attacks, which were less frequent than those against smaller, isolated villages. But inevitably, Camelot would be a target. "We will stay in our village and die together when they come," a young man vowed. Many his age had already taken up arms (contrary to the peaceful nature of the tribe) to resist the Tatmadaw, and perhaps he would, too. The sheriff, much older, took a long-term approach in his hopes for Camelot's survival. He wanted to send his eldest daughter to a hill-tribe center in Thailand so she could be the first of the villagers to learn to read and write, and return and teach them all the new script. Tall, the girl jingled with ornaments of silver rupees and cowrie shells, and at night many suitors courted her with reed pipe serenades. The Akha girls worked hard in the fields all day, then stayed up late for flirtations. They looked like young crusaders in their bead cowls and metal-studded helmets.

The oldest man sang his ancestor song that night, in which the entire family tree, reaching far back into China, was accounted for in talking blues. I taped it for friends of mine who were anthropologists working in Thailand's Akha villages. "Your tribe has foreign friends," I explained, "who know the Akha people from living in the villages on the Thai side of the border. When they learn of the Akha tribe's oppression in Keng Tung, they will bring it to the whole world's attention. Your suffering will not be unknown."

⌐ 5 ⌐

When the morning's first light seeped through the woven bamboo walls of the sheriff's front room, I sat by the hearth and drank tea, talking with old men who filed in as the women headed off to the fields. I gave the sheriff shiny copper pennies for his wife and daughters to add to their numismatic finery, if they wished. "These are of no value," I told him, "but the great man they show is one known as Lin-Khan, who taught my country that no human being should be a slave to another."

"Lady Visitor, please do not leave us," the sheriff said. "But if you must go, please promise to come back. May I perform a ceremony to make sure that you will come back and to give you safety on your way?" I agreed, and knelt by the hearth. The sheriff, his pith helmet replaced by a fuchsia turban for his *sayah* role, placed a warm boiled egg and a wad of small denomination Burmese bank notes in my right hand. Then he wound strands of orange and magenta yarn around my wrist a few times, looped and knotted it. Not having any insurance of the life and casualty sort, I relied on that sort of thing for protection. I believed in magic string, which covered acts of God and war. Despising the blind alleys of theology, philosophy, ideology, I placed my meager supply of faith in ceremonial Akha string, tied to my right wrist with a pure wish.

I rode out of Camelot on the white mule. Ashes filled the air from burnt and burning fields. The temperature rose in the shadeless black meadows. Midafternoon, we arrived in Shangri-la. No Tatmadaw had been sighted since our previous visit, so it seemed safe enough to spend the night there. The Shan soldiers and I bathed at a cold water-spout, part of the rice-pounding apparatus, an activity that seemed to bemuse the comfortably grimy Palaung villagers.

As evening fell, I was again given gifts of rice, cigars, eggs, and small packets of food wrapped in banana leaves. I accepted them, and passed them on to my troops.

"We are very happy that you have come," the grizzled headman said, "because we will have good luck now. When the other foreigners came, we had good luck."

"Other foreigners?" I asked, wondering what sinister operatives I might be crossing paths with.

"Yes, the other foreigners were very nice, too. They were two men and they came with the Kuomintang."

"When was that?"

"Oh, about ten years ago."

When I taped interviews that night, I scandalized the village elders by asking to interview women. "Look, if there are no women on the tape cassette, the foreigners will think the Palaungs are a tribe of men only," Sai Neng suggested to the crowd in the longhouse. Still no women dared move past the circle of disapproving old men to speak. "Well, I just want to interview the prettiest woman here, that's all," I said. When Sai Neng translated it into Shan, and the Shan was translated to Palaung, one lady—who had the oval face and almond eyes common to the tribe, and a beauty that would have been uncommon anywhere—edged forward a little.

The woman did not speak Shan, so one of the old men had to translate for her. He sat down in front of her facing me and shot the questions back over his shoulder to her. He tended to elaborate on her answers and Sai Neng had to remind him repeatedly to ask her the questions before giving the answers. Our taboo-busting was worthwhile, because the Palaung women knew more about the 2,4-D spraying than any of the men did; it was the women and children who worked the poppy fields.

"When the people got the smell of the chemical, they got dizzy," she said. "I don't know what kind it is. When the chemical touched the cows and the chickens, they all died. After the spraying had been done, you could not eat the vegetables if the rain didn't fall and wash the chemical away. There was no warning before the spraying, and after that the planes just flew away and disappeared."

"How do you feel about what happened?" I asked her.

"I'm still puzzled by the spraying. If I plant again I'm worried. And afraid. If I don't plant I won't have any money to buy the necessary things. I will plant again a little bit—just enough for the food. The government will not be able to satisfy all the people. But to be cruel to the people and make them poor—this is not right."

The next day, heat poured down on the trail, and salt stains outlined Ai Lo's rifle on his uniform. We snaked our way through

Palaung poppy fields. Soldiers picked pods and stripped the non-narcotic seeds out to eat. The heavy flowers nodded in the breeze and my stirrups knocked them. In the sun the blooms gave off a light, fresh fragrance. It smelled a lot like the air freshener called Poppy that Thais put in their cars. It was quite different from the decadent nocturnal aroma of seeping pods. The night smell was not at all like the perfume called Opium, or even that called Poison. Were it bottled, it could only have a name like Overdose or Abscess.

On the Thai side of the border, opium was just considered a cheap thrill for the tourists, despite a high rate of domestic heroin/morphine addiction and an incipient AIDS epidemic from shared needles. "If I see one more tourist wearing a T-shirt that says 'Opium,' I'll throw up," I'd commented to Emma when we walked through Chiang Mai. "They should have a T-shirt that says 'Heroin' showing an arm full of septic punctures instead of those pretty flowers."

The poppy fields gave way to a bamboo forest, which was partially burnt. Lahu woodcutters were culling what they could from felled trees, and collecting grasses to make into brooms. The brooms would be smuggled into Thailand, black market brooms from the Golden Triangle.

We came to the Lahu village where we'd forced (but paid) porters to work for us on the first day. The villagers greeted us cordially enough. The headman was remarkably young—twenty-eight—as all the old men had died off or left for Thailand. In the bleak village, people sat listlessly in their tiny houses, wearing ragged old Thai clothing. The young Palaung men who were now our porters were much livelier, with black pantaloons, colorful towel turbans, and single headlight earrings. All the Lahu villagers had similar faces, beyond mere tribal resemblance: thin noses, wide mouths. This suggested to me that the area was so depopulated that the tribe might have been reduced to inbreeding. The headman's sister's face was beautiful when she smiled. She smiled when I gave her son a Coca-Cola can.

Denser forest followed. Tiny orchids draped tree branches overhead. I was tempted to decorate my hat with some, but superstition prevented me. I'd had a jungle flower in my hatband when I had been arrested the year before. It was bad enough that I would be reentering Thailand a few days before Chinese New Year, just like the previous year. I'd better not trifle with flowers. And I wouldn't ride in any white pickup trucks. I now had the evidence I wanted against the 2,4-D program, and had too much to lose. I decided I'd wait days and days for a blue or red truck if I had to.

We stopped for the night at a shabby Lahu village that Sai Neng said was a TRC customs post. We had not encountered anyone in the smuggling trade: no caravans, no porters hauling Thai goods, no cattle drivers. The area seemed to have little to offer but paltry yearly opium crops and broom hay. The Tatmadaw had made southern Keng Tung Province the negative space that they wanted: a buffer zone.

I interviewed some of the Lahu tribespeople that night. They were Lahu Sheh Leh, the "black Lahu," but they no longer wore their clan's distinctive black clothing. Some Lahu men from another village came to talk to me. They had dressed in their best outfits—all of them wore the same shirts: garish, flowered, sky-blue polyester with red zippers. I'd noticed that same shirt on Palaung men as well. Some Thai manufacturer must have gotten stuck with the awful shirts, and a black market middleman must have unloaded bales of them on Keng Tung's unwitting hill tribes.

I switched on my recorder to collect the *dokka,* the heartache. An old man told me, "I am glad you have come here to listen to our troubles. Now that you are here, perhaps the British will return at last to rescue us from those infernal Burmese." As the first foreigner to arrive in this impoverished corner of the world in many years, I expected the villagers to ask for help from the outside: doctors, medicine, food. Instead, they gave *me* things. They gave me rice, chickens, candles, and lucky string. The only thing they asked of me was that I pray for the Tatmadaw not to come around anymore.

Sai Neng and I sat on the bamboo floor with the Lahus. By now I could ask some of the questions in Shan myself. The last person I interviewed was a bony, forty-seven-year-old man who wrapped a threadbare jacket around himself and coughed constantly.

"Have people you know left the area because of the Tatmadaw situation?" I asked.

"Yes, they almost all fled to Thailand. Our village had thirty households before, and now there are only six left. The Burmese come and trouble you every six months, and how can you live when you have to flee to the jungle every time?"

"Why don't the Lahus in this area wear traditional Lahu clothing and ornaments?"

"How can we have all those clothes when we cannot sell pigs and cattle? Every year the Burmese come to take the animals as food. I have nothing left." He wiped his eyes with his jacket sleeve, and spat through a crack in the floor.

"How many children do you have?"

"I have one daughter and two sons."

"How much land do you have for crops?"

"I have no paddy field. Only a hill field. I can just work only a fraction of the field. Even then because you have to flee the Burmese all of the time you cannot harvest your rice. Also when it is time to plant you cannot do so."

"How do you feel about what has happened?"

"We moved down here from near Keng Tung town because we couldn't stand the forced labor anymore. We have been here for two years and the Tatmadaw caught up with us again. And every time they come they take away all our food—pigs and chickens. We don't have the chance to sell them for cash."

Ne Win's Tatmadaw had succeeded in destroying the economy of southern Keng Tung Province, and had effectively depopulated it. Now all that was left to do was to terrorize the last tribal holdouts by raining death from above on their fields. The U.S. aid program fit the bill perfectly.

= 6 =

We spent the next morning making our way through the deep bamboo forests that surrounded the TRC base. I rode Seenuan, flattening myself to her steel saddle to avoid overhanging bamboo and thorn branches. We splashed across a river and began to climb. The hills were steep and Seenuan stepped on Ai Lo's foot. One of Ai Lo's dusty toes oozed blood. I tore a strip off my bandanna for a bandage. After ritual refusals, he tied it neatly around the injured toe. He was wearing rubber thong sandals. Like most of the Boy Scouts, he had jettisoned his Chinese army sneakers on the trail. The local villagers must have been delighted to find the discards. They wouldn't fear blisters, their feet were rock hard; they walked the mountains barefoot or in terrible plastic oxfords.

As we neared the TRC camp, I noticed other precious debris: Coke cans, plastic bags, old batteries. In the tribal zone, these things would have been scavenged and put to use. I thought of Daniel and Naomi's village in Kawthoolei and how they used the fillings of used batteries to make paint for their school blackboards. Now I was getting close to Thailand and modern, throwaway culture again.

When we ascended the last hill, the major greeted us, and over Chinese tea he asked me if the expedition had been successful.

"Yes, it was a complete success," I told him.

"Were there any problems along the way?"

"None at all," I assured him.

"I am very happy that your mission was accomplished." The major smiled. "Now, perhaps it is best that you proceed back to Thailand tonight. We have had no word that the Thais know about your Keng Tung presence yet, and there is no troop alert on the Thai side of the border. Best to go before that situation changes."

"What news of the world has come over the Thai radio during the past week?" I asked, since I hadn't my own shortwave radio.

"The main world news is that the dictator of Panama is a drug warlord," the major said, his eyebrows raised in amusement. He excused himself to send a radiogram to Khun Sa at Tiger Camp, informing him that the expedition had gone smoothly.

At the outdoor table, Sai Neng was flexing his tattooed forearms over a pad of yellow paper. He was writing a report on the expedition from notes he'd jotted down along the way.

"Everyone's sad that you will leave," he said.

"I'm sorry. I have to be sure to get the tapes and film and samples out. Evading the BPP is my main priority now."

"Thank you for making this expedition. You know I went because I followed my commander's orders, but I also went because I believe in what you are doing. That is why I was determined to get you to a place where the chemical spraying happened. Nothing would have stopped us."

The major rejoined us, with other officers, for a farewell toast. The major was an ascetic Buddhist revolutionary like Mo Heing, so he drank tea. The others poured glasses of incendiary clear rice liquor. *"Mai sung! Mai sung!"* Sai Neng and I clinked our glasses together and drained them.

"We hope you will come back here soon," the major said. "You are most welcome anytime."

In reply I pointed to a World War II China-Burma-India insignia on my leather jacket. "This is from a time when America and the frontier peoples here knew and respected and helped each other. I hope that such cooperation will be revived for good purposes, as it was on this expedition."

I bathed with heated water in a green bamboo enclosure, and dressed in civilian clothes. I would take a different route back to Ban Kong, in case the BPP was watching the way I'd come. I would go by mule, so Seenuan was saddled up again. Ai Lo would accompany me. So would a young Shan corporal and the Palaung boy who'd guided me up to the base the first night. They put on civilian shorts and shirts while I said good-bye to the major and Sai Neng.

I rode through the base, and in the daylight I could see that it was a well-fortified stronghold. It was the kind of place where Khun Sa's franchised chemists refined the year's opium crop into morphine and heroin. As we left the base, we veered off the main path and began descending a steep trail. We were to proceed slowly and cautiously, and enter Ban Kong under cover of darkness. We passed by a small village of thatched houses, and a meadow where ponies grazed.

When we reached a red dirt road we were in Thailand. The Thai Army had built such "strategic roads" along the northern border, so they could bring up troops in a hurry, if the need ever arose. Seenuan trotted on the smooth, level road as the sun began to set and the air cooled.

We left this road for a narrow, convoluted path, and it became very dark. We passed by another tribal village, where dogs barked. A man saw us, turned, and walked rapidly away. Just past the village two trails intersected. Ai Lo pulled Seenuan to a halt. The corporal and the Palaung were far ahead of us. Ai Lo whistled, but no one replied. After a few minutes, Ai Lo went ahead to look for the others. I sat there, in the dark. This is very bad, I thought. If there are BPP in the village we just passed, I can hardly claim to be an innocent tourist who's just lost her way—how would I explain the mule?

After what seemed a long time, my escort reemerged from the gloom and we took what could only have been the worse of the two trails: It quickly deteriorated into a network of steep, dry streambeds. Seenuan stumbled down the bone-white watercourse, kicked and cursed all the way. We plunged down. Darkness was total and Ai Lo, ahead of me, was conserving his flashlight batteries. I felt as though I was being pushed blindfolded down an endless flight of stairs.

After ricocheting through the gullies for about an hour, we found ourselves in the flat fields of Ban Kong's surrounding valley. Ai Lo kept flipping his flashlight on and off, and the strobe effect was intensely disorienting, so I took out my own flashlight. When I shined it to illuminate the path ahead, it cast a monstrous donkey-head shadow, just like the shadow puppets children make on bedroom walls with their hands. I found the shadow disturbing and wanted to close my eyes. But if I closed my eyes, I knew I would sleep.

As I rode by small villages, I leaned forward in the saddle, so that if we were stopped I could claim to be a sick tourist being brought down from some tribal village for medical treatment in Ban Kong. Field-clearing fires burned in the night. I rode through a flaming stand of bamboo that sparked and crackled. Firelight illuminated a stone tower that might have been a guard post. We seemed to be on the edge of Ban Kong. The Palaung boy rushed back to us and whispered urgently to Ai Lo. Seenuan halted. My heart halted. It appeared the BPP *were* coming after us. Then the corporal doubled back to join us. More whispers and Ai Lo yanked on Seenuan's bridle and my mule resumed her jaunty walk through smoke and embers.

I dismounted when we entered Ban Kong. We had entered from a side of the village I'd not seen before, and the dirt road flanked by dragon-decorated shophouses seemed to stretch forever. Foreigners were not infrequent visitors there, but entering on a mule from the wrong direction was altogether too conspicuous. So I tried to walk like a tourist. Walking at all was not easy after the ten hours I'd spent in the saddle that day.

The young corporal signaled that I'd reached my contact's house, which I failed to recognize in the dark. My contact came out to meet me at the gate, and he hurried me inside. I sent him back out with an envelope in which I'd enclosed some Thai money for Ai Lo and the others to buy themselves food and cigarettes.

"They will stay in another house tonight, and go back to the camp with your mule tomorrow," my contact told me when he returned to his kitchen. "Your mule-boy has the fine old-fashioned Shan courtesy. When I gave him the envelope he bowed formally and clicked his heels. You can spend what's left of the night here safely, the Border Patrol Police do not seem to be looking for you. Tomorrow morning, you can leave for town in a truck." It would be a shiny new blue pickup truck, with a tape deck blaring a Mandarin version of Madonna's "La Isla Bonita," which happened to be my favorite song that winter.

"Have you had your dinner?" my contact inquired. "Would you like to eat some rice?"

"No, thank you, I'm really not hungry, but some water would be great."

He brought me ice water in a tall glass, and said, "Excuse me a moment. I must go turn off the generator."

When he returned from his task, I still had not moved to drink the water. I was sitting there, too tired, staring at the clear glass that gleamed in the candlelight.

A
RADIANT
OBSTACLE

⹁ 1 ⹁

Three days after I crossed unscathed from Keng Tung Province into Thailand, I found myself in another border town, holed up in the Fang Hotel (a favorite abode of brigands) waiting to cross into the Shan State again, this time with the Shan State Army, Khun Sa's rivals. At the last minute, the SSA decided, without explanation, that they couldn't take me into their territory after all, so I returned to

Chiang Mai. There I found a translator for my Keng Tung tapes, and I made the transcriptions into a report called *The Victim Zone*. Chiang Mai being what it was, I was sometimes in the same room with Thai intelligence types, but they did not know about my Keng Tung trip, or were not interested in it. I was home free.

When I slept, I kept dreaming of escaping Burma, fleeing it like a Keng Tung refugee. In the dream, I searched for a thorn tree with yellow flowers, which would mean I'd reached safety. Waking, I tried to picture the remote TRC camp. Soldiers would be coding radiograms, washing uniforms, eating red rice. I tried to imagine that tranquil, isolated place. I wondered about the looking-glass world the camp was gateway to: how fared the Palaungs in their red sarongs, the coin-spangled Akhas, and the forlorn Lahus?

Early in March, I went south. The two main Mon rebel factions were united now. They were attacking Tatmadaw posts along the Andaman Sea, and intimations of ancient Mon imperialism were making their National Democratic Front allies—the Karens—nervous. I began my southern travels with a visit to a third, renegade, Mon group. I got a ride to their base with Dr. Pongsri, the Mon I'd met at Khun Sa's Tiger Camp festival, and another Mon from Bangkok. It was an all-night drive along Thai highways and through coconut plantations, until we reached the Thailand/Burma border and the base commanded by Pakomon.

The fortified front gate faced the Thai border with signs that read NO PERMISSION TO ENTRANCE and ANTI BURMA AND COMMUNIST, accentuated with two human skulls mounted Jolly Roger–fashion above crossed femurs. "They were Burmese spies," Pakomon commented as he waved us in. He was a young warlord—an anomaly in Burma. Pakomon, trained and educated in Taiwan in the 1970s, was in his thirties, and he had an Afro hairstyle and a goatee. Wearing a green beret, he was a hipster in tight camouflage. His army, a mere hundred troops or so, wore expensive camouflage uniforms, and had long, rock-and-roll hairdos.

"They have long hair so we can tell them from the Tatmadaw in combat," Pakomon told me.

Their insignia proclaimed them troops of the "Mon K. Army."

"What does the *K* stand for?" I asked.

"*K* is for Kingdom," Pakomon replied.

"If there was a Mon kingdom, who would be the Mon king?"

"Oh, it's just something our KMT patron thought up for us. Now we're actually switching to patches that say 'Mon D. Army.' "

"And *D* is for . . . ?"

"Either Defense or Democracy, I haven't decided yet." From what I had heard about Pakomon's operation, the *D* could have stood for Drugs, too. A new route for narcotics moved south through Burma, with Tatmadaw assistance, and then entered Thailand and Malaysia along the coast. Pakomon was rumored to have a hand in that, which certainly meshed with his KMT connection.

A few Thais were staying at the camp: a truck mechanic working on Pakomon's vehicles and the mechanic's lady friend who wore a black-and-blue velvet dress; and officials from Ranong, the seaport that was the southernmost spot on the Thailand/Burma border. A corrupt network known as the "police Mafia" made Ranong the Marseilles of Thailand. We sat on the floor of a bamboo barrack beneath a hissing pressure lamp, and drank fresh bear's blood mixed with Dewar's White Label. The blood gave the Scotch a salty aftertaste.

Cocktail chat consisted of speculation about leaders and armies, border talk. Someone asked me if I knew how the Kachin rebel chairman, Brang Seng, was able to travel to Europe and Japan, promoting his proposed solutions to frontier problems.

"I know about his travel documents, but it's a secret," I said.

"Secrets!" a Ranong official, who was quite drunk, snorted. "Who keeps secrets anymore? You are behind the times! Secrets are made to be divulged! I myself rented helicopters to your CIA for their Secret War in Laos!" He proceeded to divest himself of a burden of classified Laos information, reeling it off in slurred, semicoherent English.

Not to be outdone, Dr. Pongsri told a secret story about Khun Sa.

"I probably shouldn't tell anyone this, but General Khun Sa commissioned a precious jade Buddha statue to be made in the Shan State, so that he could present it to the King of Thailand in honor of His Royal Majesty's sixtieth birthday last December. Of course, General Khun Sa had no way to present the statue directly, so he handed it over to a certain Thai general who has been known to visit Tiger Camp. The Thai general gave assurances that he would present it to the king on General Khun Sa's behalf. But he has not done so! He keeps the statue on a shelf full of precious Buddha images in his very own home! He tells General Khun Sa's men that he is just waiting for the right moment for the presentation, but I do not think he will ever give it away."

I laughed appreciatively, blood on my lips. I had been in Southeast Asia long enough to know that even the high and mighty got ripped off.

"What do you think about the Karen leader, Bo Mya, going to Tiger Camp to meet with Khun Sa last month?" Pakomon asked me. "Not so good for the Karen image, is it?"

"In America we have a story about a clever rabbit," I replied, "who catches his enemy by making a figure out of sticky tar. He puts the tar figure out on the road and hides behind a bush shouting insults at his enemy. The enemy thinks the tar figure is shouting at him and fights him, but he gets all stuck in the tar! Khun Sa is like the tar figure, and Ne Win is the clever rabbit. Whoever goes to deal with Khun Sa gets stuck to him with the tar, and Ne Win just laughs."

The next day, I got a ride from Pakomon's camp to Ranong with a shadowy Thai operative who wore plain green fatigues. He dropped me off at a hotel in the center of town. I registered as "Rita Falcone," occupation: meteorologist (investigating the effects of certain high-pressure fronts from the west on the climate in southern Thailand). The Thai operative came by my hotel in the morning to give me a lift to the pier, where Thailand's part of the Isthmus of Kra met the Andaman Sea. On the way, we made brief stops at the Ranong police station; a brothel adorned with Happy

New Year banners; and an empty shop where we had tea in the back room with a languid Chinese man who, although still in his pajamas, wore a gold watch, a gold bracelet, gold rings and gold chains, and flourished a gold cigarette holder.

A variety of small wooden boats were running passengers back and forth to the Burma side of the channel, but the Karen boat-boys said they couldn't take me, a foreigner, there. I went back to the town's center, where the market sold Burmese garlic and seashells. Men in plaid sarongs strolled the town's two main streets. They were Arakanese, Karens, Mons, Burmese—crews from fishing and smuggling boats.

I returned to the pier, alone, in the afternoon. It stank from a massive influx of Burmese fish. Ancient, brown fishing junks with Mon crews bobbed at the dock while bright plastic bins of every sort of seafood, from crabs to sharks, were unloaded. Tubs of Thai ice for keeping the fish fresh were loaded onto the boats because in Burma's degraded economy, ice manufacture was prohibitively expensive. When I was about to leave, a Karen boy offered to take me in his boat to "see Burma city." I climbed into his car engine–powered longboat, and we sped off, waving to Thai customs and Immigration officials as we passed their stilt-house checkpoints. We cruised out of the harbor, stopped at a tiny uninhabited island, and then veered close to the Burma coast. I got a look at Burma's southernmost town, Kawthaung, which had palm trees and old houses with faded paint along a promontory. The British had called it Victoria Point. I took a few pictures, and we zoomed back to the Ranong pier with its black market ice.

⌐ 2 ⌐

While I was in Ranong, the National Democratic Front held a press conference at Three Pagodas Pass. I'd intentionally avoided it because I wanted to keep my presence on the border out of the

consciousness of Thai officialdom, and because I had little interest
in such events. I only wanted to see how the soldiers and civilians
lived, not their leaders' ceremonies and pronouncements. I went
back to Bangkok from Ranong, and then headed for the familiar
territory of Three Pagodas Pass. I planned to stay only a short time
and then make a trip to the Karens' Tenasserim district.

After an all-night ride in a Mon smuggler's elephantine ten-
wheeler (an excursion notable for purported bird's nest soup and
bad coffee), I arrived in Sangklaburi. At a house in town, the Mon
leader Nai Shwe Kyin greeted me cordially in splendid English. I
had not met him before. He had been the leader of a Mon faction
that had been in conflict with another led by Nai Non La, whom I
had met on my trip to Three Pagodas with Spin. Since their
reunification, the Mon rebels were increasing their troop strength
considerably.

The National Democratic Front had brought the Mon factions
together, but the NDF was in a way contributing to Mon conflict
with the Karens. The NDF divided Burma into ethnic entities
with a "Mon State" and a "Karen State." But Nai Shwe Kyin
produced old maps to show that Mon rule had extended far
beyond the narrow strip of land the NDF allotted them and well
over much of the designated Karen territory. I tended to agree
that the NDF divisions were too neat and unrealistic. Burma's
ethnic groups were mixed together all over the country, not in
separate homelands. There were thousands of Shans in the Kachin
State, and thousands of Kachins in the Shan State, for example.
And many smaller groups like the Lahus and Palaungs didn't
have specified territories.

Nai Shwe Kyin, a small, bright-eyed man in his late seventies,
brought me to his camp, which he planned to move nearer to Nai
Non La's base. Nai Shwe Kyin turned on his shortwave and got
Bulgarian opera on the BBC. We drank tea in thin cups embossed
with gold dragons in his thatched-roof bungalow. He told me
stories about fighting the Japanese in World War II. Later, the
radio gave cricket scores.

When I left the camp the next day, a Mon whispered to me, "Be
careful of the Karens. Some foreign journalists went to Manerplaw

and would only meet with NDF representatives. So the Karens gave them poisoned oranges that made them sick." I nodded politely, knowing that the Mons were genuinely concerned for my safety, but I did not believe the story.

I visited the Karen missionary family near Sangklaburi, and stayed with one of the daughters, who was a nurse. Although a Karen, she was glad the Mon rebels were united because she had assisted in stitching up far too many casualties of the Nai Shwe Kyin versus Nai Non La conflict. She was sick of the whole war in Burma. She told me a story from a past rainy season: "I was walking back to Three Pagodas from a Karen village on the Burma side, with the American doctor from our hospital. Many porters with loads strapped on their backs were struggling through the mud. We saw one of them slip. His load was so heavy that he couldn't get up again by himself. The doctor went to help him, but the porter was so weighed down, the doctor—who was a big, strong man—couldn't lift him. We had to undo the pack first. When he got up, the porter put the muddy pack back on. I think he was coming down with fever. We walked along with him, slowly, until we reached Three Pagodas and he joined the other porters. I couldn't get it out of my mind. The poor man down in the mud, just like an insect. That night I told my father about it. And my father said, *'That's what war does to people.'* "

I went to Three Pagodas' bazaar by *songtaow,* on a paved road that now ran there from Sangklaburi. The old, muddy slog was now a twenty-minute ride. Among the passengers was a young tourist couple, choking on the dust that blew in off the new road. Three Pagodas had finally been featured in the guidebooks for budget backpackers. Whatever attraction it offered, the ultimate draw was that the Karens, in their innocent tribal tradition, offered free accommodations to the tourists.

Three Pagodas' bazaar was booming in this hot, dry season. Black market goods poured in and out by ox cart, as well as on the backs of porter throngs. I found Joshua, my old World War II veteran friend, and we ate greasy chop suey outside the new cinema hall. The movies were Thai action-adventure films, Rambo rip-offs that could be understood without subtitles. The young Karen soldiers perusing the movie posters were third generation rebels, combat hardened, with cropped hair, rag headbands, and washed-out, tiger-stripe fatigues.

The Tatmadaw hadn't gotten close enough to shell the bazaar in a long time, so Three Pagodas seethed with sleazy, boom town energy. The black market thrived, along with a Thai-run illicit lottery. The Mons had erected elaborate signs proclaiming the town Mon territory and the Karens had built archways calling it part of Kawthoolei. They fought for their shares of the smuggling income by offering discounts and rebates at their separate customs posts.

Joshua and I crossed his new "parking lot" (a pasture where he charged ox cart drivers a small fee to rest their oxen) on our way to one of the Pakistani coffee shops. Joshua translated the BBC news as the Burmese-language broadcast played in the shop. When Ne Win had demonetized the currency six months before, some students in the city had mounted demonstrations. Now, student anger exploded as street-fighting in Rangoon. Here on the border, we were hoping that the time had come for the urban Burmese, so repressed, to finally rise up against Ne Win's tyranny.

A Mon doctor brought me on his motorcycle to the camp of Nai Non La, who had only nice things to say about the Karens. Mild-mannered, white-haired Nai Non La's English was not bad, but he felt more comfortable with a fluent translator, so he called Nai Tin Aung up to his rustic headquarters. Nai Tin Aung had curly, steel gray hair and wore a gun belt strapped around his thick, saronged waist. We discussed the recent press conference. The Karens had boycotted it, but otherwise it had gone well. And the Thais had not caused any trouble for the foreign attendees.

"Many foreigners attended the press conference," Nai Tin Aung told me, "including a film crew from Germany. We were going to allow them to go on a long trip with our soldiers, but one of the

Germans fell ill with stomach trouble, so they all packed up and went back to Bangkok instead."

Poisoned oranges? I wondered, and asked, "Where had they been planning to go?"

"Oh, we were going to send them from here to the coast of the Andaman Sea."

I had never heard of any foreigner, even Thai Mons, making that trip before.

"I'd go in a minute," I said.

Nai Tin Aung and Nai Non La exchanged surprised glances and said something in Mon. "But you would have to walk too far. Over very high mountains, for many days," Nai Tin Aung said.

"But I have just gone far into the Shan State, where the mountains are much higher," I pointed out, leaving out the fact that I'd ridden mules the whole way.

Nai Non La grimaced. "This is too much. Too far. Too much hard walking for you," he said.

I let the subject change, all the while scheming to get myself on this terrible march to the sea. Now that I'd found it was possible, there was nothing I wanted more than to explore the utterly hidden world of Mon seacoast villages. We talked for a while about my meetings with Pakomon and Nai Shwe Kyin.

"If you wish, we will put you up at Three Pagodas Resort," Nai Tin Aung translated for Nai Non La. "It will be more convenient and comfortable for you than staying in the bazaar."

Three Pagodas Resort, which I'd dubbed The Last Resort, had recently sprouted on the Thai border not far from Nai Non La's camp.

"No thank you. I always stay with Joshua," I said as an inspiration hit me. He was being possessive. The Mons didn't like the idea of me staying with a Karen. "I just had an idea. If I decided not to go to Karen Sixth Battalion headquarters in the Tenasserim, where I've been before, then I'd have time to go to the Andaman Sea with your Mon soldiers instead."

A few words were exchanged in rapid Mon.

"We will send some of our women soldiers to accompany you,"

said Nai Tin Aung, "and you will visit many villages on your way. You can make human rights interviews." It would take at least four days to reach the sea. My Thai visa would expire in about three weeks, so I had just enough time to make the trip and return to Bangkok in order to *properly* exit Thailand.

⸗ 3 ⸗

Nai Tin Aung picked me up in a Jeep at Joshua's house the next morning. On the way to the Mon camp, we stopped at a shack near the pagodas so I could interview a young couple who'd been captured by Burmese police. The husband was a Mon from the seacoast of Burma, and the wife was a Thai from Kanchanaburi. They'd gone to Burma intending to visit his family. Just outside of Ye City the train they were on broke down, so they got off to continue by bus. At the bus stop, Burmese police arrested them, accusing the husband of being a Mon rebel soldier. He was not, but a Mon bird tattoo on his forearm was considered sufficient evidence of his rebel sympathies. The couple was brought to a prison camp.

The gifts they had brought for the family—cash, wristwatches, gold chains—were confiscated. The young man was tortured for several days in an effort to force a confession. The police burned him with cigars, hung him upside down in a well, buried him in dirt up to his neck. He showed me shiny scars on his legs where the police had rolled metal bars to wear the flesh off. His wife had been severely beaten. She opened her mouth to show me where molars had been knocked out. Her remaining teeth were, like those of most young Thais, white and healthy.

"When I went to Burma I was two months pregnant," she said.

"What happened to the child?" I asked.

"When the Burmese beat me, it came out in blood."

"When you were arrested, did you tell them you were from Thailand?"

"Yes, I told them. They did not care. I heard that some Burmese people from the city heard that I, a foreigner, was in the prison. They came with food for me, but the police turned them away."

Eventually the couple had escaped with a few other prisoners. Near starvation, they had made their way through the jungled mountains until they had reached Thailand.

Many people—Shans, Palaungs, Karens, Burmese—had told me of their mistreatment by Burmese soldiers and police. They described their beatings and tortures quietly, aggrieved but matter-of-fact. To them, it was the norm in Burma. The young Thai was different. She hissed her words, her eyes burning hatred and bitterness. Her abuse by foreigners had been a shock, a fate she'd never imagined.

At Nai Non La's camp, I met Nyundthun, a nineteen-year-old Mon soldier who would be my interpreter on the seacoast expedition. No English speakers were available, but Nyundthun had gone to school in Bangkok for two years and spoke Thai well. "When you reach the coast you will meet a general who speaks English," Nai Tin Aung assured me. "And he will arrange for your interview translation."

"Would you like a small firearm to take with you?" Nai Non La inquired. I declined, much as I was fond of guns and would have liked to swagger past the tourists in the bazaar with one on my belt. I'd have plenty of well-armed soldiers around for protection, and in the event of capture by the Tatmadaw, carrying a gun would only make things worse for me. Nai Non La gave me a can of lychees in heavy syrup (which weighed as much as a pistol), some dried fish wrapped in newspaper, and a bag of melon candies.

I was accompanying an expedition delivering a Chinese rocket-launcher and a dozen or so rockets to troops on the seacoast. We went to the bazaar and waited around while porters' back-baskets were loaded with the heavy, finned rockets. One of the three women soldiers who would be going along brought me iced sugar-cane juice, presenting it to me with a wonderful smile.

The officer in charge was a young sergeant ("Sarge") with a light beard. He wore a broad-brimmed hat and had slung a pink Karen shoulder bag beside his M-16. Sarge led us off through the bazaar and down a dusty gulch. I marched in line with nine soldiers and four porters. One of the women soldiers slipped and slid down the gulch, her carbine clattering. She got up, laughing, and brushed the dust off her green fatigues.

We climbed into the hills, sweating. Our pace was slow. The two younger women soldiers paused frequently, gasping for breath. Like the men, who were mostly in their thirties and forties, the women (early twenties) carried rifles, packs, and ammo pouches. In a fire zone where fields were being burnt from jungle, black ash radiated heat and cinders blew in our faces. Eventually the trail leveled off, and we walked through fields at dusk until we arrived at a small village. Sarge, Nyundthun, the women, and I were billeted at a farmhouse. The men would sleep on the veranda, we women on the floor of the front room.

I went with the women soldiers to the river to bathe. We had a new cake of red perfumed soap to share. I learned their names. The serious one, who was a couple of years older than the other two and had no problem with hill climbing, was Pakuson. The youngest—shy, with short hair and muscular legs—was Rad Aung. And the third, a dreamy-eyed soldier with a lovely big smile, was Chu Win.

Back at the farmhouse, Nyundthun told me we'd leave early in the morning. Nyundthun was the youngest in our party. He had a fashionable haircut, a complicated digital watch, and new black leather Thai Army boots. He and Sarge sat up talking while the rest of us settled on the floor to sleep. The women lay down on either side of me, their rifles stacked against the wall within easy reach. Pakuson had an M-16 (the American status symbol), Chu Win had an AK-47 (practical, lightweight), and Rad Aung had an old, worn carbine. They slept under red-and-white Thai cotton sarong material, and they'd brought a sheet of maroon plaid Burmese cotton for me. The night was cold, and we slept fitfully, shivering. I wished I'd brought my sleeping bag, which I'd left in Bangkok. I had not expected to end up sleeping in such cold mountain air.

At five A.M. we woke up, strapped on gear, and moved out—breakfastless, coffeeless. With the dawn's light came the realization that I was not going to get any special treatment. In Keng Tung, I'd been the visiting Chinese princess, with mules to ride and cans of Coca-Cola at every stop. Now I was a foot soldier: no sleeping bag, no blankets, no porter for my gear.

We marched noisily through thick jungle and crossed several streams. I was wearing Reebok high-tops, which were soft inside and had decent traction. But my socks absorbed water when we waded through streams. The wet socks chafed my feet, starting blisters. All the Mon soldiers wore rubber thong sandals, except Nyundthun and Sarge, who had new Chinese canvas jungle boots (with socks). After a few hours, we stopped for rice and curry at a cluster of bamboo shacks, and I took my Reeboks off. I put the soggy shoes in my daypack and buckled on my silver plastic sandals, but my raw, red toes showed that the damage had already been done.

We climbed. We hoisted ourselves from root to root, rut to rut, rock to rock. Midday on the mountain, sweat made mud of the dust caked on our skin. The women soldiers and I rolled our trouser legs up; the porters and some of the older, male soldiers who wore sarongs hitched them up for coolness, revealing thighs tattooed with magic blue whorls.

We reached a summit and rested in the breeze. Descending the other side of the mountain strained my knees and ankles, so I went slowly. The effort made my legs tremble when we stopped on the trail to rest. Finally we reached a valley and marched through cool ravines. Refugees were building huts by a river. They had ice buckets full of weak Chinese tea to refresh passing smugglers and soldiers. We stopped and drank glass after glass. We rested in a refugee woman's open hut. Her husband, although feverish with malaria, was hard at work clearing the jungle beside the hut, chopping down saplings with mad energy, burning the foliage.

Our own madness was apparent as we continued on our way by

night, climbing another mountain. My knees were buckling, but I managed not to fall. The wet shoes sagged in the bag on my back. The mountain was on fire. Burning bamboo exploded in loud reports. Sparks dive-bombed us. Smoke billowed across our path as we trudged upward. We pulled ourselves along, grasping whatever branches weren't thorny or on fire.

One of the rocket porters collapsed in a mountaintop clearing. Sarge decided that we should sleep there, in the hope that a rest would help the man survive the night. Nyundthun gave the porter some quinine and one of my Fansidar antimalarial tablets.

The women soldiers spread out a plastic sheet to sleep on, at the foot of a huge tree. They said their evening Buddhist prayers, *wai*-ing and bowing to the tree. Wrapped in our cotton sheets like mummies, we lay among rifles, canteens, and ammo clips. We got thorns in our feet from a bush at the bottom of the plastic. Sarge and Nyundthun gathered the thorn branches into a bonfire and hunkered down to talk all night. The crackling of bamboo on the mountain below us did not abate, but the stars above were brilliant as the jungle's smoke began to drift away.

⹀ 4 ⹀

Sarge roused us in the dark and we marched on, with the malaria-stricken porter tramping far behind. Hours dragged by.

"You are tired," Nyundthun observed sympathetically as I staggered along. "If we had our Mon nation, you could go to the seacoast by airplane. Now we don't have a nation. We don't have anything. I don't care if I have to die fighting to get us a nation."

We kept walking. Chu Win was in bad shape, leaning on a bamboo staff. I noticed a tear or a drop of sweat rolling down her cheek as I passed her. All day, smuggling porters scurried past us on the trail. Their loads—stacked cans of Aji-no-moto, bicycle wheels, bags of rubber sandals—towered above their heads. They clambered nimbly up and down the trail, gleaming with sweat. Most were men, but women and even children carried heavy loads as well. Often the porters would call out to me in Thai, cheerfully, as if it were all great holiday fun. When I was looking particularly worn out, a porter told me, "Don't worry! In just half an hour you'll be there!" *Be where?* I wondered.

An hour and a half later, we reached a riverside resting place. Porters were stronger than soldiers and carried more. Soldiers walked slower, but kept going longer—they walked until they dropped. Porters walked fast, stopped often, and did not walk at night. At the river, porters and soldiers all took a break. Like everyone else, I drank the river water. I had never fallen ill from drinking or eating anything in Asia (including tap water, river water, unpeeled fruit, salads, and monkey), so I figured my resistance was up to it.

A boulder had been adorned with squares of gold leaf and small Buddha pictures. Candles burned on it to honor travel spirits. We dumped our gear and sat with porters on a stretch of muddy riverbank. When Chu Win shuffled up long after the rest of us, dragging her AK-47 by its strap, some of the porters laughed, but not unkindly.

Instead of breakfasting by the river, we continued until we reached another river (or a bend in the same one), where some shacks sold coffee, candy, batteries, candles—things porters or soldiers might need. We ate rice and canned sardines. I took a baby portion, using the fork and spoon the Mons had brought for me. The others scooped gummy, chalky rice right from the pot with their hands and ate like there was no tomorrow. Even if there really was no tomorrow, I couldn't get enthusiastic about that megadose of congealed starch.

Late in the afternoon some new Mon troops arrived from the west, the direction of the sea, and we jumped up and followed them back the way they'd come. We marched quickly on rocky paths to a village. There I met the local officer in charge and his radio operator, a boy who looked like some Chinese kung fu movie actor.

That night we slept in a village house that provided little shelter from the cold. Sarge and the local commander talked all night on the veranda. Whenever I woke from the cold, they were still telling stories in loud Mon.

We made our usual frantic departure before dawn. Nothing seemed to be calm or quiet with the Mon Army. Having slept in uniform, all they had to do was take a quick pee in the bushes, strap on their packs, and sling their rifles over their shoulders. But this was always done with such commotion that it looked like we were being ambushed. We marched off and immediately waded through a river, and then we all sat around at a tea shop on the riverbank. Nyundthun brought me tea in a hopelessly genteel rose-patterned cup and saucer. I supposed "hurry up and wait" was the nature of all armies, but the Mons had it down to a fine art.

Then our route was on the coastal plain. We followed the Ye River and sometimes forded it, up to our waists in the cool, brownish water. We entered plantations: coconut palms, the slender areca palms that produced betel nuts, and fruit trees. The soldiers helped themselves. Someone handed me a mango and a small yellow guava. The fruit sugar fooled our stomachs into thinking we'd had breakfast.

The quiet, shady plantations abruptly gave way to a large village with wide streets for ox-cart traffic and big, two-story woven bamboo houses on wooden stilts. We stopped for a few minutes and our expedition was joined by some more troops, commanded by Captain Min Kyaw Soe, a thin, handsome university graduate.

We stopped just after noon at another village, where we were given big green coconuts, lopped off at the top so we could drink the sweet, clear "water" inside. The village was drab and dry, the people bone thin. But the women and girls were all dressed in vivid blues and purples—violet, lavender, hyacinth, heliotrope, periwinkle—and smiled bravely. As we marched out, I heard a gong-and-xylophone orchestra playing a frenzied tune that was somehow familiar. When we passed the house where the music was coming from, a woman swathed in bright rags came reeling out in a trance. I recognized the hot season Ghost Dance. I'd once seen it, in

Lampang, a northern Thai town that had once been part of a Mon empire. Once a year, offerings were made and, as an orchestra played, mothers and grandmothers entered a trance. Possessed by ancestral ghosts, they danced wildly. This Mon woman maintained her trance very well, apparently oblivious to the rebel army marching past her house. Giving the ghosts their yearly chance to manifest themselves was obviously more important to her than checking on the progress of the war. All the war did was produce more ghosts, anyway.

On we marched, up another mountain. We double-timed it up a slope and along a ridge. Then we went downhill and we all had to move fast because a bamboo grove was on fire right beside the trail. We ran downhill through the flames. Chu Win fell, slid, laughed, and kept running. Then we climbed again, munching red jungle fruit. We ripped along mountain paths, cooled at last by a stiff breeze.

When night fell, we descended to a plantation. The fruit foraging did not cease, but now weapons were carried at the ready, safeties off. We were now very close to the Tatmadaw positions on the outskirts of Ye City. To reach the sea, we would have to sneak past the Tatmadaw and cross a paved road that ran south to Kawthaung. Captain Min Kyaw Soe and Sarge gave orders to extinguish cigars, cigarettes, flashlights. Any flicker of light could tip-off enemy patrols or sentries to our presence. With local villagers guiding us, we moved on—camouflaged, alert. We were invisible, but we were also crashing through the underbrush, making noise that could only be taken for a rebel army on the loose—or perhaps a herd of wild elephants, if elephants were given to cursing loudly in Mon every time they tripped on something.

No moonlight revealed us, and little starlight shone. We cut through orchards and went in what seemed like circles on ever-narrowing trails. We made a wrong turn, and Sarge "thanked" our village guides in a voice thick with sarcasm. After hours of pointless wandering in the dark, we finally managed to hit the "motorcar road." The two-lane thoroughfare glowed eerily white in the night. We marched quickly along it for a mile or so. Perhaps Tatmadaw truck convoys owned it by day, but now, at midnight, the road was ours.

We cut off from the road, on an ox-cart track, into brushland. The track consisted of two parallel ruts of very uneven depth, with scraggly bushes growing down the center. I had poor night vision, and I began to stumble over things—roots? stones? I didn't quite fall, but I was about to, so Sarge told Pakuson to guide me. She took my hand in hers, which was reassuringly dry, and led me along.

The scrubland spread out all around us, dark cover perfect for an enemy ambush. This would be quite a place to die, I thought. A Tatmadaw force of superior size could be tracking us through this bush, about to cut us to shreds. I thought the Tatmadaw would be shocked to find me among the Mon casualties.

We stopped suddenly and everyone sat down on the trail. Sarge whispered jokes. We ate the last orange candies from a jumbo bag the soldiers had brought from Three Pagodas' bazaar and spat in the dust. We sat and whispered and laughed quietly at nothing, waiting for our guides to figure out where the hell we were.

At last the guides appeared from farther up the trail, with a Mon Army scout who reported that we were safe. No Tatmadaw patrols were out hunting that night, so Sarge told me I could use my flashlight. We all went crashing off cross-country through patches of thorny scrub. The batteries in my delicate plastic flashlight died, so Pakuson (who had natural infrared vision) handed me hers, a big, heavy, Tiger Head model.

We crossed dried-up rice paddies and then a field of vegetables. Chu Win and Rad Aung pulled up fistfuls of leafy greens. Then they ripped off a pineapple, but threw it away because it was unripe. I didn't think that whoever had planted the field would be exactly delighted. But it had been a long night and a long day; we had been on the march for fourteen hours.

Adjacent to the vegetable field was a palm plantation, our shelter for the rest of the night. It was about two in the morning when the women soldiers and I took over a rickety, derelict stilted hut. Nyundthun and "Radio Boy" climbed up with a bowl of water and some limes and made limeade for us. I put Bactine on Chu Win's knees, which were scraped from several falls that night. My feet were grotesque with puffy blisters (top and bottom), as were Nyundthun's and Sarge's. Before I could sleep I had to massage my legs to stop them from twitching. Outside, Sarge and the area commander were warming their posteriors by a bonfire, up all night talking, as usual.

⸗ 5 ⸗

For once it was daylight when I awoke, and soldiers were just stirring from sleep in nests they'd made of fallen palm fronds. The women soldiers set to work preparing the looted vegetables for breakfast. Some local people appeared and sold the Mon Army a couple of chickens, which the men grilled on a camp fire. That morning it all felt like we were just children having an adventure, playing games in an abandoned house, playing war in a vacant lot. We had survived the night, forgotten the war, slept. We woke up and ate chicken.

We marched away through a stretch of green rice fields. When we reached a village, some people came up to me and said, "Please take a group photo of us, to show the world that we Mon people really exist. Ne Win tells the world that we do not exist anymore." I took their picture—lined-up, barefoot, underfed, proud. The Burmese government liked to claim that the Mons were completely assimilated into Burmese culture. It was accepted by the rest of the world that they were a vanished race. I had half believed it myself before I saw such Mon villages of two hundred houses, three hundred houses, more. Village after village resounding with Mon speech, full of Mon people of all ages wearing their Mon National Day T-shirts smuggled from Three Pagodas' bazaar.

When we left, girls in their best sarongs were standing by the roadside with glasses of perfumed water. They dipped orchids in the water to sprinkle it on us as we marched by, and a village elder handed each of us a Shan cigar. Even though we were fruit stealers and vegetable looters, they seemed to like having us around.

We hiked down an ox-cart track in blazing sun until we reached a town near the sea. The streets were lined with fine two-story teak houses, shops, and covered market stalls. Mon soldiers were everywhere, and I was taken to the home of the coastal area's commander, a thin, older man with a bristly beard. The launcher and rockets were handed over to him, and he was very pleased.

I was given a lemon barley soda and told to sit on the veranda. Some old ladies brought me dishes of fruit—too much fruit. Children came to stare at me, and then adults stood in front of the veranda and stared at me, too. Pale yellow *thanaka* powder coated their faces. They were silent, almost unblinking. It was like being surrounded by an audience of mimes.

When I got up to leave, I realized that blisters had formed under the balls of my feet. The sun was searing. During a rest halt in a scrap of shade, Captain Min Kyaw Soe politely asked me, "Would you like to listen to a Mon song?"

"No, thank you, perhaps later," I said, not in the best mood. He played it anyway, on a small tape deck. It was nice music, soft and strange, and it helped me walk the rest of the way to the beach.

This was, as I had suspected, *a war with a great beach*. The Mon soldiers marched along the sand, ocean shimmering in the background, tropical islands offshore, azure sky above. My mood went swinging up. I had reached the Andaman Sea! I had walked and walked and walked. Now there would be boats.

The entire population of a small fishing village crowded around to look at me, but the troops pushed through the tumult, and soon we were on longboats heading out to a fishing junk moored in the bay. The soldiers made a lot of commotion boarding the junk. It rocked a bit, which turned several of them very green at the gills. Sarge and Chu Win were definitely the worst sailors of the group. Before we'd even hoisted anchor, they were vomiting their guts out over the side. I gave them each a Dramamine tablet. Chu Win promptly puked that out, too. Sarge fell asleep. The more seaworthy, like Pakuson, Radio Boy, and me, loved the cruise; we were out on the open sea, the air was perfect, the light divine.

Our weathered old junk had a Japanese engine with Rambo stickers plastered on it. We cruised past tough Mon fishermen rowing their wooden boats. Then a shot rang out and everyone started yelling and scanning the horizon for Burmese gunboats. It turned out that Nyundthun's M-16, lying on the roof with its safety still off from the night before, had been jarred by the engine vibrations and had fired.

The next crisis was more serious. Black smoke began pouring out of the Rambo engine. This is an interesting way to die, I thought. I figured the boat would explode before we'd have to worry about drowning or shark attacks. The Mons were, naturally, all shouting at each other (except for one very seasick boy who seemed to be quietly praying for a quick end to it all). They were throwing on their packs and rifles, which I thought was a sure way to make every one of them sink like a stone when the boat went down. Then someone simply cut the engine. We drifted into a bay. The crew dropped anchor there, and Radio Boy made some calls.

The soldiers were still panicky, but quieter. Chu Win and Sarge went out on deck to await rescue and continue vomiting. Slowly a rowboat headed our way from the beach and collected the sickest soldiers. Eventually all the troops were transferred ashore.

The sun was setting into the Andaman Sea as we headed down the beach. The troops looked grim. They're not even enjoying this, I thought. Don't they know how many Americans list "long walks on the beach at sunset" as a favorite pastime? The trouble was, it became an *extremely* long walk on the beach. Fatigue set in and my blistered feet were killing me. At first I'd been thinking, ha, ha, German film crew, eat your hearts out! But I soon decided that the ordeal-by-long-walk-on-the-beach-at-sunset was the Germans' revenge.

The sun bulged and glowed and cast ruby sparkles over the waves. It was beautiful, it was awful, it was endless. Back in the mountains, I had decided that the only way I could deal with the hard march was to keep complaints to myself and just keep going, however slowly. On the flat sand I would not complain and I would keep going. I began to repeat to myself a phrase I'd seen on a Japanese lady wrestler's T-shirt in a newspaper photo. It made a good Zen koan for walking meditation or walking death. I repeated it to myself fifty, one hundred, one hundred and fifty times. It was everything I wanted. It was a cool breeze and a warm blanket. *A Radiant Obstacle in the Path of the Obvious,* I chanted. It was everything I wanted to be, that night and forever.

Pakuson began to sing as she walked beside me, slowing her strong steps to match my faltering pace. I hadn't heard her sing before. It was a strange, pretty song, like the ones on Captain Min Kyaw Soe's tape. The Mons sang ethereally, in contrast to the harsh tones of their spoken language.

At the far end of the beach we found a fishing village and collapsed at a shack on the sand. I examined my feet by oil lamp. The blisters had gone septic. They oozed yellow fluid and were embedded with sand. Nyundthun and Sarge had big, disgusting blisters, too, like mushrooms after a rain. We were all dead tired. Even insomniac Sarge stopped talking and slept that night.

⹀ 6 ⹀

"We will have to walk for a while, to reach a boat," Nyundthun told me in the morning. I wrapped my blisters with gauze and tape, jammed my swollen feet into the plastic sandals, and hobbled down the trail like an old Chinese lady with bound feet. We descended a gray mud bank to a small boat that reeked of rotting shrimp. It brought us to a mangrove swamp. We squished through the mud to a hut whose owner let us use his well water to rinse our feet. The gauze bandages on mine were now gray, salt-soaked tatters. One of the Mon officers hired an ox cart to bring me, Chu Win, and Rad Aung to the next village. The cart jolted along uneven ruts. When we had to go downhill, the oxen would break into a gallop, throwing us into the air.

In a large village we were greeted by dozens of women soldiers resting on shady verandas. I met General Htaw Mon at last, and he did speak English well, in a slow, deliberate voice. He had startlingly light brown eyes and an ironic, feline smile.

"We will arrange for you to visit coastal villages," the general said, "but I don't think you can walk anymore."

"Sure, I can walk, but slowly," I said. "I am starting to think that my country couldn't win in Vietnam because the American soldiers had very good boots, but they wore them in the jungle and got blisters—while the Vietcong had only rubber sandals and didn't get blisters."

The general laughed and said, "Well, you won't have to walk much now. We shall proceed by boat."

The general introduced me to Nai Aung Shein, a World War II veteran with a silver crew cut who was a New Mon State Party central committee member and a reserve army officer. Then Mi Chon De, the ranking women's unit officer in the area, strode in with her aide, Mi Kyide Soi Mon. Mi Chon De, young and slim, wore a belt of gleaming M-79 grenades around her hips. Her shiny black hair was cut short, revealing rhinestone earrings.

When Pakuson and I went to the village well for a bucket bath, Mi Kyide Soi Mon, who spoke some English, came along. "Sister, let me fix your shoes," she said, and scrubbed my foul Reeboks thoroughly with laundry soap. Mi Kyide Soi Mon had paler skin than most of the soldiers, and light brown curly hair.

The village headman invited me to his house, and we located the village on my map. He told me I was the first Western visitor in twenty years. We drank Dragon American Special Cream Soda and ate bowls of watermelon pulp mixed with sweet, condensed milk. Then I went to the village monastery to meet its abbot. He asked me to take his photograph and arranged his red robes. He sat on a baroque, gilded throne. It seemed very Mon to me that a dirt-poor village would spend whatever money it had making an ornate throne for the head monk, to evoke the ancient Mon civilization.

All around the village, women soldiers mingled with the local girls, chatting and giggling. Many of the houses had a tiny "shop" in the front room: a few shelves stocked with lipsticks, soda pop, cigars. One of the lady shopkeepers invited me and a few of the women soldiers for a dinner she'd cooked specially for us.

After dinner I taped interviews with three older women. Two of them had been captured by the Tatmadaw and forced to be porters. The other's husband, a farmer, had been shot and killed by the Tatmadaw.

Then we left, Mi Kyide Soi Mon and I riding in an ox cart with wooden ox bells jangling. At least forty women soldiers were marching with us—an extraordinary spectacle, a female army. Civilian girls accompanied them out of the village, holding their hands, kissing them, giving them flowers. Mi Chon De, laden with her heavy weaponry, gripped the hand of a local beauty. "Take our picture!" she called to me.

Our evening march ended up at a Buddhist monastery. Most of the soldiers bedded down in the monastery yard, but the general and his staff would sleep in the main temple building. So would Mi Kyide Soi Mon, Pakuson, and I, with rifles stacked at our feet. I was amazed. In Thailand it was utterly taboo for women to sleep in temples. I found the Mon Army as socially subversive as it was politically insurgent.

When I awoke, another ox cart had arrived to give me an hour's ride to a town with a large market place and a Buddhist pagoda. The townspeople poured out of their houses to watch the women soldiers march in and were astounded to see me with them. I was installed at a small house, and people crowded around the porch to gawk at me. I caused bedlam when I walked over to the market, escorted by a mob of incredulous children. I tried to ignore my audience as I sat down for a coffee.

A man came along who spoke Thai. He turned out to be a Mon from Cambodia, which had a sizable Mon minority—or had before the Khmer Rouge, anyway. He had escaped Pol Pot's genocide to a refugee camp in Thailand, and then escaped that, and ended up with these Mons on Burma's war-torn coast. Out of the frying pan, into the fire, I thought.

As visitors to Three Pagodas Pass always noticed, many Mons were strikingly beautiful. In their impoverished elegance they wore their colorful sarongs and huge rattan sun hats with panache. Shirtless old men displayed Jack LaLanne builds, from lifetimes of rowing boats on the sea. Market ladies held trays of cakes and bunches of tamarind leaf on their heads, with the posture of caryatids.

I interviewed ten men who had been captured and tortured by the Tatmadaw. The last time the Burmese forces had come through, they had suspected the men of aiding the Mon rebels and had beat them, hung them down wells, and slashed them with bayonets. One man's daughter had been shot dead by the Tatmadaw in front of his house. The Tatmadaw used the same antici-vilian counterinsurgency tactics, and the same torture methods, all over Burma, but for different purposes, depending on the victims. The hill-tribespeople I had talked with in Keng Tung understood very little about politics and insurgency, and the Tatmadaw tormented them to drive them off their land. For the Mons—literate people with a strong nationalistic sentiment—the Tatmadaw used torture to procure information.

When it was time to move out, three young captains joined us. Captain Sai Htaw was the liveliest, with shaggy hair, and mustache, and a big, crooked smile. Captain Rai Chia was a Moulmein University graduate, and Captain Chan Rot had a degree in veterinary science. All three had been in Nai Shwe Kyin's Mon rebel faction prior to the recent unification.

At the Ye River we boarded boats, and Captain Sai Htaw stood in the front of mine, George Washington style. "You will see many beautiful views of our Mon land!" he shouted to me. A flotilla of longboats, each flying a brightly colored pennant, carried us down the river. Thick palmettos lined the shore. The boats overtook each other as if it were a race, and the women soldiers cheered. The sun set, reflecting on the river in vibrating lines.

We changed over to bigger, open motorboats, and took to the sea. The troops had their usual yelling crisis, this time over hitching up a boat to be towed. By now I understood that when everyone started shouting, it did not *necessarily* mean the boat was sinking. The Mon soldiers argued, they raged, they talked back to their officers. Nobody seemed to mind. General Htaw Mon had the master plan. He was decisive, calm, and organized. I thought he put up with a lot from the ranks.

I could see fires burning on distant mountainsides when we went ashore. We had walking to do—"About three furlongs," old Nai Aung Shein informed me—but I had no idea how long a furlong was. It turned out to be an hour's painful hike along rice paddy embankments. The reward at the end was a magical little village suffused with the heady scent of frangipani.

Pakuson, Mi Kyide Soi Mon, and I were billeted in the candle-lit front room of a big teak house. Captain Sai Htaw dropped in to work on my blisters.

"I am a front-line doctor," he announced. "I have cured many cases like this." He snipped off the puffed skin with scissors. It didn't hurt, but after a while he got carried away and cut the unblistered skin.

"Stop that!" I snapped.

"Okay, okay, I am only a *barefoot doctor,*" he laughed. He then insisted on painting the soles of my feet liberally with iodine, so they looked like the hennaed feet of a Bedouin bride. He gave me an Ampicillin capsule and many assurances that the blisters would be dried up completely the next day. Then Nyundthun came in and asked to borrow my tape player. I could hear Mon ballads playing on it in a nearby house as I fell asleep. I had two layers of springy woven palm mat to sleep on, and for once the night was not cold.

When I awoke, my blisters did seem much reduced under the coat of crimson iodine. We weren't going anywhere for a while. The women soldiers washed their uniforms and relaxed in sarongs, powdering their faces with *thanaka.* They managed to carry plenty of cosmetics with them in the field: jars of *thanaka,* lipsticks, vials of black "Chum" (labeled "made from the finest chemicals, this eye liner is the best beautifier for modern girls"). The men used *thanaka,* too, sometimes, and even tough Sarge packed a glass spray bottle of cologne. Although a respected guerilla force, the Mon Army was not given to Rambo commando machismo. One of the older men had a decal on his M-16 stock with the tacky Vietnam-era slogan "Kill 'Em All, Let God Sort 'Em Out," but ribbons, flowers, and magic duck emblems were more the norm.

I did a group interview with some of the women soldiers, with Captain Sai Htaw as my English translator. We sat in a circle on the teak floor: Pakuson, Rad Aung, Chu Win, Mi Kyide Soi Mon, Mi Chon De, and two others. Their ages, I found, ranged from nine-teen (Mi Kyide Soi Mon) to twenty-three (Pakuson). Most were from farming families; only Chu Win and Mi Kyide Soi Mon had middle-class town backgrounds. Mi Chon De and Mi Kyide Soi Mon were the only ones with substantial educations. The others had been educated only in makeshift independent Mon schools.

I asked why they had joined up. Nobody said it was for fun, travel, or adventure. They said they'd joined because the Burmese government overtaxed their parents, confiscated goods, and abused people. They joined because they wanted to fight the Tatmadaw, often to avenge an abused or killed relative. Most of their parents had originally opposed their enlisting, saying "It's not women's work," but were now reconciled to it.

Mon women in the towns and villages always "congratulated" them for joining the army, they said. Civilian men asked them questions: Were they carrying the same gear as men? (yes), were they marching the same amount as men? (yes), were they sleeping with the male soldiers? (no). Regulations stated that enlistees must stay in the army for five years. After three years, they were allowed to marry. None was married, so I asked if they had boyfriends. "No, no, we don't want boyfriends!" they chorused, possibly for Captain Sai Htaw's benefit.

In basic training they'd found drill and weapons easy, but rope-climbing and using a cable to cross a river difficult. I asked what they liked and disliked about the army.

"I like my grenade launcher, and the other equipment, and the uniform," Mi Chon De replied. "What I *don't* like is when men in the villages make rude remarks!"

The others said they liked their guns and the marching, but detested boat trips on the ocean. Pakuson alone, from a fishing village, was an enthusiastic sailor.

Only Mi Chon De and another young officer had been in combat. They had taken part in a predawn attack on a Tatmadaw-held bridge, firing with rifles on full-auto at an unseen enemy. "I was not afraid," Mi Chon De said, her jaw set. "I was angry, and I wanted to kill them." The other officer nodded and said, "I was happy, because I wanted to kill the enemy." Two Tatmadaw soldiers had been killed in the attack, but no one knew by whose gun.

"How long do you think you will have to fight before the revolution is won?" I asked. They believed the war would last just another two or three years. The National Democratic Front was united, the Mons were united, Ne Win was weakening. Two or three years seemed reasonable after the forty the war had already lasted. But soldiers probably always thought a war was going to last just two or three years.

"And after the revolution, what do you want to do then?" I asked.

"Oh, I want to stay in the army!"

"I want to stay a soldier."

"If I can't be a soldier, I'll go back and take care of my parents, but I really want to stay in the army."

A revolution is definitely going on here, I thought.

Then they asked me questions, leading off with, "How tall is the tallest building in your country?" Mi Kyide Soi Mon had several social studies–type inquiries about the U.S. economy, employment, and education; the others asked about my parents and where my silver bracelets came from.

In the afternoon, we hiked back to the boats and then cruised the glorious sea, past perfect, empty, white sand beaches. At one point Captain Sai Htaw, risking being washed overboard, climbed back to the stern where I sat, just to declare, "We are now over the boundary from Ye Province to Tavoy Province!" and then climbed back to his lookout in the bow.

We put in at a fishing village, a strip of rickety stilt shacks facing each other across a narrow lane on the sand. Most functioned as shops, selling low-ticket smuggled items like Chinese cigarettes and Thai soap. The headman served me palm-fruit juice at his house, where the general was billeted. He told us that five years before some Germans had come there exploring for petroleum.

"Like the Germans, I have come here looking for something," I said. "But not petroleum. I am here to look for the Mon people and how they really live, so I can tell the outside world about you."

Unfortunately, when I reached the shack where Pakuson, Mi Kyide Soi Mon, and I would stay, the Mon people had all turned out to look at me. After a while, I did a Miles Davis—turning my back to the audience—but they didn't lose interest. They stayed. They gaped at me, eyes wide, mouths ajar, silent. I started to identify with the Padaung women, put on display at the Pai River because of their deforming brass neck rings.

I was rescued by the captains three. I went for a walk with the captains through the village, where fishermen were mending nets, and out onto the broad beach. I learned that some of the villagers were not Mons, but Tavoyans, a Burmese ethnic subgroup with its own dialect. They were tall, handsome people.

I slept well and awoke to drops of rain dripping through the ragged thatch roof. It was raining hard—a surprise, since the monsoon wasn't due for a month. The rain kept the audience away, and I had tea and biscuits on the porch. Children played in the downpour, naked except for palm-leaf hats. Captain Sai Htaw appeared and asked me what I'd like for breakfast. The catch of the day was in.

"Eat seafood a lot!" he said. "Whatever sort you like."

"Maybe crab, or shrimp?" I ventured. A soldier walked by with a clutch of big lobsters dangling from strings. "And those . . . ," I added hurriedly. Lobster was cheap on the Mon coast, as it turned out. At the captains' table, it was the Lobster Quadrille: lobster for breakfast, prepared four ways, accompanied by crab, shrimp, sweet slabs of fish, and fried potatoes. The amount I ate was rather shocking to my companions from Three Pagodas.

I gave my feet a rest and recovered from the lobster overdose. We didn't seem to be going anywhere. Reports were coming in about Mon attacks near Ye City. The rebels had burned a government fishery office, killed a Chinese fishing industry advisor, and captured some Tatmadaw guns.

The sky cleared and the gapers resumed their positions, leaning on the porch railing, enthralled. I turned to Captain Sai Htaw and asked, "How do you say 'Go away' in Mon?" Without hesitating, he told me.

I turned to the assembled multitude. *"Aha hoo hoo ah,"* I said. The many pairs of staring eyes grew even wider. The captains and Pakuson echoed me.

"Aha HOO HOO AH!" I said, in a louder, more Mon voice.

It worked. The crowd thinned, then dispersed altogether. The soldiers roared with laughter. The Mons had finally gotten me to be rude, and they loved it.

An excursion to the local monastery was scheduled. It was about two miles away, so transport was arranged to spare my feet. The fishing village had no ox carts, just a big cart pulled by a pair of buffalo. The team was yoked up, and Pakuson, Mi Kyide Soi Mon, and I climbed onto the cart, and we clattered off down the beach. Only Fellini could have come up with this scene, I thought, sitting under a green parasol in the high cart pulled by two great snorting black water-buffalo. My two lady bodyguards in sarongs held their assault rifles ready as we rode down a pristine ivory crescent of beach at high noon.

The monastery had a generator, so electric lights illuminated the golden Buddha images. The general told me he thought that the abbot, an austere-looking, birdlike old man, had a television set in his monastic quarters, and that the fishing village had a VCR—but only one videotape, a spy movie that everyone was quite bored with.

When we returned to the village, I photographed a small boy holding a freshly killed monitor lizard by its tail. He cried when I snapped the picture. A boy not much taller came by, in Mon uniform, carrying an AK-47. He was a thirteen-year-old rebel soldier. I asked him when he thought the revolution would be won. "In one or two years, I suppose," he answered. When the revolution was over, he wanted to be a policeman. He had run away from home to enlist. I photographed him and said I'd send a copy for him to give to his parents.

We left the village at sunset. Most of the troops marched, but a few of us went in an old wooden boat, property of the unofficial "Mon Navy," which zipped over the Andaman Sea like a cigarette speedboat. I sat in the bow, lifted up over the water. With waves curling silver in our wake, we entered the Ye River channel. We were near the island where Tavoy's Tatmadaw commander had installed troops in order "to smell the news" about my presence, as General Htaw Mon put it.

We stopped at a muddy riverbank and Captain Sai Htaw proclaimed, "I am going to find you an ox cart!" and disappeared into the dark. The rest of us walked inland a short way and sat down to wait. Captain Rai Chia asked me if it was true that an entire underground city was built under the Rocky Mountains in America in case of nuclear war. I said I didn't think so.

An ox cart rumbled up, and Captain Sai Htaw introduced the driver with, "This is my lovely friend! He is a bachelor boy like us!" In the moonlight we found our way to an empty teak house at the edge of a village. Somewhere, out in the night, a crazy person howled and sang.

I saw a village of tall wooden houses among groves of areca and coconut palms when I awoke. I interviewed people who had been captured by the Tatmadaw and lived to tell about it. I explained to the villagers why I wanted to tape their stories, and I noticed that Captain Chan Rot was translating the words "human rights" into what sounded like *am-nes-dee*. I stopped him and explained that

Amnesty International had its own staff investigators, and that I
was not working for that organization, although my reports would
be sent to it. He told me that *am-nes-dee* had simply become the
word for *human rights* in vernacular Mon. I considered it a tribute to
Amnesty International's power for good in the world that such an
isolated area was given hope by Amnesty's unstinting efforts.

We left for another pretty village under palm trees. The people
there were very thin. Children's bellies were bloated, their ribs
stuck out. I met some teenage girls who helped the Mon Army by
warning it of Tatmadaw movements. The networks of villagers
providing reliable intelligence were one of the Mon rebellion's great
strengths. Combined with radio communications, the village grape-
vine allowed the Mon Army to range through open country and
choose when to confront the enemy.

"Come back and stay a long time with us," the teenagers said to
me. I would have liked to at least stay overnight, but we moved out
at eight in the evening. Most marched, but a few of us went by boat.

The moonlight was bright, and the sea was high. Spray hit us
hard as we sped north out of Tavoy Province, back to Ye. We
passed a *chedi* gleaming white on a point of land, the Mon equivalent of a lighthouse, and stopped at a small island with a rock-
strewn beach. The women found a shelter of sticks and leaves that
someone had left and spread plastic sheets beneath it. The men
arranged themselves among the boulders on the beach. A bonfire
would have dried our spray-soaked clothes, but we didn't want to
give any sign of our presence to Burmese government boats that
might patrol the night, so we slept in our wet clothes, pretending to
be lumps of stone and clumps of leaf.

It might have been a pirate camp. Brigands, often Thai, roamed the
seas of Southeast Asia, preying on fishing fleets, cargo ships, and
boatloads of Vietnamese refugees. Theirs was a cruel trade of rape
and murder as well as plunder. En route to Pieng Luang by
songtaow, I had realized that I looked like a bandit, sinisterly
wrapped up against the road dust. Indeed, I was going to Pieng

Luang to meet with outlaws and steal the news of Tatmadaw abuse in the Shan State. When I dodged in and out of Keng Tung Province, I was in the company of smugglers, on their secret nocturnal routes. Then I, too, was a smuggler, of information about tribal villagers and a deadly chemical mist. Now the Mons and I camped like buccaneers on an obscure island in the Andaman Sea. We were pirates, our treasure the interviews, images, information. Established, respected human rights groups could not go to those places. Government agents did not tread there. I had become a pirate, a human rights pirate, raiding the coast for all the information I could thieve from Ne Win's Burma.

= 7 =

When light hit the beach, Pakuson and Mi Kyide Soi Mon built a little fire and we drank coffee from a mess tin. We got back in our boat and entered the Ye River channel. The water level was very low, and the boat kept getting stuck. Captain Chan Rot took advantage of our frequent strandings to jump out and look for shellfish on the river bottom with his bare feet. He found dozens of purple-shelled bivalves by shuffling around in the knee-high water. We ended up leaving the boat and walking inland to a small town.

General Htaw Mon was already there, on the veranda of a teak house. The house's front room was decorated with pages from an Italian men's fashion magazine and framed portraits of the King and Queen of Thailand. All the other Mon houses I'd been in were decorated only with Mon and Burmese calendars. A teenage Mon girl rushed up to me, speaking Thai.

"I am so happy to meet you!" she exclaimed. "I have gone many times over the border to Thailand to buy things to sell here. The trails are awful! Sometimes I just stop and cry." A few children came up and gazed at me. "These people are very provincial," the girl said. "When I come back from Thailand with a Thai hairstyle and some Thai clothes, they all come to stare at me. In the other villages they ask me what country I come from."

The girl's mother had also acquired Thai ways. She greeted me with a graceful *wai,* and spoke Thai not only to me, but to the Mon officers as well. That amused the general, but he was impressed with her house. "Very smart place," he commented. We sat at a folding table, on cushioned chairs, rather than on the floor Mon style. Coconut water was served in a polished aluminum tureen, instead of in its own heavy husk. I ate a last breakfast of shellfish with the captains, who were going off to raid a Tatmadaw outpost farther south. I rode out in an ox cart driven by Nyundthun, whose boots were raising a new crop of blisters in the pits of the old ones. While he drove he talked about wanting to visit America as a representative of the Mon revolution. "I want to see New York and Washington," he said, "and Hollywood!"

Arriving in a dusty little town, we stopped at a house with a cold drinks concession, which was raking in money selling iced sugarcane juice to soldiers coming in off the midday march. A bath seemed like an equally refreshing idea, so Pakuson and I went off to bathe at the well in the town center. Most of the town stopped what they were doing, and stood transfixed, to watch me pour water over my blond hair, pale skin, Karen sarong.

I went back to the sugarcane house and sat in a corner of the kitchen, in a snit.

"It's just that they haven't seen anyone like you before," Nyundthun said.

"Well, so what?" I retorted. "It's incredibly rude. What if a Mon woman went to a foreign country and everyone watched her take a bath? How would she feel?"

Mi Chon De and another woman officer walked in, ranting about what disgusting louts the men in town were for watching me bathe. "If it happens again, we will shoot them," Mi Chon De offered. She didn't seem to be joking.

One of the sugarcane grinders brought me a cold glass of juice, and I went out on the veranda. A crowd gathered there, and

Pakuson filled them in on what I was doing on the seacoast. An old woman felt my red-stained feet and said, "No wonder they're all ripped up—they're softer than our hands."

"Of course her feet are soft," one of the women soldiers said. "In America they go everywhere by motorcar!"

Having made friends with the townspeople after all, I left in another ox cart, and in the evening reached the large town where I'd first met the general. Pakuson, Mi Kyide Soi Mon, and I went to a hillside house with a veranda high up on the second story. Nobody could stare at me up there. Pakuson field-stripped her M-16 and gave it a loving, careful cleaning. I kept thinking our departure was imminent and we'd soon be out creeping around in the moonlight. But it got later and later, and I fell asleep. A loud report—gunshot or burning bamboo—woke me. Some soldiers ran down the street, but no one else stirred, so I went back to sleep.

At sunrise, women of the town waited at the roadside to dole out rice to a procession of red-robed novice monks on their morning alms rounds. The general told me we'd be crossing the motorcar road that night.

"Can you walk?" he asked.

"Yes, my feet are all better now," I answered.

"Good. You will have to walk this evening. But first you will go by motorcycle."

I envisioned some sturdy, high-powered trail bike churning up the dirt tracks, but it turned out to be the area commander's little Honda motorbike. He gave me a ride to the next town. The Honda was barely alive, coughing and spluttering, but it was the only motorized land transport I'd seen since Three Pagodas.

I was dropped off at a quiet old house. I studied the calendars. Every Mon house had its calendars, and this set went back five years. Each cover was a color photo of a Burmese movie-star couple posed with foreign accoutrements. The latest, 1988, featured such objects of socialist envy as a Plymouth Duster, a big Kawasaki motorcycle, and a plastic picnic cooler. Beneath the glossy calendar covers were blurry group photos of Burmese Socialist Program Party People's Councils, Farmers' Cooperatives, Youth Brigades, Defense Corps. Twelve months of Ne Win's bureaucratic power base.

A civilian boy took me on the Honda down an ox-cart track and left me where a path veered away. I waited as Mon soldiers—young and old, men and women—trooped by, their sandals slapping the dust. I marched with them through a field, where farmers stood to watch us pass. An old man reached out to shake soldiers' hands. He grasped my fingers and yelped, *"Ingelei!"* (English) delightedly. My Gurkha hat and khaki shirt probably resembled the garb of the last foreigners he'd seen: World War II British soldiers.

On the other side of the field, an entire village had turned out to see us come through, about a hundred people eager for a look at the Mon Army, thrilled by the women soldiers and amazed by me. Pakuson, Mi Kyide Soi Mon, and I went into one of the stilted houses, eased out of our gear, and accepted glasses of hot tea.

A commotion arose outside—shrieking voices, the sound of running feet. The villagers who had just been serving us tea ran down the steps, out of their house, without a look back. My companions scrambled for their rifles and frantically buckled their packs and ammo pouches on. I threw my bags onto my shoulders. Then we, too, were out the door and down the steps. Except for knots of Mon soldiers conferring with officers, the village was deserted. A cloud of dust had risen, and the civilian population had vanished. Soldiers were still rushing out of the houses, bumping into each other, cursing, coughing. Pakuson pulled me toward Radio Boy, who was shouting into his transmitter. Nyundthun trotted up to tell me that the Tatmadaw had been sighted by villagers. The enemy was nearby. We strained to hear the crackling voice Radio Boy had called up.

Suddenly General Htaw Mon appeared with the tiger-stripe-uniformed corporal who operated his radio and carried his maps. The general smiled.

"False alarm," he drawled. "Some villagers saw our advance guard out there and mistook them for Tatmadaw. Never mind, never mind."

The rumor of attack was quickly dispelled. The villagers reappeared, as if at the hands of a conjurer. At the first word of the Tatmadaw, they had grabbed their children and run for the jungle. They'd wanted no part of what was going to happen. The Tatmadaw meant murder, torture, rape, slavery. The Mon Army meant crossfire, and the possibly fatal stigma of being a village that helped the rebels. The villagers had run for their lives. From Kawthoolei to Keng Tung, civilians had told me how they emptied their villages in terror of the war. Now I had seen it, so fast, so terrible.

We filed out of the village, smiling, smiling, sorry to cause trouble. Some village ladies handed us pieces of sweet, spicy cake. They had somehow managed to bake cakes for the women soldiers. I couldn't imagine what they used for an oven, or where they'd gotten the flour, the recipe, or the idea. But there it was, cake for their own Mon rebel soldier girls. The soldiers would risk their lives fighting for them, and the civilians would risk everything to be a village that helped the rebels.

Along the narrow embankments of rice paddies, we marched in close ranks, halting and proceeding, quiet for once. The general had us well in hand. We went through scrubland, low bushes, open country, and forded a river. We reached the motorcar road and ran across it, two or three at a time, diving into the brush at the other side. We regrouped and kept moving fast. We aimed ourselves at the mountains. The moon rose, but bamboo arched over us, blocking out its light. One of the Three Pagodas contingent, an old soldier who looked like Buster Keaton, commenced complaining, a ratchet-jawed harangue. Sarge found a porter to carry Buster's pack and rifle. We continued, complaints and curses continuing and multiplying in the night, providing a Mon cadence as we climbed.

We descended to a humid valley, where we found a plantation in which to camp. Mi Kyide Soi Mon, Pakuson, Chu Win, and I were awarded the plantation house, a rotting old shack with a floor full of holes. Pakuson, ever resourceful, built a fire in the sand-filled hearth and cooked rice. We sent a girl recruit down to a nearby stream to fill our canteens. Half a dozen teenage girls and two

young boys were accompanying us from the seacoast to Three
Pagodas, where they would begin basic training.

⊃ 8 ⊃

The next day was extremely hot, and we marched craving wind and
shade. The sun sizzled the heavy air around us, hour after hour. In
the afternoon we forded a river and stopped in a palm grove.

"It is too hot to go on," the general told me. "We will wait until
evening. I myself feel dizzy." He went off to rest in the shade, and a
medic gave him a shot of quinine for his chronic malaria.

The rest of us spread out under the palms. One of the men
climbed the tallest tree, hitching himself up the ridged trunk with
his feet, and sent big green coconuts crashing down from the crest.
Mi Kyide Soi Mon was ill—probably malaria—and she slept,
looking frail.

I took advantage of the rest period to perform *kata,* formal karate
exercises. I moved slowly. I didn't want to sweat in the hot afternoon, I just wanted to stretch and remember: look at the enemy,
then strike; follow the compass points; kick harder; let the muscles
remember; be smooth. I worked my way up to the most advanced
kata I knew, *Matsukaze,* "the pine tree in the wind." I imagined the
enemies and reacted, swaying and striking like the pine, a pine
under palms.

When it was dark, General Htaw Mon told me that my Three
Pagodas group would continue back to headquarters with the
recruits, but that he would be taking the rest of the troops north-
west of Ye City the next day. My group was leaving immediately
with Nai Aung Shein, the old veteran, who was to attend a central
committee meeting at headquarters. I said good-bye to Mi Kyide

Soi Mon, giving her my compass. "Good luck, Sister," she said, pressing a green, flowered handkerchief into my hand. I shook hands with Mi Chon De and the general, and then my contingent marched off into the dark.

According to Nyundthun, we had four hours' walk ahead of us that night, but after a mere two hours of trudging up a mountain, Buster let loose with a fierce burst of invective. Sarge reacted by hissing, "So! I see! You're tired! Okay. Fine. We'll sleep *here,* then!" A jungled mountainside with no clearing, it was hardly a suitable camp site. We edged off the trail and threw down plastic sheets in the underbrush. It was cold, and twigs and stones poked through the plastic. Shifting around to avoid them threatened to pitch us down the slope. The soldiers griped themselves to sleep. Ne Win devised this bed for me, I thought, echoing the sentiment prevailing among the Mon soldiers. When things were that bad, one could blame it all directly on Ne Win, the despot, the killer, with his Swiss bank accounts, his doctors and necromancers, the evil troll.

Around four A.M. we arose from a poor excuse for sleep, and walked on for two and a half hours, with a few green mangoes to sustain us. We stopped to rest by a stream. A hunter happened by, carrying the carcass of a dark, striped civet cat with a long, pointed snout. The soldiers bought it from him. Nyundthun referred to it as a "rat" in Thai and said happily that we'd now be having "rat soup" for breakfast. It wasn't at all bad.

Hour after hour, we marched. After a river crossing, we began walking on paths of loose, round stones. The gray lumps slipped and shifted underfoot, crunching my toes. "This is the Ne Win Highway!" I remarked. I was stumbling along in the fourteenth hour of walking since we'd awoken on the wretched mountainside.

I walked stupidly, myopically. I walked slowly, reluctantly. Crossing the river again, I could not see the bottom, and my balance was thrown off by the sharp pain of each footstep. Sarge gripped my wrist and led me through the water. He lent me his Tiger Head flashlight after mine had eaten through my last set of batteries.

At last we reached a village, and I recovered quickly. Pakuson and I went to a bend in the river and bathed in the deep, warm water. Our red perfumed soap had become just a sliver. A glass mug of Nescafé awaited me at a bamboo house. No curious crowds gathered to see me. We were on the trade route to Thailand now, and people had seen plenty of foreigners on trips to Three Pagodas. A radio in the house played Tammy Wynette's "Stand By Your Man," and then crackled into impenetrable static. I went to sleep. The radio, its signal lost, made a faint sound like surf.

The radio came back to life in the morning with the Burmese government radio station broadcasting in English about the new pagoda Ne Win was building for his own eternal glory and honor in Rangoon. It would contain Buddhist relics donated by the King of Nepal (from one tyrant to another, I thought). Burmese pop music, full of wild echo and razor-sharp reverb, followed the news-in-Newspeak. Rock's development in Burma had seemingly stopped at the Gene Pitney and Roy Orbison stage, which was not a bad place to stagnate. An instrumental version of "I Walk the Line" rang out. I liked that song. I had been to the Andaman Sea. I had no questions about what I was doing. I did not stop and think "What am I doing here, in a war nobody cares about, in the middle of nowhere?" I knew what I was doing: I was *walking the line*. I put myself on the line. I cared about the war. And after you've been there, it is no longer the middle of nowhere; it is the middle of somewhere.

"Tonight we will climb the mountain," Nai Aung Shein said.

I flashed my knife blade over a newly blistered toe. "I will now cut off my toe," I announced. "Or . . . I will cut the sandal." I sliced away some of the silver plastic, freeing the swollen toe. Nyundthun had oozing sacs of pain on his heels, soles, each toe. I tried to cushion them with gauze and tape.

It was Easter Sunday. Jim Thompson had been missing for twenty-one years.

At around three in the afternoon, we marched off into the hot, flat fields. We passed a group of villagers who'd been hunting in the mountains with old flintlock rifles and gathering rattan. I dubbed them "The Gentlemen's Hunting and Caning Society," which amused me keenly for several miles.

We entered the mountains in moonlight. I had thought the climbing would intimidate the recruits (*that will separate the women from the girls!*), but they were relentlessly cheerful and energetic. The slender teenagers kept our bags and ammo pouches balanced on their heads as they raced up the mountain trails, talking, giggling, and singing all the way. Their high voices were eerie in the night jungle. I followed the Merlinesque figure of silver-haired Nai Aung Shein, the fairy chorus just below us.

We came to the riverside resting place, where candles burned on a spirit rock. Now candles twinkled along the riverbank as well, and a bonfire of thornbushes blazed. We joined the porters there and drank limeade made with the river water. One of the porters had fallen in the dark. I bandaged his scraped knee.

Sarge gave the order to keep marching, so we crossed the river and filed around the spirit rock, passing a porter who waited patiently on the narrow trail for us to go by. With his load of Aji-no-moto tins towering above him, he loomed in the night like some Aztec idol, his face wet and golden in candlelight.

We took to a mountain-ridge trail, climbing quickly, surefooted. The fairy chorus sang Mon songs. Sarge kept up a running commentary in a piercing Minnie Mouse falsetto, parodying the giggly girl recruits.

The moon frosted the trees. The night jungle smelled like a doctor's office, a Chinese apothecary's shop, a barber shop. Things bloomed at night, and whistled, and flew.

In moonlit meadows, we stopped to rest, not to sleep. Chu Win was fatigued from the climb, struggling to keep walking. "She's a real *commando*," one of the men said sarcastically. We waited for her, and then went on again. We gained ground, leaving Chu Win behind with a recruit who carried her AK-47 for her. We were covering a whole day's worth of mountain in a few hours of night. Our previous mountaintop camp amid tall trees was occupied by slumbering porters. Just beyond it we found some open ground on which to spread our plastic sheets.

It was podiatry time. I cut debris off my toes and taped what was left. I sterilized a pin with a cigarette lighter and persuaded Nyundthun that it would hurt less to dig into his blisters and drain them than to keep walking on them. I used the last of the adhesive tape on Sarge's shredded soles.

The mountaintop was cold, but even under thin cotton I fell asleep fast. I dreamed that I was sleeping on the sidewalk in a big American city. I was asleep when Chu Win reached our camp.

When we set off in the morning, the recruits carried all the packs and most of the guns. It was not terribly reassuring that nearly all of our weapons were now in the hands of kids who would have no idea how to use them, should we be attacked. The women soldiers were wearing sarongs, hitched up to miniskirt length. In Ne Win's Burma, men and women wore ankle-length sarongs—the dictator's idea of cultural purity, tradition, conformity. But rebellion was in the air. One of the first signs of student unrest in the cities was the university girls' wearing their sarongs shorter. How could the regime survive? The Mon women soldiers marched through the jungle with their trousers rolled up to their knees, their sarongs hitched up to their thighs. They exposed their subversive legs in the towns and villages. How could Ne Win's vision of Burma survive?

As we descended the mountain, my sandal straps cut into my feet, and I was grateful when we stopped for a rest. I planned my return to Bangkok: I would pick up a kilo of ripe, juicy, yellow mangoes at the market near my town house. I would eat the mangoes and read through a stack of mail and newspapers. I would sleep in blue silk Dior lingerie. I said the word *lingerie* to myself a few times. It was always like that. I could be a "soldier" for a few days, and then leave. I could live in the sophisticated city and then head back to the jungle's green mysteries. I could have rat soup and I could have Mister Donut double-chocolate doughnuts. It was very different from really being a soldier in this war. A soldier would just keep going, year after year. A few hours' rest and a bath in a river would be a soldier's only respite. A cotton sheet would be all a soldier could expect against the cold night air. A soldier would eat as much rice as she could. A soldier would want camaraderie, not privacy. She would have a heavy rifle as her most precious possession. And she would think the war was just going to last about two more years.

We climbed again. The girls sang. I followed Nai Aung Shein and stopped only when he did, which wasn't often. Once we went through a clearing where some porters with particularly heavy loads waited for us to pass. One was a little girl, about ten years old. She wore a faded flowered sarong. Two big tins of Aji-no-moto strained her bare shoulders and were anchored by a strap around her forehead. She smiled at me. I took a pink elastic band from my hair and slipped it onto her wrist, and I held her hand for a moment. When most of the soldiers had gone by, the porters began to file off, bound for the coast. The little girl turned stiffly, and walked away with them, her motions robotized by the burden on her back.

The trail sloped down, steeply. I pulled off my sandals. We were walking on ruts pounded smooth by thousands of porters and soldiers.

"Your feet hurt very much," Nai Aung Shein observed.

"No, really, it's okay," I insisted. "I started out with good shoes from America, then Chinese sandals, and at last I have the Ne Win shoes: barefoot!"

When darkness fell, I put on my Reeboks. We went straight into a river. We kept crossing and recrossing it. We were slogging through this river, we'd been up since five A.M., we'd gone up and down the mountain, my feet hurt, my shoes were wet, I was slipping on wet rocks. We followed a beam of light far ahead that lured us from bank to bank. We assumed it belonged to one of our soldiers. I didn't remember this endless River Styx from the route in. Were we lost? The soldiers were cursing and grumbling. It was sickeningly exhausting. To make it even worse, one of the soldiers, in an effort to cheer himself up, began singing "We Are the World," a song I loathed. Splash, crash, goddamn it, splash, crash, bang, *ayah!,* we are the world. On we went.

Then the light was waiting for us atop a muddy embankment.

Reaching it, the soldiers exclaimed in surprise, because a soldier not from our group but from headquarters held it. And then a portly, uniformed figure appeared from the jungle and said, "Miss Mirante, we have come to fetch you. If you will walk just a little bit farther, we have a motorcar waiting." A Tiger Head beam revealed that this miracle man was Nai Tin Aung, from headquarters. After a remarkably quick exit from the jungle, we came to a shop where Nai Tin Aung bought mugs of iced sugar-cane juice for our whole Mon army.

The "motorcar" turned out to be a white truck. I jettisoned my superstition about crossing the border in white trucks and climbed in the front seat. The women soldiers jumped in the back. The male soldiers would walk to Three Pagodas the next day. The truck's air-conditioning was at frostbite level. A rearview mirror ornament of plastic flowers swung back and forth hypnotically.

"What news has there been of Burma proper?" I asked Nai Tin Aung, who sat next to me.

"Oh, very many things have been happening," he replied. "In the cities, civil unrest is widespread. We hear that students, monks, and Moslems have made demonstrations. In the international world, your Americans seem to be understanding that we have a dictator who is like that Noriega man." At that moment, with the air-conditioning making me shiver, I realized that I would get what I wanted in life. After all, a motorcar had magically appeared for me.

The year before, I'd had the goldfish dress dream. I had dreamed it the last morning of a visit to Kawthoolei, my last border violation before I'd returned to the U.S. in 1987. I had dreamed that Diane Brill, an avant-garde New York fashion designer, had created the dress for me. It was a strapless party dress of copper-colored metallic lace. The short skirt, flounced over petticoats, was in the shape of a goldfish. I had earrings to go with it: clear globes containing plastic goldfish. In the dream, Spin was hiding out in one room of an abandoned, decaying mansion in the jungle. He was on the run from the law, a fugitive from injustice. Wearing the goldfish dress, I went to Spin's lair for breakfast, which happened to be mango pancakes.

"The law is closing in on me," Spin said. "I'll have to leave right away. I'm going to take the train to Costa Rica." (From the Southeast Asian jungle.)

"I'll go with you," I said.

"Would you really?"

"Sure. It's on my way back to the States." So then we boarded the train to Costa Rica, which was just like the narrow-gauge railway that rode the death tracks of the River Kwai from Kanchanaburi.

I had woken up from the goldfish dress dream with the conviction that if I followed three simple precepts, everything would be wonderful. I would have to dye my hair flaming red, buy a goldfish, and carry something copper with me while I was in America. So I had obeyed the dream's instructions, and for a while things did look suspiciously good. But it soon went back to the usual mess: my paintings wouldn't sell, I had no money, the U.S. was massively boring, Burma was a lost cause. Anyway, the red washed out of my hair, I lost the Tibetan coin I'd carried for an amulet, and the goldfish went to Davy Jones's locker.

This time, in the white truck en route to Mon headquarters at Three Pagodas Pass, my sense of impending good fortune was even stronger than after the goldfish dress dream. I had no instructions to follow (no acrid dyes, no fishbowls to clean). It would just happen. I would get what I wanted. I wanted the 2,4-D spraying of the Shan State to end. I wanted Spin to emerge from the Khyber Pass, or wherever he was, to tell me tales of the Pathans, to run his fingers through my hair. And right now, tonight, I wanted a *blanket*: a thick, heavy, Chinese-made "Flying Horse" or "Tiger and Jewel" or "Air Ship" blanket; or at least a plain old Thai blanket of soft gray wool.

We drove through Three Pagodas' bazaar, where the shophouses were all shut up tight at ten P.M. We passed by the Thai border checkpoint and nobody was awake in the guardhouse. At Mon headquarters, I drank coffee and reported to Nai Non La on the success of the expedition.

I would sleep in the barrack of women soldiers who worked in headquarters offices. The walls of the long building were covered with posters and photos. Dozens of women were asleep on mats, surrounded by stacks of their books, folded uniforms, and sarongs. A typist found me a space on the floor. She showed me her English lesson book, a 1930s edition of *Oxford English for Adult Learners*. It was a very odd book. It progressed rapidly from the normal "This is a chair," "This is a table," to a discussion of frogs squashed flat by motorcars: "That will happen to you, my lad, if you're not careful crossing the road."

"We have every mosquito with malaria here, sister," the typist said, as she hung a mosquito net over my sleeping space. I recalled the Soi Suan Phlu Immigration detention center in Bangkok, where a Cambodian prisoner had called me "sister" and mosquito nets had given an illusion of privacy at night in the crowded ward.

The Bangkok jail had been incredibly noisy, and electric lights had stayed on all night. In the Mon barrack it was dark and quiet. I entered the mosquito net, my domain alone, and found there a blanket, gray with red and yellow stripes, soft.

KATA

- 1 -

The war in Burma had made many people refugees, and some people rich. It had made me a connoisseur of corruption. After my expedition to the Mon seacoast, I got another visa in Penang and then went to Chiang Mai to find out about timber contracts recently awarded to Thai businessmen by the Burmese government. Thailand's forests had been logged out to the point of no return, so Thai logging companies routinely bought valuable hardwoods like teak from the Karens and other border rebels. Government-controlled teak forests in Burma had been severely depleted, but the rebel territory of the frontier included mainland Asia's largest remaining tropical forest tracts. The Karens' logging operations were small-scale and selective. Teak trees had to reach a certain girth before they were cut, and the teak was always replanted. The Thai method was simply to clear-cut every tree in a concession area and extract as much timber as possible in the shortest amount of time.

283

In the spring of 1988, the Burmese government had allowed a
Thai company to take a consignment of teak logs out of Burma.
The Thais had to pay off Khun Sa, whose troops occupied the log
transport route. Thai officials were involved in the deal. The same
players ran the wood business and the heroin business in the north
of Thailand.

An American friend, a former fighter pilot, drove me north of
Chiang Mai in his pickup truck for a look at the teak logs moving
out of Burma. We sped up the paved road, singing along with a tape
of "Flower Drum Song," until a Ranger checkpoint stopped us.

"Who are those police bastards?" my friend asked.

"They're not police, they're Rangers. Paramilitary," I said.

"Police bastards all the same. The curse of fair Thailand."

We managed to sweet-talk our way past the black-uniformed
Rangers and drove to within a kilometer or so of the Burma border.
We saw no logs, only a pathetic fringe of teak trees preserved by the
Thai government in a futile gesture of conservation.

From Chiang Mai I made a brief trip to the embarkation village for
Manerplaw. I would stay firmly on the Thai side of the Salween
River border, but I arranged a meeting with some National Democratic Front representatives. Kachin, Lahu, Shan, and Wa delegates
of the NDF boated over from Manerplaw to meet me in a safe
house in the village. They brought with them a twenty-two-year-
old mathematics student who had been involved in demonstrations
in Rangoon the month before (March 1988).

The student told me how a fight in a tea shop had led to campus
demonstrations, which had been ruthlessly suppressed by security
police and the Tatmadaw.

"Some students were beaten and killed in the clash," he said, "and
we students saved their blood-stained clothes and we kept the clothes
in our campus. Since then, the news has spread to other places."

For several days, students, joined by Buddhist monks and Moslems, had fought to take over the streets from the armed forces.
Protesters were drowned, shot, suffocated in prison vans; tortured,
raped, and executed in prison. The universities had been shut

down, and now a student underground was organizing—in the cities and in rebel frontier camps—for the next round of demonstrations.

"I had always had the idea to come to Manerplaw after I finished my studies," said the student, who was of Karen and Karenni parentage. "I haven't graduated yet, but now the situation compels me to come to the revolutionary area." He told me that students of all ethnic groups had joined the demonstrations, with Burmese protesters the majority. The student, thin and recovering from malaria, clenched his fists and said, "The students who stay in the cities, they can never support the government. So whenever they get a chance, they will continue their demonstrations against the regime. They have their organizations also."

I spoke for a while with the NDF representatives about their goals and tactics. I would soon be leaving for the U.S., I told them, to present my 2,4-D report and other human rights documentation in Washington.

I returned to Bangkok. Spin was back from far-flung war zones: Afghanistan and Sri Lanka. He was renting a room in a concrete high rise at Bangkok's epicenter, and a teenage Danish tourist, Trinka, occupied a corner of it with her backpack. Spin had met Trinka in Sri Lanka (only Scandinavians were beach-desperate enough to still consider that beleaguered isle a vacation spot). He had taken her along on a visit to Three Pagodas Pass, introducing her to Mon leaders as his "secretary."

I had shown my slides of Mon women soldiers on the unknown seacoast to an Asian newsmagazine, which considered the pictures good enough to feature in "Eyewitness," its photo-essay section. Getting one's photographs in "Eyewitness" was an honor, and paid well. Spin, the professional photographer, had never had an "Eyewitness" spread. The photo essay, and Trinka, distanced us from each other like coils of barbed wire.

Even in the last days in Bangkok, I loved Spin. Feverish Spin, wearing tropical patterned shorts and a few strings of red beads, gluing rice paper over his windows to block out the sun. Malarious

Spin, writing his Afghan stories, making bebop music on his typewriter. His weird eyes, deep North Atlantic blue with epicanthic folds, stopped me in my tracks. Like Bangkok's massage battalions, I walked on Spin's aching back. But someone you love should make you feel beautiful, and Spin was starting to make me feel leprous. I walked out into the night. The noise of the city was maddening. The city heaved and spewed. Horrifying noise, poisonous air. The city choked on itself. The city rang in my ears.

I planned one more border trip to Three Pagodas Pass and the Tenasserim. The Border Patrol Police didn't mind foreign visitors in those places, and I had made a promise to Nai Non La that I intended to keep: I would teach a short course in unarmed self-defense to some of the women soldiers at headquarters. I had learned that their basic training lacked any martial arts lessons, so it was a small way in which I could show my gratitude for the seacoast expedition.

Three days before leaving for Three Pagodas, I had lunch with Dr. Pongsri and Nai Shwe Kyin, who was in Bangkok for an eye operation. Dr. Pongsri let it slip that Spin had just left on a secret trip to Khun Sa's camp. An American magazine was paying his way, and he'd brought Trinka with him. They'd flown up to Mae Hong Son. It was all news to me, bad news. What a fool, I thought. Flying into tiny Mae Hong Son airport, to be identified by every cop around. Returning to the scene of the crime. For the next couple of days, as I shopped for gifts to bring Joshua and the Mons, I felt sick with foreboding. If Dr. Pongsri is spilling the beans about it, word of Spin's trip must be all over town, I thought.

⌐ 2 ⌐

On the bus to Sangklaburi, I saw a foreign journalist and two tourists. I sat with the journalist, Crosby, a suntanned British freelancer I'd met in Chiang Mai. Crosby and I talked border talk. I

told him about the teakwood and the mathematics student. He
wanted to know if a trip to the Andaman Sea was possible. "Only if
you want to drown in mud," I told him, for the monsoon was
underway.

The lapis lazuli necklace I wore suddenly broke, scattering beads
all over the bus. I was horrified—Spin had brought me the necklace
from Afghanistan. I crawled down the filthy aisle of the bus as it
swerved along the mountain road and managed to retrieve most of
the glittering blue beads.

We took a *songtaow* to Three Pagodas' bazaar as rain began. The
tourists were delivered to Iris, who had become the doyenne of
budget travelers. She sold toast and coffee to backpackers, and put
up with their endless questions. I brought her stacks of photocopies
to keep her charges occupied: a summary of Tatmadaw human
rights violations, compiled by Britain's venerable Anti-Slavery Society, and a page suggesting things foreigners could do to help stop
such abuses. They could write to their governments to urge cessa-
tion of aid to Burma, and they could join organizations like the
Anti-Slavery Society and Amnesty International. Amnesty had just
released a report based on testimony of Karen, Mon, and Kachin
refugees, documenting what Amnesty termed "a consistent pattern
of gross violations of human rights."

Crosby and I went to Joshua's house. Joshua's hacking cough had
been subdued with medicine from the mission hospital. He was
now making some money selling lottery tickets in the bazaar. It
rained all night. Frogs croaked and bats flew in and out of the open
windows of Joshua's house.

I reported to the Mon base to begin my self-defense course. It would
last five days, with an hour's instruction each morning and another
hour in the afternoon. I had written out a lesson plan (similar to the
karate classes I'd taken in the U.S.) that included basic punches,
kicks, and blocks. Ever since I had begun studying karate, I'd had
something like the self-defense class in mind. Women were considered easy victims by the Tatmadaw, which sought out the defense-
less and used rape as a terror tactic. I wanted to teach the Mon

women soldiers some unarmed self-defense techniques so they
could teach them to other—civilian—women.

My class was to be held in the spacious front room of the Supply
Division building, which had a smooth teak floor. Seventeen
women appeared for the first class. As I'd specified, they were
barefoot and wearing their loose fatigue trousers with T-shirts or
cotton blouses. Only one of my students spoke any English, so Nai
Tin Aung acted as my interpreter, lounging back in a sling chair,
puffing cigarettes.

I told the students to line up, and I showed them how to bow to
their teacher in the traditional Japanese manner. Then I explained
to them that they would not be learning to do the feats they saw in
kung fu movies at the Three Pagodas' bazaar cinema hall. They
would not learn to vanquish throngs of ninjas by somersaulting in
the air. I would teach them simple, useful, unarmed combat techniques, and a *kata* that they could use for exercise when they were
encamped.

From the very first hour, I could tell that I was lucky: my
students were enthusiastic and adept. With an age range of eighteen
to twenty-nine, all were enviably fit. They were used to following
orders of the "turn left, turn right" sort. They were respectful to me
as their teacher, but in the Mon style they were still cheerfully
insubordinate: they took orders, but they had to discuss them a bit
first. They giggled far too much for a proper martial arts class, but I
didn't mind.

A few of the women were about three minutes late for the
second, afternoon class, which prompted Nai Tin Aung to deliver a
five-minute lecture on the virtues of punctuality. That made the
class eight minutes delayed. After that, the women showed up early
and we would start early and let the classes run overtime. Their
energy did not lag.

In between classes, I drank coffee with Nai Tin Aung and
lunched with two other foreigners working at the Mon base: Dr.
Valerie and Mr. Ian. Dr. Valerie was a Scot with long blond hair.
She had just arrived at Three Pagodas, sponsored by a British
medical relief group. She had done emergency-room work in

London, so Mon war casualties didn't faze her, but she was disturbed by the scruffiness of the dirt-floored headquarters hospital.

"I saw that big new temple in Sangklaburi," Dr. Valerie said, "and it has a beautiful inlaid parquet floor. I don't see why it didn't occur to its donors that they could have spent some of the funds on a simple concrete floor for this hospital full of malaria cases and war wounded instead."

"It's because they're on the other side of the border, so they don't have to care about all this," I said cynically. "And a hospital floor isn't nearly as effective as a temple floor in getting them a big score for their next incarnations. Or maybe nobody thought to ask them for a hospital floor."

Mr. Ian, an Australian social worker, had happened into Three Pagodas Pass and become enchanted. He looked after the Mon orphanage and taught English classes for Mons and Karens. He wore a big round wicker hat and draped a Mon sarong on his bony frame. Mr. Ian was teaching self-defense against isolation and Dr. Valerie was teaching self-defense against disease.

My class sweated. They kicked. They yelled. The yell, forced out with the breath when one kicked or punched, was essential. "Ja!" they would yell at first, which over the next few days evolved into a deafening "YAI!"

A couple of my students dropped out, taking to their beds with malaria attacks, among them Rad Aung, my friend from the seacoast expedition. The others progressed, even the worst of them. A major change took place on the second day when I began to let them spar with each other. Having been bashed in sparring matches myself, I emphasized to the class that they must attack and block effectively, but *gently*. They giggled all through it, but they were terrific. Those who had been awkward at performing individual techniques were suddenly able to use them well to defend themselves.

My class punched and kicked and blocked. They moved swiftly in their green trousers and bright blouses. They wore *thanaka* powder and red lipstick, and left clunky wristwatches and cheap rings in a heap on a table while they worked out. Among them was a "natural," a potential champion by any standard. The Champ was small, agile, and very strong. She was an officer (a section leader) with short hair and big, brown eyes. Two of her brothers were Mon boxers, she said. From what I'd seen of it, Mon boxing was a vicious sport, even bloodier than Thai kickboxing. The Champ had learned a few things from her brothers before she'd gone off to join the Mon rebels. Mostly it was great style. She faced her opponents with a perfect stance and deadly concentration. And her kicks meant business.

A tall, pretty girl changed the most. For the first two days, everything had to be explained to her long after the rest of the class had caught on. She smiled apologetically, confused. Then, on the third day, I began to teach the class the most basic *kata*. They weren't doing as well with it as I had come to expect. They made wrong turns, rushed and stumbled. Only the tall one had the right stuff. She must have practiced between classes. Her *kata* performance was smooth, zeroing in on her invisible enemies, punching and blocking them. Some innate grace conquered her hesitance and clumsiness.

General Htaw Mon arrived at headquarters from the campaign he'd been waging on the seacoast. "We've made a series of attacks on the railway line," he told me. "I want to cut it, to cut off Tatmadaw supplies to the whole south. Just recently we exploded a locomotive." The general smiled. "The women soldiers demanded to be put in combat. They said they refused to return to headquarters until they all got a chance to shoot at the enemy! I made sure they got their battle. They did well. Now they all want your martial arts training."

We decided to select two or three of the best students in my class to be sent to Bangkok for extensive karate instruction. The Champ was an obvious choice, along with the tall girl who was good at *kata*. They would stay with Mons in Bangkok, and return to train other soldiers, male and female, at headquarters. The Mon rebels appreciated foreign aid, such as it was (Dr. Valerie, Mr. Ian, and me), but mainly they wanted to be self-sufficient. Above all, they wanted their people to be educated, so they would have a knowledge of history and be able to plan for the future.

Each morning I commuted to the camp from Three Pagodas' bazaar on the back of a Mon doctor's motorcycle. The trail from the paved Thai road down to the camp became a deeper gully of mud with each night's rain, so I dismounted and walked that part. I was happy in my work. I'd finally had enough of the conflicts and corruptions of the border; I knew far too much about heroin, teakwood, and factional disputes. With karate—teaching it or learning it—such concentration was required that for an hour at a time everything else in the world vanished. After the afternoon classes I did my own *kata*s, gliding through eight of them, finishing with *Matsukaze*.

Crosby spent his days gauging the zeitgeist in the bazaar, talking to Bengali shopkeepers, Mon smugglers, Karen officers. Three Pagodas' bazaar now had two "town councils": one for the Mons, the other for Karens, Chinese, Indians, and everyone else. Neither council managed to do anything worthwhile. The road through the bazaar was still a garbage-strewn mud ditch.

In the evenings, Joshua cooked us meals of rice and *dal* with a splendid mango chutney (a dish from his days as a soldier of the Raj). With his lottery commissions, Joshua had realized one of his longtime dreams by starting a fish farm. When it was about to rain, he would set out candles around his fish pond so flying termites, lured and bedazzled, would fall into the water to become fish food. After the rain came, he'd return to the pond, "to check on the fish," wearing a World War II Japanese helmet as a rain hat. At night, Joshua twirled the dials of a shortwave radio Crosby had brought him, searching for the Burmese edition of the BBC World Service.

Crosby bought a Golden Bee mosquito net in the bazaar. When he put it up, something that may or may not have been a scorpion fell out and bit him on the hand, painfully ("Bloody hell!") but to no serious effect. I purchased a Tiger Head flashlight, made of heavy gleaming steel. The switch button was a ruby of red plastic.

I fixed the binding of Joshua's worn Guest Book with gaffer's tape. Some recent entries had actually been addressed to me. "You're very brave," someone I'd never met had written. So I wrote in the book to the other border aficionados: "When you start getting 'mail' here, it's probably time to find another war zone. Anyone for Kurdistan or Eritrea?"

Meanwhile, hordes of backpackers seduced by the Three Pagodas Pass blurb in a budget traveler guidebook were arriving at the Karens' free guest house. For now, tourist traffic was permitted. Busloads of Thais came up on weekends to shop for Mon hats and Karen textiles and pose for pictures by the *chedi*s. The Thai border checkpoint was so casual it remained unstaffed most of the time. I went past it on my way to work and back every day.

European and Australian tourists, in shorts and neon T-shirts, ate breakfast at Iris's place. Her sylphlike children and her husband (who was quiet for a Mon) waited on them. She kept the earnings from the breakfast trade, along with occasional small winnings from the lottery, in a zippered pouch around her waist. When her good nature needed a break, I'd sit at Iris's roadside table to answer questions.

"How far can I go without running into the soldiers?" a British tourist asked.

"Just to the end of the bazaar," I told him. "There's a Karen checkpoint there."

"Is that all? That's not very far at all!"

"Well, *there is a war on,* you know . . ."

Nai Tin Aung was absent with a fever on the last day of my self-defense course. The class had reached the point where I could manage without an interpreter, anyway. I demonstrated the moves, my students imitated them, I corrected, they ran through the techniques admirably. They sparred very well. I tested them on the basic kicks, punches, blocks, and the *kata*. The good ones were now excellent, and had the bright lights of Bangkok in their eyes. The worst ones were passable, although the one left-hander in the class could not throw a left punch to save her life.

In the afternoon class, I covered "dirty" self-defense. Until then, I'd been teaching pure karate, departing from what I studied in the U.S. only in encouraging the Mon women to aim some kicks below the belt. During the last class I indicated vulnerable body parts to target: temples, jaw, eyes, nose, windpipe, stomach, groin, kidneys, knees, shins, ankles. Then I showed what they could do: a knee to the groin (wild giggling from the students), a sidekick to the knee.

I showed them karate techniques using everyday objects as weapons. We used things they happened to carry around with them: the ballpoint pen jabbed at the eye, the Tiger Head flashlight back-fisted to the windpipe, the AK-47 clip used to "load" a punch. The women soldiers carried spare ammo on their belts, so it was conceivable that they might have the clip but not the rifle handy.

The class ended with a fairly presentable rendition of the basic *kata,* and then a last flurry of ten punches, ten kicks, ten more punches, the loudest yells of "YAI!" Afterward, my students brought me a mug of coffee and gathered around while Dr. Valerie took our pictures.

⚊ 3 ⚊

The next day I said good-bye to Joshua and Iris. Crosby and I went to Mon headquarters. It was raining heavily. I was wearing camouflage trousers and a military-style shirt with cryptic insignia embroidered on the epaulets. A Mon soldier, one of the older guys, stopped on the muddy path and saluted me. I returned his salute. "Did you see that?" I exclaimed to Crosby. "That soldier saluted me! Spin would be *so* jealous!"

I found General Htaw Mon, Nai Tin Aung, and Nai Aung Shein for farewells. The general gave me a Women's Unit shoulder insignia and Nai Aung Shein presented me with his wicker helmet. Then Crosby, Dr. Valerie, Mr. Ian, and I caught a *songtaow* to Sangklaburi. I needed to telephone the newsmagazine's Bangkok bureau to check on captions for my photo essay, then I would go to the mission hospital village, and proceed to the Tenasserim from there. Dr. Valerie would come along to have a look at the mission hospital, and Crosby would meet Uncle Benny. Mr. Ian had some errands to do in Sangklaburi. But our first priority was what I termed "a fabulous lunch," at a Thai restaurant near the Sangklaburi bus depot. I ordered the meal: chicken with cashews and chilis, garlic-fried pork, beef in red curry, pork with mushrooms and ginger.

After lunch, Dr. Valerie went to the post office and happened to meet an American who worked at the mission hospital. He offered us a ride there, but he had to do some shopping first, and I had to make my call to Bangkok. I went to the long-distance telephone office, which was in a side-street shophouse. The clerk dialed the number, and I picked up the phone in the booth. A receptionist answered at the magazine. The editor was out for a few minutes, but he had said that if I telephoned, I was to be sure to call back. So I waited, perusing movie ads in a day-old copy of a Thai newspaper.

When I phoned again, the editor was there.

"I'm afraid I have bad news for you," he said. "Spin's been arrested."

"Where? In Mae Hong Son?"

"No, in Bangkok, at his apartment. Weren't you with him at Khun Sa's camp this time?"

"No, I wasn't. What happened? Why was he arrested?"

"I really don't know any details about it, but he's apparently at the Immigration jail in Bangkok, Soi Suan Phlu, now. I've heard that the police were looking for you, too."

"But I've only been at Three Pagodas, and that's quite legal."

"Anyway, do try to be careful."

Shuddering, I left the booth and scanned the Thai newspaper for any mention of Spin's arrest. I found no reference to it. I assumed that Spin had been detected crossing into or out of Tiger Camp, then tracked down and picked up in Bangkok by Special Branch and/or the Immigration police. His rotten luck. I can't very well just leave Thailand, I thought. If the police are after me, they'll just arrest me at the airport or the Malaysian border. Anyway, Spin's the one who went to see Khun Sa this time, not me. The police would have no reason to arrest me. Spin will need a plane ticket to get out of Soi Suan Phlu, and money, and contacts.

I wanted to go to Bangkok at once, to get Spin out of jail. I told Crosby and Dr. Valerie what had happened, and they went to the mission hospital without me. I walked over to the bus depot, but all transport in the direction of Kanchanaburi and Bangkok had left hours ago. I would have to wait until morning.

I took a *songtaow* to Uncle Benny's house, which was near the mission hospital. He listened gravely to the news of Spin's arrest. "I will pray for him," he assured me. He gave me a cup of milky tea and I tried to relax.

My Karen nurse friend put me up for the night. She heated a bucket of water for my bath. "Soon this village will be getting electricity," she told me. I poured the hot water over my shoulders by kerosene lamplight. I killed a scorpion in the bathroom, mashing it against the wall with my Tiger Head flashlight.

I slept on white sheets under a Mudon blanket (Burmese cotton) that I'd bought in Three Pagodas' bazaar. I decided I would bring the Mudon blanket to Spin because it would be good for sleeping under on the jail floor.

I slept, without tears. A Thai nurse who had been at the house when I arrived had told me, "You must put a piece of ice in your heart." But ice would melt. Maybe a piece of diamond would be better, or a ruby from the Shan mines. I felt like my love for Spin created a laser force-field to protect us both, a talisman. It was like a ruby Uncle Benny claimed had been found by Karen hunters long ago, so big that it turned the jungle red with its glow.

My days and nights in the jungle had made me the untrammeled creature of Uncle Benny's fairy tales, denizen of a world where war, love, and magic fed off each other. As I slept, I held my broken lapis necklace, wrapped in paper, in my hand. When the necklace had broken on the bus, it was telling me, "It's over with Spin." But I hadn't heard the necklace speak—I was too intent on searching for its beads on the floor.

THE
SPIDER'S
WEB

⹀ 1 ⹀

Just before dawn, I left the jungle border village. It was a dark, rainy day. In Sangklaburi, I caught a minibus for Kanchanaburi. I sat in front next to the driver's girlfriend, who wore red shorts. Between gear changes the driver stroked the girl's thigh.

I decided to go directly to the Immigration jail, to see what I could do to get Spin out. I doubted that the Thai authorities were

looking for me, but if they were, I didn't want them to find me at
the town house in Bangkok. My 2,4-D reports and other files of
documents, letters, and news articles were there, and I did not want
them to fall into the hands of the Ministry of the Interior. Also, I
didn't want to get my friends who owned the town house in
trouble.

My last night at Joshua's place, I had dreamt that I had gotten
away with murder. In the dream I flew to Los Angeles on New
Year's Eve, brutally murdered someone (a blurred, unrecognizable
figure) with repeated knife thrusts to the gut, then flew to New
York. I was undetected, unsuspected. My crimes against the Burma
border—illicit penetrations, multiple stab wounds—I had gotten
away with them.

I felt sure that the Thai police could not make a case against me
for border crossing. The Keng Tung expedition had not drawn
attention, and Three Pagodas Pass was a permitted crossing point.
On my current, Penang-issued visa, I had not crossed the border at
any other places. I convinced myself that I had played by the rules. I
had acquired the spurious innocence of the true criminal, the kind
cool enough to pass polygraph tests.

Just in case I did run into some trouble at the jail, I jotted down a
list of phone numbers—the U.S. embassy, reporters, influential
contacts—to be called in an emergency; and I wrote the embassy
phone number on my arm in ballpoint pen. Instead of my camouflage trousers, I wore the black pants I'd taught karate in; and
instead of my army shirt with the World War II insignia, I wore my
only other shirt—the one with the arcane symbols on the epaulets. I
belted it tightly. I wore arrogant purple nail polish and black Ray-
Bans.

I was following the libretto of *Fidelio* (heroine rescues unjustly
imprisoned hero), but the soundtrack in my headphones wasn't
opera; it was the Four Tops' greatest hits tape. With Vietnam-era
classics like "Reach Out, I'll Be There" pounding in my ears, I was
ready to face the music at Soi Suan Phlu.

On the bus from Kanchanaburi to Bangkok I read the latest
Bangkok Post, amazed not to find any mention of Spin's arrest. In

Bangkok I took a taxi to the Immigration complex and had it drop me off in back, at the jail entrance. I told the guard that I'd come to see Spin.

"Visiting hours are over. Come back tomorrow morning, bring your passport, and you can visit," the guard said.

An Immigration officer walked in and asked who I was there to see. I told him, and he asked to see my passport. I asked him if Spin was being held there.

"I think so," he said. "You'd better come to the office to check." He didn't return my passport. I went with him to an office in the main, front building, which turned out to be the illegal aliens section. I asked to see Captain Chun, who had pretended to be nice to Spin and me the year before. The officer told me that Captain Chun was not in. My passport was handed across the room, and one of the tan-uniformed officers at one of the gray metal desks produced a thick file of documents.

"You were here last year," the officer who had brought me in said. "The officer in charge wants to speak with you."

The officer in charge did not introduce himself to me, but I read his name on the badge pinned to his crisp uniform: Col. Satapon Thong-On. His office walls were decorated with an assortment of gilt and brass clocks, and some photographs of himself hobnobbing with Thai royalty. Colonel Satapon looked up from the paperwork on his desk and glared at me.

"Why did you come back to this country?" he asked in English.

"I came to Thailand for cultural reasons. I paint. And I'm interested in the minority people from Burma—hill tribes, refugees."

"You got in trouble last year." Colonel Satapon smiled.

I smiled back. "I did. But now I play by the rules. I just talk to people in Thailand." I stared at the colonel through my Ray-Bans and smiled ingratiatingly. "What about Spin? Where was he arrested? Why is he being held here?"

"You go everywhere with him, don't you? You go together."

"No, actually, not since last year. Why is he here? What are the charges?"

"Maybe I'll put you in with him."

I laughed. "But there's a men's ward and a women's ward here."

"Maybe we'll put you in a special room together. Where we can watch you."

I didn't like the way this was going. Black lenses hiding my eyes, I kept my voice calm and friendly. "How long has Spin been here, anyway?"

"I can throw you in detention, too," the colonel said, his eyes narrowing.

"I don't see how. I've got a valid visa, and I haven't done anything wrong. Last year we were specifically told to buy round-trip tickets and come back. I've been given visas in New York and Penang."

"No. You're on the blacklist. You're not supposed to be here."

"If I'm blacklisted, why did the Thai consulates give me a visa?" My voice was low and even.

Colonel Satapon leaned back in his chair. "What's that in your pocket? Film?"

I remembered how Immigration police—the colonel's under-lings—had been interested in film the year before. I unbuttoned my shirt pocket and showed the colonel that it contained not film but a little fold-up alarm clock with a device for calculating time around the world. Colonel Satapon had one just like it in the collection on his desk. After that he ignored me, turning his attention to the files of hapless illegal aliens. He got up and left his office. I sat there and read the *Bangkok Post*.

The colonel returned. "Go with him," he told me, pointing his chin at an Immigration officer who stood in the doorway.

I walked slowly, and the officer told me to hurry up. I was looking for a foreigner to whom I could pass the list of phone numbers. Unfortunately, it was now late afternoon, and the lines of tourists waiting for visa extensions were gone. Just as we reached the gate of the jail, I saw a blond man carrying a briefcase with a "Jesus is Love" sticker on it. I supposed he was one of the mission-aries who were allowed to visit detainees. I managed to hand the note to him as I passed, unnoticed by my escort.

I was brought to the downstairs office of the jail. A few Immigration police were still there late in the day.

"We have to search your bags before we bring you upstairs to detention," one told me.

"What are the charges?" I asked. "*Why* am I being put in detention? What reason?"

"It's just our chief's orders," the oldest officer replied.

"I can't believe this! All I did was come here to see my husband and they put me in detention, too." Even though Spin and I were far from married, I used a Thai word that implied "husband" to add some weight to the complaint.

"And who is your husband?" the officers asked. I told them.

"Oh, *him!* He is very famous here!"

They gave me my detainee identification to sign.

"Before I sign this, I must call my embassy," I said firmly. To my surprise, they let me use the phone in the office. I was supposed to dial zero, and then the number. Nothing happened; the line was dead. I kept trying. The Immigration police rummaged aimlessly through my two shoulder bags. They found my malaria medicine. They ignored the white, unmarked chloroquine tablets, but were intrigued by the Fansidar, which was sealed in silver foil with mosquitoes pictured on it.

"Yah gun malaria" (medicine against malaria), I explained.

Then an officer turned up an aerosol plunger of nonoxynol 9. Mystified, he tried to open it. I stopped dialing the phone.

"That's *yah gun look*" (medicine against offspring), I said, "and don't touch it!" The cop dropped it back in the bag and rushed off to wash his hands. His cohorts laughed at him.

I asked one of the younger officers to dial the phone for me. He got a busy signal. I leaned close to him, to encourage him to keep trying.

"When the line is open, we'll come up and get you, but now you've got to go up to the detention ward," the oldest officer said.

"No way," I said. "I've been here before, remember. I know once upstairs, you're dead to the world. I have got to call my embassy first."

This time I reached a busy signal at the embassy. I dialed the magazine editor and told him what had happened to me. I asked him to call the embassy, and local journalists. "Visiting hours are in the morning, should anyone feel so inclined," I said.

I thanked the officers for letting me use the telephone. "See if my husband needs any help," I suggested. I went upstairs. One of the guards was a fat Cambodian trusty whom I recognized from the year before, a creep who did the cops' dirty work, like fingerprinting and beating prisoners.

Feeling mean, I said, "You must really like it here. I guess you're *never* going to leave."

"Never say never," the trusty shot back.

He brought me to the same ward, which was still crammed with women, children, and their belongings. The steel door slammed and the guards left. A dark-skinned young woman in shorts and a man's shirt swaggered up.

"You can stay in the smaller room," she told me in English. "There's another European there for you to talk to. It's all so crowded now, but tomorrow a lot of Vietnamese are leaving. Where are you from? Did you overstay?"

"I'm American," I replied. "No, I didn't overstay my visa. I didn't do anything at all. It's political."

We went to the small room. "The other people in here are from Burma," the young woman said. "I am from Malaysia. I'm called Boy." Amid the people from Burma, a thin European with long brown hair was sitting on a straw mat. "And that is Caroline. She is French."

"Here, have a seat," Caroline said. "So, you are here because you overstayed?"

I sat on the straw mat and explained how I'd ended up in the ward for the second time. We ate oranges. The ward was excruciatingly noisy, with about 120 voices echoing off the concrete at once and loud Thai music blaring from a cassette player. Kids were yelling and babies crying. Caroline and I traded stories at the top of our lungs. She had just been released from criminal prison and had to stay in the Immigration jail for a few days before being deported to France.

"My little sister and I and a friend of ours got busted for a few kilos of heroin in Chiang Mai. I was a stupid junkie then. We were going to bring it back to Europe. I made the run a couple of times before. This time, my boyfriend was in jail in Bali. The jailers there were beating him up. I wanted to make enough money to buy him out. So I went up to Fang, north of Chiang Mai, to score, but my usual connection was gone. I got the stuff from another guy, and he informed on me. My sister and my friend made big bribes and got out after a year. I did two years in Chiang Mai prison, and another two years in the big prison down here. Then they decided to let me go."

Caroline seemed pretty straight. I saw no tracks on her hands, arms, or legs. Her family was Irish-French, and her English was excellent. So was her jail Thai, full of scabrous idioms. She made a cup of coffee for me, with water from a pot hooked up to the lighting system. I told her about Burma.

"These girls come from Burma," Caroline said, indicating a cluster of fair-skinned teenagers who were gazing at me among the larger group of dark-skinned Bengalis.

"Nai Mon ha?" I said, managing to ask them in Mon if they were Mons. They were. I ran through my Mon vocabulary and then told them in Thai, which they understood, about the places in Ye and Tavoy provinces I had visited. They were from Ye. They could read Burmese, so I gave them some Burmese magazines I'd bought in Three Pagodas' bazaar full of poems and stories and movie gossip. They'd had nothing else to read since they'd been in jail, a stretch of months.

"So you know Khun Sa?" Caroline said. "I *adore* Khun Sa. I kept a magazine cover with his picture on my wall in prison." Spin had taken that photo the year before, at Tiger Camp. "I want to be the wife of Khun Sa," Caroline sighed.

"Oh, I think Khun Sa would love to have a French wife," I told her. "I'll have to send him your photo."

A pale-skinned, chubby Englishwoman came by and sat down with us. She wore a red batik dress and a leopard-skin headband. Her face was caked in sweaty makeup. She had been in the jail for four months, she said. She spoke in childlike broken English: "My embassy will get me out, but they want to give me injection to get me on the plane. Every time I go to airport, I run away." Abruptly, in a tiny voice, she asked, "Do I look English to you?"

"Well, you don't look Thai," I said.

"Oh, good! I don't want to look Thai!" she exclaimed.

The missionary to whom I'd passed the note appeared at the ward and I spoke to him through the bars. "I was surprised you weren't handcuffed when they brought you in," he said. "They always use handcuffs here." He told me that Spin was in Ward 4. I asked him if he could go over and tell Spin I was in Ward 5, but he said he couldn't go back that evening. He'd just been over there when the guards were beating the prisoners with sticks, and they didn't like the missionaries around when that sort of thing was going on, so he wouldn't go back until morning. But he assured me he'd make my telephone calls.

The Mon girls were quiet, absorbed in reading the Burmese magazines. But the Bengalis were like a demented tribe of gypsies, arguing, slapping their children, stepping on each other. Caroline told me how one group of them had ended up in the Soi Suan Phlu jail: "That little girl in the white dress was taken by a gang that steals Thai and Indian children to sell for illegal adoption in Malaysia. When it happened, the family ran to the police station in their neighborhood in Bangkok, yelling and screaming, even though they couldn't speak much Thai. The police caught the gangsters and came back with the little girl. But they also have come to understand this whole family is illegal, from Burma, and they don't have bribe money, so they all got put in here."

A corner of the room belonged to Boy. She had decorated it with cut-out pictures from fashion magazines. She had also set up a little library of paperbacks in English and a pantry holding Nescafé, sugar, and Coffeemate. The cassette player was hers, and she and the Bengali mothers used its cord to whack the children when they got out of hand. "I don't like that," Caroline said, "but Boy loves it. She is the 'father' here." Boy had adopted the Bengalis, whom she called "Burmese," and had tried to make them more orderly and disciplined. The ward was much cleaner than it had been the year before, although it was even more crowded.

Though she longed for order and peace, Boy thrived on the

emotional chaos of the ward. She had scrawled graffiti on the wall proclaiming her undying love for some girl named Zizi, but she had half a dozen others in her "harem." It was an ongoing, improvised soap opera. The day before, a morose Nepalese girl had threatened to kill herself with a knife, over unrequited love for Boy. Now the Nepalese crouched against the wall, absorbed in her usual pursuit— writing long letters to her husband who was locked up over in one of the men's wards. What could she come up with to fill five pages every day? I wondered. "Dear Beloved Husband, Yesterday I attempted to end my life because that Malay bitch doesn't love me . . ."

I wrote a note to Spin. I told him I'd been "thrown in" with no charges and had contacted the media. I asked what had happened to him, how long he'd been there, did he need anything, did he have a plane ticket to leave Thailand? I made an envelope for it from a magazine page, and Caroline handed it through the bars to a kid who would deliver it.

As the evening wore noisily on, I drank coffee with Boy, who had donned gold silk pajamas. Like Caroline, she had been in criminal prison. She had been studying Thai in Bangkok and dealing heroin on the side. She had stabbed a girlfriend, with a pair of scissors, in a fight over money. "I just wanted to hurt her, not to kill her," Boy said. She was convicted of attempted murder anyway. She had done a couple of years in prison, and was to be deported, but the Immigration officials were in no hurry to let her go. They wouldn't let her use her plane ticket to Malaysia. It looked to me like she was too useful to them, keeping the ward reasonably orderly and clean.

Vietnamese women who were to leave the next morning invited me to their going-away party in the next room. They sat in two facing rows and drank soda pop, and sang plaintive Vietnamese songs. One of the women played drums on a plastic bucket with a pair of chopsticks to accompany the singing. The Englishwoman regaled them with a rendition of "Leaving on a Jet Plane." It would be some time before the Vietnamese would see an airport, though. They were only getting trucked to a refugee camp on the Cambodian border. But this move was still cause for celebration. Refugees lived on hope. The next place, whatever it was, would be better, they believed. These women had come to Thailand on boats, and ended up in jail in Bangkok. They thought that from the refugee camp they could eventually resettle in America, Australia, Canada, Europe. It would take years, but leaving Soi Suan Phlu was a step on the way, they believed.

They poured soda pop for me, and gave me cookies. "We're so happy you could come to our party!" a Viet-Chinese lady told me in Thai.

"Oh yes, I'm glad I could make it," I said politely. "If I had not been sent here until tomorrow, I would have missed you."

I returned to the Burma Suite. It was nearly midnight. Some of the prisoners were hunkered down to sleep, shrouded in thin blankets. Children were still awake and chattering, though, and the Bengalis talked loudly and played Bengali music on Boy's tape player. I decided to sleep and took my place on Caroline's straw mat, with my Mudon blanket. Boy handed me a black eye-mask (with "United Airlines" printed on it) to block out the fluorescent light.

But I couldn't sleep. Twenty-six of us were squashed into the twelve-by-fifteen-foot room, and quite a few were still talking. The eye-mask only increased the claustrophobic feeling. A sleeping Bengali child kept flinging his arms onto my head. Disentangling his hands from my hair, I sat up and leaned against the wall. A sympathetic Bengali woman offered me a sleeping pill, which I declined, preferring wakefulness to sedation. I read instead. I had just started Graham Greene's *Getting to Know the General*, about Torrijos of Panama. Reading Graham Greene in jail—the year before it had been Mishima. Eventually, I got under the Mudon blanket again and slept.

⌐ 2 ⌐

I awoke at six in the morning, still on the border schedule. The Burma Suite slumbered on, nowhere to go, nothing to do. The big room was full of activity as most of the Vietnamese and some

Cambodians packed to leave. I started writing an account of my being put in detention. I made three copies: one titled "Statement," to give to embassy representatives; the others titled "Press Release," for reporters who I was sure would appear when visiting hours started at 9:30.

A French lady came to see Caroline, and Caroline told her about me. She asked what she could do to help and I gave her a copy of the list of phone numbers. But visiting hours went by and nobody came to see me. I was appalled that no one from the embassy had come. They weren't even confined to normal visiting hours. By noon I was genuinely depressed. I hadn't gotten a reply to the note I'd sent Spin, and my lists of phone numbers had not produced any results. I tried to read the Graham Greene book, but it was too noisy to concentrate. I kept reading the same paragraphs over and over again.

A charity's delivery of little cartons of milk—plain, chocolate, and strawberry flavored—arrived. Boy had cleverly told the charity people that the same number of prisoners were in the ward as the day before (it had actually decreased from 120 to a still crowded but breathable 89), so we had a milk surplus. Boy tossed me three cartons of chocolate milk.

Caroline insisted I eat some of the bread and butter her French visitor had brought. She told me prison stories. Her last three months had been spent in the prison hospital. "They tested the whole prison for AIDS. A lot of the men had it, but only two women were positive for HIV. A Thai girl and me had it. They put us in isolation in a hospital room. It was terrible; they were idiots. They would slip our food under the door. And we weren't even sick. They kept us there because they were afraid of it, of us. Then suddenly they let me go." Caroline told me about her family, seven brothers and sisters: "Three of us were junkies. And one of my sisters has AIDS and she had a baby. The baby has AIDS." She showed me family snapshots. I saw something familiar about the photo of a sister, who was sitting with a group of Asian men in green uniforms. "This is my sister when she was in a movie in Thailand, years ago. She played the part of a journalist who talks to Khun Sa." I told Caroline how I had seen that movie, in Mo Heing's rebel camp, one winter night.

I showed the Mon girls some photographs of the seacoast and the women soldiers. They examined the pictures for a long time. I wondered if they would be better off joining the Mon Army. Was war better than jail? Was war better than the enslaved prostitution that was the fate of pretty young illegal aliens in Thailand?

A major fight erupted in the afternoon. Small fights had occurred all day, at least one every half hour. The Bengalis argued to let off steam. In the afternoon's squabble, a Burmese girl accused one of the Bengalis of stealing a packet of salt and a lime. She slapped the Bengali girl across the face. Boy stepped in, furious that they'd been fighting over such a trivial matter. Boy's Malay idea of proper behavior, which involved cooperation and a little peace and quiet, was totally at odds with the culturally ingrained behavior of the rest of the Burma Suite. Boy took it personally. "I've done everything for you Burma people," Boy harangued the room. "Boy gets you medicine when the Burma children are sick, Boy gets you clothes, Boy gets you extra cartons of milk. And all you do is steal from each other and fight!" The Bengalis enjoyed provoking Boy. It made an ordinary fight even more exciting.

Predictably, Boy decided that both teenage girls needed a whipping. She brought out the electric cord.

"She should really be dressed in black leather and studs for this," I remarked to Caroline.

"Yes, with high-heeled boots," Caroline said.

Boy cracked the cord in the air to create suspense. Then she smacked it across the girls' saronged bottoms, one smack each. The Burmese accuser took it stoically; the Bengali accusee burst into tears.

About twenty minutes later, another punishment session, for some Bengali children who'd been fighting—more electric cord whacks and more tears. A child brought a copy of the *Bangkok Post* to Caroline and me, providing us with a better diversion than watching Boy whip the Bengalis. The paper contained nothing about Spin and me being in jail. It did have a piece detailing the Burmese government's objections to the Amnesty International report of human rights abuse by the Tatmadaw. The *Post* quoted a

Burmese state-owned newspaper called *One Thousand Officers* that had called Amnesty's charges "fabrications" that "emanated from jealousy against establishment of a peaceful and prosperous socialist state."

Food arrived: rice with a spicy beef curry and fruit. An evening meal was donated each day by "some Moslem embassy," Boy explained. It was certainly an improvement over the sickening fare the jail had provided. I supposed the Saudis or others had found out that the Moslems in jail—Iranians, Afghans, Bengalis, Malays— had been served a diet based on pork fat. With charities contributing the food, the Thai Immigration authorities really had to spend very little on the upkeep of the jail. They paid the electric bill—that was about all. With all the payoffs, it was probably a profit-making operation for the officials involved.

A letter from Spin came with the food. "No charges, no questions, no nothing," Spin wrote. He had been in jail for a week, and had no ticket out. Spin's letter ended with a defiant "Long live free-lance photojournalists and human rights workers." His familiar and profane style raised my spirits immediately. I ate some of the Moslem curry.

At four in the afternoon, someone called out that I had a visitor in the corridor. He was an American-educated Thai who worked for the consular section of the American embassy. I stood at the window and the consular representative passed forms through the bars, releases for me to sign, giving the State Department permission to dispense information about my "arrest." I explained that there had been no arrest, I was detained without charges, and gave him a copy of my statement. I also showed the man a letter I carried from a U.S. congressman that said my efforts "to preserve the dignity of the Burmese people while simultaneously working to curtail opium poppy production are commendable."

"You should not be in jail," the consular representative said, his brow furrowed with concern. "This would never happen in the States!" I wasn't so sure—I'd heard of Immigration cases in the U.S. that were similarly lacking in due process. I gave him my Visa card and asked him to use it to buy a ticket to Hong Kong for me, and one to Penang for Spin (who would be on his way to New Zealand). The representative assured me that he'd do so, but it might take another day to get us out. He said again that my detention was an outrage and told me he would lodge a protest with the Immigration division chief.

Not long after the consular representative left, the missionary appeared with a note from Spin. "So you got busted in the spider's web," Spin wrote. "You're crazy. Why didn't you just split?" He went on to speculate that Immigration had been "waiting to have the pair bagged before action's taken." In that case, Spin would have sat in jail until I appeared. Finding the "why" of my detention incomprehensible, I concentrated instead on the probability that Spin and I would soon be getting out of jail and out of Thailand. I wrote him a letter telling of the consular representative's visit.

I found enough space to do some karate practice. With all the cat fights in the ward, I decided I wouldn't be teaching anyone the techniques of "unarmed self-defense." I stretched and kicked and went through a rather constricted version of the *kata*s. Looking at it one way, knowing martial arts didn't do much good in jail: you'd always be outnumbered and outgunned. But it wasn't the usage of karate that mattered, it was the knowledge of it. The knowledge gave you strength, even if you held the strength back.

That night one of the Immigration police entered the ward on the pretext of supervising the garbage-emptying detail. Normally, garbage was brought downstairs in the morning by male prisoners with wives in Ward 5. They bribed the guards for the privilege so they could get glimpses of their wives. With so many prisoners leaving that morning, the garbage had gone uncollected. Officer Chitapon, with a big belly and self-satisfied demeanor, prowled the ward.

Chitapon squeezed an Afghan woman's arm as she walked by. He cornered Caroline and examined the black cat tattooed on her shoulder. Looking distastefully at Caroline's clothes—a man's checked sarong and undershirt—he asked, "What are you, a girl or a boy?"

"Oh, I am absolutely a boy," Caroline replied, and he lost interest in her.

Chitapon was really looking for two of the Mon girls, the prettiest, seventeen and nineteen years old. "Where are they?" he bellowed. "Are they in the shower? Get them out here!"

"*I'll* take the garbage downstairs, all of it," Boy said.

"I don't want you, I want them," Chitapon said, brushing past Boy. "Hurry up and pick up those pails, come on." The Mon girls followed him downstairs.

About twenty minutes later, the Mon teenagers came back, weeping convulsively. They ran into the bathroom. Boy dragged them out and made them tell what had happened. Downstairs, Chitapon had backed each of the girls against the wall, rubbing against them, fondling, grabbing. He told them they must give in to him or stay in jail forever. Then he let them go back upstairs, having enjoyed enough power over the powerless for the time being.

"These things happen here all the time," Boy told me. "Last month he brought two girls from Laos downstairs. They didn't come back 'til two in the morning. He said he would kill them if they spoke of it. Later they got bought out by the whorehouse man. That's how girls leave here, if they're not lucky."

The Mon girls were horrified and angry. They took showers to wash away the contamination of Chitapon's pawing. "I have a tape recorder," I told them. "If you wish, I'll make a recording about what happened to you. I won't use your names. The tape will show the outside world how prisoners are treated here." The girls agreed to make the tape, but they were still too upset to speak coherently.

While waiting for them to calm down, I decided to take some pictures with my flash-equipped Minolta. When I used up a roll of film, Boy asked if she could buy another roll and take some photos, which she would secretly send out to be developed. I handed Boy the reloaded camera. The Mon girls cheered up and started putting on makeup and their best clothes. The other women dressed up to pose as well. They put on jeans and shoes and lipstick, and hung purses over their shoulders as if they were actually going somewhere. The first roll went by fast, and Boy asked to buy another. I tried to refuse payment, but Caroline said, "Take the money—it's very rare that anybody offers to pay for anything in here."

The women laughed with delight every time the flash went off. None remembered pictures having been taken in the ward before. It made them happy. It was something to get dressed up for, a way to show the outside world—faraway friends, families, husbands in the men's wards—that they were still alive, and beautiful.

After things had settled down from the photo session, I heard the commotion of greeting a new arrival in the main room. Cries of "Overstay? Overstay?" meant it must be a Westerner, so Caroline and I went out to investigate. The new arrival was about my age and height, with blond hair and glasses, like me. She wore a very nice green cotton dress and had only a small leather purse with her. For a moment I wondered if she had been taken in because she fit some description of me the Thai police might have been circulating. Then she told a disjointed story about having been caught on a bus without the two baht fare, being taken to the police station, and then being brought to the Immigration jail because she hadn't had her passport with her.

Caroline and I found her rather suspicious. Something about the lady said "American intelligence operative" to me. I couldn't imagine Thais getting that worked up over a two-baht bus fare, particularly if it was a blonde foreigner stiffing the conductor. And it was not illegal for foreigners to leave their passports at their home or hotel. The American was very interested in me and kept asking about the situation in Burma. For once, I was not in the mood to expound. "Give me your card and I'll send you some material," I offered, but she did not have a card to give me. She was vague about where she worked.

By then it was 11:30 at night. The steel door opened once again, and an Immigration officer appeared with three hefty Cambodian trustys. They told me to come out into the corridor and bring my bags with me. I thought the consular representative or other outside connections of mine had convinced Immigration to release me—it had all been a misunderstanding, time to go.

Instead, the trustys directed me to put my bags on a table in the corridor so they could search them. The trustys spoke English. One of them rooted through my shoulder bags. He was looking for my tape recorder. When he found it, I told him that the cassette in it was completely empty. He listened to it anyway. No sound came out of it, and—clumsy and frustrated—he broke the headphones, taking them off. He tossed the tape recorder back in the bag and continued his search. He located my two cameras, and three boxes of apparently unused film. Since the year before, I'd gotten in the habit of putting exposed film rolls back in the boxes and gluing them shut so they would look unused. The Cambodian put the film boxes and my cameras on the table. I figured someone in the ward had informed them about my plan to tape the Mon girls' story. It wouldn't have been Boy or Caroline, because they knew I hadn't made the tape. It was probably someone from the main room who'd been listening in.

The Cambodian found some photos of the Mon seacoast, none with me in the picture.

"From last year," I said. It would be a hell of a long shot to prosecute me on that basis, I thought.

The trusty put the photos with the cameras and film boxes. He scowled down at me. "You're in big trouble now," he said.

"Come on, I am not," I said with an amused smile.

The Cambodian found the kyat notes given to me by the Akha sheriff of Camelot.

"What money is this?" he asked.

"It's Burma money," I replied. He grunted and put it back in the shoulder bag. Then he dug out my lock knife and decided to add that to the pile for confiscation. The Immigration officer told me to take my bags and go back in the ward.

I dropped my bags back on the floor of the Burma Suite. I rolled my eyes at Caroline and said, "Déjà vu. They come in at night and try to psych you out. I'm sure they're mad at me because the consulate guy probably gave them hell, and because I could expose what's going on here with the girls."

"That scumbag jailer was yelling at Boy in here while they were searching you," Caroline said.

"What was he yelling at you for?" I asked Boy.

"Because I took pictures, and because I let you take pictures. And he tells me not to hang around with you because you're a big drug trafficker. He says that's why you go to Burma so much. I told him, 'That's shit. She doesn't even smoke or drink! She's no drug dealer.' "

I laughed, but I got a sinking feeling that perhaps the Ministry of the Interior had decided to play rough and frame me.

Be cool, I told myself. The Thais can't frame me unless the Americans are in on it. And I'm obviously in the good graces of the embassy at the moment. After all, I'll give State a free briefing on parts of Burma they can't reach, when I'm in Washington. Gloom descended. If I get to Washington! I thought. I did a better search of my bags than the Cambodians had and found some items to burn: a Karen border pass, a letter from a Mon leader, a photo of me with a Kachin revolutionary. I gave my Mon Women's Unit insignia to the Mon girls whom Chitapon had taken downstairs, girls who deserved medals and combat pay for resisting his advances.

Caroline and I went back to chat with the American lady, who kept asking me about Burma and the 2,4-D spraying. I was by then in such a bad mood that I blurted out, "You're not with the embassy, are you?"

"No, of course not! I hate this administration!" she protested.

It rang false to me.

"When I get out tomorrow, I can call people for you," the American offered.

I gave her the name of a friend of mine at a wire service.

"Isn't he CIA, though?" the American said.

I sighed in disgust. "Look," I said, "he's a friend of mine. Some of my friends may have Agency connections. *So what?* If you don't want to call him, just say so. Anyway, you might not be getting out of here all that fast. As you may have noticed, unexpected things happen around here."

Suddenly, the American decided she felt tired, and asked if there was anything to sleep on. I brought her my army poncho, and a Karen sarong to use as a blanket. She slept near the door in the big room, just as I had the year before.

In the Burma Suite, Boy and Caroline were drinking smuggled-in beer. I declined it and drank a chocolate milk instead. I sank into a sound sleep under my Mudon blanket in spite of the noise and the light, and in spite of the fact that I still didn't understand why I was in jail.

⸗ 3 ⸗

Waking at 6:30, I wrote a new press release, incorporating incidents from the night before. I ended the statement by asserting that my detention without charges and any further harassment were an "arbitrary, capricious and willful abuse of the Immigration Authority's jurisdiction."

I wrote out copies of the press release. Again, I was expecting visitors. I was also expecting another night in jail, and probably some stiff interrogation about the confiscated film, which—if developed—would show scenes of martial arts training at Three Pagodas.

At nine o'clock, before visiting hours had even started, the consular representative appeared in the corridor with a plane ticket to Hong Kong for me. He handed me my Visa card and told me I was booked on a flight leaving at one-thirty that afternoon. Apologetically, he told me he couldn't obtain a ticket for Spin because the U.S. embassy could not provide such services to a New Zealand citizen.

The other American detainee came up then, asking if my visitor was from the embassy. He said that he was, and she started in about her passport being at a police station (it had been at her house when she'd told her story the night before). She was so on edge that I decided she might actually not be an intelligence agent. I asked her, politely, to back off for a minute while I finished speaking with the consular representative.

I told the representative what had happened with the Mon girls, and about the search and threats. He shook his head. "They cannot do that to you," he said. "Don't worry, you will get all your things back." I thanked him for his help and *wai*'d. He *wai*'d back, and said, "Our position is that you can go wherever you want and write whatever you want. This should never have happened."

A visitor brought Caroline some clothes her family had sent for her to wear on her flight back to Paris. They were so French: a chic black suit, white tights, black velvet hair bow. Caroline would leave the next night. We sat on the straw mat, listening to her tape of Willie DeVille. "He is a junkie," she said admiringly. She still had that Beat fascination with the romantic heroes of Junkiedom, like Khun Sa, the opium warlord, and Willie DeVille, the Puerto Rican addict/street balladeer.

I received another letter from Spin, who had enclosed some envelopes so I could send him more letters without tearing out magazine pages to put them in. Spin wrote that no one from the New Zealand embassy had bothered to visit him during the whole week he'd been in jail. He had managed to speak to them twice on the telephone. That was all. They weren't helping him get a plane ticket. Spin's cellmates in Ward 4 included "a few Burmese-Chinese, two and three years here, sentenced to rot. One claims he paid the demanded five G's but no release, was raging bull today. Total fury. Need avenging angel to settle accounts."

At around ten o'clock, the guards brought me downstairs to run through arrest procedures, since I was about to be deported. A Cambodian squashed several sets of prints off my fingers. I smiled a big smile for the camera when my mug shot was taken. The police typed out their sets of forms: age, place of birth, address in Thailand (I gave them a hotel in Sangklaburi as my residence). I helped myself to glasses of water from their office cooler and stretched into karate stances. I was terribly pleasant to the Immigration officers. I asked if I could see Spin for a few minutes, and offered to pay for the privilege. "No need for payment," the officer in charge said, "you are to see him for five minutes after we finish this paperwork. It is the chief's orders."

The officer brought me to the wing of the building where the men's wards were located, and we climbed the stairs to Ward 4. I saw some Middle Eastern faces pressed against the barred corridor window. I called Spin's name. He was near the door.

"You really look like hell," I said when I saw him. His face was scruffy with whiskers, his eyes were red-rimmed, and a muscle jumped in his creased cheek. He looked like a Charles Bukowski poem illustrated by Ralph Steadman. His sweaty hands clutched the bars. There must be some deep-seated impulse in primates that makes us clutch the bars of our cages. I held his hands over the bars.

I was not Spin's only visitor. Trinka and a European boy were there with a kilo of oranges they had brought Spin. I ignored them. They could wait. I was the one with a five-minute time limit. I told Spin that I was sorry my embassy couldn't get him a plane ticket, but I would contact a New Zealand businessman I knew in Bangkok, who I was positive could make arrangements. I said I'd make sure the New Zealand consul came to see him.

"Don't worry, you'll be out of here soon," I assured him.

Spin coughed, and his eyes glittered. "Bloody incredible things go on in here," he said. "Terrible stuff. I'm taking notes on the sly."

An Australian came up and thrust a tattooed arm through the bars to shake my hand. "Hello, sister!" he said.

"Yes, I am your sister," I said. "I came from Ward 5."

"Oh, this is the one who's been sending you the letters," he exclaimed to Spin. "Well, well, then." He shook my hand again, and disappeared into the ward.

The Immigration officer tapped me on the shoulder. "That's five minutes," he said.

Spin's blue eyes darted about anxiously. I caught them, gazed in as far as I could, and saw nothing.

"Mondana bashen," I said.

"Zenda ba," Spin replied. It was the poetic exchange of Afghan freedom fighters meeting on mountain trails in the Hindu Kush: "May you live long," "May you keep your strength."

And as we had once shouted the Shan slogan "Grow and prosper" with the soldier boys in Khun Sa's revels at Tiger Camp I said *"Mai sung."*

Spin's eyes pierced mine. *"Mai sung!"* he echoed, and he watched me walk away.

The guards brought me back to Ward 5. The American was gone, and Caroline had gone to the tax office with a French embassy escort. Even if you'd spent four years in prison, Thailand required your tax records to be in order before you could leave the country. Boy was staging another punishment tableau, elaborate and tiresome. She lined up all the children to get light whacks on the hand with the electric cord, in order to impress upon them their obligation to be quiet and orderly. A charity had delivered a parcel of books to the ward, which included a full set of *Remembrance of Things Past* in French. That would be just the perfect way to spend a couple of months in Immigration jail, I thought. Get a pair of earplugs and go for total immersion in the lives of the Guermantes.

I had one more visitor, a wire service reporter. She told me that the officer who had put me in detention, Satapon Thong-On, had been "on holiday," unavailable for comment to the press, ever since. "Fled the scene," I said. The wire service would have to be content with "a senior immigration official who refused to be named declined comment on the charges." The charges were that they had detained Spin and me without just cause, since our visas had been legitimately issued. I talked to the reporter for a while, and gave her my latest press release.

On the wall behind the straw mat where I had slept, I'd found a tiny ballpointed graffito that read "The Kachin State." I imagined the prisoner who had written that, longing for the pine-clad mountains of her north Burma homeland. I stacked the volumes of Proust and stood on them to inscribe, high on the wall in red marker, "Freedom for Burma! Death to Ne Win!"

The Cambodian trustys came to fetch me. "Promise you'll send us a postcard," Boy called as I waved good-bye. In the downstairs office, the police gave me back my cameras, and film, and photos, all tied in a plastic bag. A roll of film was missing from the Minolta, but it had been unexposed anyway. The rest of the film was intact. "What about my knife?" I asked. It took considerable hunting around in desk drawers, but they located it and handed that over, too.

I saw my passport, with new Thai writing opposite my visa, in red ink.

"What does it say?" I asked.

"That you're the prettiest lady in jail," said the young officer who'd helped me call the embassy.

God, Thailand! I thought.

Actually, it said that the Ministry of the Interior had declared, as of August of the previous year (when I'd been nowhere near Thailand), that I was not to be issued a visa or allowed to enter the country.

Leaving the office, I really turned on the charm, thanking the police for being so helpful and kindhearted. I smiled graciously and *wai*'d and said sweetly, "Please do whatever you can to help my husband. If he needs anything—phone calls or whatever—please help him."

The young officer went to the airport with me in a cab I paid for. He checked me in at the Thai International counter, and brought me past the Immigration lines. When he saw the gate number for my Hong Kong flight, he groaned, "Gate 44, too far to walk. You can go by yourself now."

"Just a minute," I said. "Please, when you go back to Soi Suan Phlu, do anything you can to help my husband in Ward 4." The officer assured me that he would try to be of assistance to Spin.

I had time to make some phone calls. I found a pay phone near the gate and fed it my remaining baht coins. I telephoned the New Zealand businessman first. I asked him to encourage the New Zealand consul to visit Spin and to procure a plane ticket if necessary. Then I phoned some journalists and other friends in Bangkok.

The airline's obsequious Thai hospitality left me cold. I stuck their proffered sprig of purple orchids into the seat pocket in front of me, out of my sight. I read the *Bangkok Post*. Again it lacked any mention of Spin and me in jail. It *did* have a very self-righteous editorial criticizing Singapore's detention without charges of political opponents, though.

⚬ 4 ⚬

It was evening when I landed in Hong Kong. I caught a swift ferry to Lantau Island, where a college friend welcomed me into her antique-strewn beachfront condo. I slept on the sofa, which was made up with pristine, white sheets. It was so quiet. It was quiet enough to think straight, at last, but I slept instead of thinking.

Deportation was like being shipwrecked, and I had washed up in Hong Kong with only my moldy jungle clothes. First thing in the morning, I raided my friend's closet and borrowed a demure lavender dress. Then I took the ferry over to Central, Hong Kong's business hub. I quickly covered the short distance from the ferry pier to the Connaught Centre, a dominolike edifice overlooking Hong Kong harbor with row upon row of round windows (the Chinese were said to call it "the house of a thousand assholes"). Several of the windows belonged to my destination, the New Zealand legation.

I explained to the receptionist that I was there with information about a New Zealand journalist who was being detained in Bangkok. An aging diplomat in some sort of old school tie brought me into his office. After I explained Spin's situation, the diplomat launched into a speech about foreign sovereignty, saying that if someone was arrested, New Zealand couldn't interfere, "because it is up to the law of the land how they are to deal with the miscreant."

"But he's not a *miscreant*," I protested, remembering to smile my Thai smile. "He wasn't even arrested. He's been held without charges for over a week just because he's a journalist."

The diplomat absorbed that, and cleared his throat. "All right, then, let's see what we can do for the fellow." First he looked Spin up on a computer. Apparently New Zealand was such a small country that all passport holders were in an immediately accessible computer file. The screen showed that Spin had a clean record, at least as far as New Zealand was concerned.

"Passport issued in Singapore, 1984," the diplomat read. "Must be one of these chaps that've been knocking about Asia a long time."

Yes, I thought, knocking about (burnt out by wars, compassion fatigue, survivor guilt, hepatitis) Asia a long time.

"Came here from Fiji, myself," the diplomat said. "And Korea before that."

Then the diplomat placed a call to the New Zealand consul in Bangkok. After some opening banter, he said, "I say, about this fellow in jail in Bangkok, seems like a detention without charges, human rights sort of thing." He handed me the phone so I could speak with the consul.

"Just saw Spin this morning," the consul told me. "Would have thought he'd want to stay in there a bit longer, to get a really good story! But he's going to be deported tomorrow. A friend of his seems to have obtained a plane ticket for him."

As I left the Legation, the diplomat said, "Thank you for being so concerned about one of our nationals. We do appreciate it."

I had been transported from Three Pagodas Pass and jail, and Central's legions of stylish young professionals were rather daunting. I felt strange in the crowds. I turned around and took the ferry back to Lantau. At my friend's condo, the Filipina maid asked me, "What does Mem want for lunch?"

"Oh, I'll have anything," I stammered.

What I got was Campbell's alphabet soup. I lunched with my friend's seven-year-old daughter and two of her schoolmates. The conversation was about ballet lessons, ponies, and finding our names in the soup.

After lunch I went out and vegetated on the beach, something I hadn't done in years (marching down the Mon seacoast didn't count). The afternoon was sunny and quiet. The warm air held no humidity. The water was polluted but the sand was clean. I read Sun Tzu's *The Art of War*.

In the evening I telephoned the New Zealand businessman in

Bangkok. He told me that Spin would be on a morning flight to Penang, and that the *Bangkok Post* had dared to print my wire service interview that day. "You really raked the Immigration Department over the coals," he said. Some newspaper reporters telephoned from the U.S. to interview me. Between phone calls I watched television. A newscaster said, "Yesterday, another two hundred and forty Vietnamese refugees arrived here by boat." They would be indefinitely detained in one of Hong Kong's "closed camps." I had arrived by airplane, and I was free.

~ 5 ~

Awaking early from another night on the soft, white-sheeted sofa, I drank Mr. Juicy orange juice and direct-dialed Bangkok's airport. I gave Spin's name to an information clerk, and the number of his flight to Penang. "He is on the plane," she confirmed. Now Spin was free.

My love would turn from ruby to copper to ice. Soon after my return to the United States, I would be doing office temp work in the relentlessly monotonous confines of an engineering firm. The day before my thirty-fifth birthday, early in August 1988, I would be sitting in a beige cubicle typing the words *chargeable service* over and over again on forms:

> Chargeable service
> Chargeable service
> Chargeable service

Mesmerized at the Selectric, I would, that day, fall out of love with Spin with the inevitability and decisiveness of gravitational pull. I would suddenly acquire the prescience of the lapis beads. Within the week, Burma would explode: a massive combustion with millions demonstrating in the cities; a shadow play of Ne

Win's henchmen; Tatmadaw massacres of Burmese students, monks, and children. Burma would be on the network news every night, and on CNN all day. Burma would achieve the reality of the world's front pages. I would have no time to spend on Spin. The U.S. would cut off all aid to Burma, and Senator Moynihan of New York, with my Keng Tung report in hand, would force a high-level investigation of the 2,4-D program.

I would practice the art of collating, and other menial tasks, at the engineering firm by day and the art of revolution by telephone and typewriter by night. I would urge the rebels to take advantage of the urban uprising, to be real armies of liberation, to take towns, seize territory. But, for the most part, the rebels would sit on their hands. Immobilized by the monsoon season and years of black market inertia, they would fail to act until it was too late and the Tatmadaw would have overpowered the resistance of the cities with a reign of terror.

Additionally, the rebel armies would turn on each other at Three Pagodas Pass. Karen civilians would flee deeper into Kawthoolei, Mons and others would cross the Thai border, and then the Karen and Mon forces would go at each other with their expensive black market weaponry, obliterating the whole Three Pagodas bazaar with their shells until nothing was left and a National Democratic Front team came down from Manerplaw to contrive a truce. Over three hundred people would die in the weeks of fighting, including Iris's husband, who was captured by Mon soldiers and executed. As far as anyone could tell, he was killed because he was married to a Karen.

At the height of the demonstrations in Burma's cities, Khun Sa would prepare to move his operations into corrupt, authoritarian Laos, and refuse outright to fight the Tatmadaw. One day in September, Prince George would appear at the British Council in Chiang Mai, an English school in an imposing colonial-style building. Appearing "mentally deranged" to the director, Prince George would plead to be taken to the British embassy, then to the Burmese embassy. He was drunk beyond reason and terminally ill. The Tailand Revolutionary Council said the prince had a brain tumor. He died within the month and they cremated him with full honors.

Still, hope held on in Burma. Burmese students and other urban dissidents fled to the frontier areas by the thousands. Those who survived waves of malaria stayed on in rebel camps, and hundreds fought side by side with the NDF troops. The young idealists gave the rebellion a much needed infusion of urgency and an infiltration network for the cities. The war went on in the muddy trenches of Kawthoolei, the Mon seacoast, the Kachin mountains, but it was no longer unknown. That fall, the Karennis finally attacked the Loikaw power plant. The commandos' rockets damaged relay transformers enough to shut the lights off all the way down in Rangoon for twenty-four hours.

I belonged in the thick of the revolution, but, blacklisted by Thailand, I could not return to the frontier. I realized I had taken the rap for Trinka's trip to Tiger Camp. I found Reuters and *Agence France Presse* reports indicating that the Thai authorities had assumed it was me who'd gone back there with Spin. Since there were no charges, no trial, I was not given a chance to prove otherwise.

And that September, while calls for democracy could still be heard from Rangoon, I was in a New York library one day, trying to track down a news story quoting a Drug Enforcement Administration spokesman calling the doomed 2,4-D program "a disaster." As I left, I stepped aside to let a Tibetan monk into the elevator ahead of me. Outside, sunlight warmed the air, and I took off my tweed jacket as I walked. I heard a clink of metal on the pavement and a passerby said, "You dropped something." On the sidewalk was the old Tibetan copper coin that was the amulet from the goldfish dress dream. I'd been sure I'd lost it, but it reappeared, just like that. With copper in my pocket, ice in my heart, and a head full of revolution, I knew now that everything would end up well. Cracking open a fortune cookie, I found the motto "Hell is paved with good intentions" with a smiling face printed next to it. Not the *road* to Hell, but Hell itself. With my copper coin and my good intentions, I would be ready to walk through Hell, or dance through it, or ride through it on a white mule.

* * *

In Hong Kong, that post-deportation June morning, I drank all the
orange juice I wanted. I thought of Spin's plane, now flying over the
Isthmus of Kra to Malaysia, and of the pine trees in the Kachin
mountains. I had lost Spin, I had lost Thailand, but I would never
lose Burma. Then thoughts left me, and I looked out the glass doors
at the path to the beach. The path was shaded by tall casurina pines
that swayed slightly in the sea wind. The breeze stirred two gauze
goldfish, remnants of a Chinese lantern festival, that hung just
beyond the doors. Barefoot on the polished floor I performed *kata,*
reaching my best, *Matsukaze,* becoming calligraphy, turning like
the pine tree in the wind. I had to be ready.

AFTERWORD

Burma continues to be a nation in chains. In September 1988, a junta of Ne Win's trusted officers took charge as the State Law and Order Restoration Council, known by its sinister acronym, Slorc. The junta included Saw Maung (a long-winded authoritarian), Than Shwe (a taciturn authoritarian), and Khin Nyunt (the epicene, manipulative chief of Military Intelligience). Ne Win, more reclusive than ever, pulled the strings of the Slorc puppet show from behind the scenes. The junta changed the name of the country to Myanmar (an archaic, grammatically incorrect, Slorc-ish spelling of "Burma") to satisfy Ne Win's advisory wizards.

Aung San Suu Kyi became known and loved throughout Burma in 1989. The Oxford-educated daughter of Aung San, Burma's assassinated anticolonial leader, Suu Kyi galvanized huge crowds with her eloquent prodemocracy speeches. A firm believer in nonviolent resistance, she bravely faced down the Tatmadaw until the Slorc put her under house arrest in July 1989. There she has remained, incommunicado. Her political party won a 1990 national election with over 80 percent of the vote, but it has not been allowed to take office. The Slorc has jailed many of the winning prodemocracy candidates.

When it was formed during the brutal crackdown on the prodemocracy uprising of 1988, the Slorc regime was deeply in debt

and had no foreign exchange reserves to speak of. Some observers
thought the Slorc's Tatmadaw would simply run out of bullets. But
the Slorc turned to the sale of Burma's natural resources to gain
hard cash for military expenditures. Thai Army officers greased a
large-scale logging deal by returning Burmese student refugees to
the gaping maw of the Slorc, and a great wood frenzy commenced.
Thai timber firms clear-cut the Burma side of the border from the
Shan State to the Tenasserim, making sawdust of the rich forest
habitats in a few short years. The wild elephant and rhinoceros all
but vanished into myth, and the monkeys, apes, and bears (with no
place to hide) and the hornbills (lacking tall trees for nesting)
became scarcer than ever. Foreign trawler fleets, mostly Thai, and
tin-dredging barges decimated marine life in the Andaman Sea.
The Slorc forcibly relocated Mon fishing villages away from the
coast, destroying their livelihood. When the rebels fought back for
control of the forests and sea, the Slorc launched a rampage called
"the Teak War." Thai logging trucks were used to transport
Tatmadaw troops to battles, including the capture of Three Pagodas Pass. General Htaw Mon was held hostage in a Thai jail by a
logging company with designs on the hardwood of the Mon territory. Thai jails, including Soi Suan Phlu, were full of Burmese
refugees—many of whom were dissident students—who were
often forcibly repatriated to Burma or bought out by Thai businessmen and used as unpaid laborers or prostitutes.

The tribal troops of the Burmese Communist Party revolted
against their commissars in 1989. The Slorc made deals with the
newly fragmented BCP, reviving its old Ka Kwe Ye opium warlord
franchise arrangement. Eventually Slorc agents convinced Pa-O
and Palaung rebel leaders to surrender as well. With the Shan State
pacified, opium production actually increased. Heroin refineries
multiplied in Burma, and the narcotics flowed out to Thailand,
China, and elsewhere. The drug cargo traveled by Tatmadaw
trucks along roads refurbished by the Tatmadaw's unpaid tribal
laborers. AIDS began to stalk Burma's mountains, when tribal
children were brought to Chiang Mai and advertised as "AIDS-
free" prostitutes. They did not remain AIDS-free for long, and

when they returned home, the disease spread through their villages. Heroin addiction burgeoned among the young people of Burma's towns and cities.

The Slorc grew wealthy from its hand-over-iron-fist sale of Burma's heritage. It parceled out oil exploration concessions to companies like Amoco and Unocal, and set up a joint venture with Pepsi Cola. It raked in narcotics money beyond the wildest dreams of Manuel Noriega. The Slorc rearmed with Yugoslav and Chinese bombers, gunboats, and vehicles. The Tatmadaw bulged to over 280,000 strong. But its position astride the nation was insecure. In late 1991, Karen and Burmese student rebels infiltrated the Irrawaddy delta, coming within forty miles of Rangoon. Kachin rebels took and held mountain terrain, and Mons hit along the southern railway line. Against all odds, civil disobedience continued in the cities with students and Buddhist monks staging demonstrations— risking imprisonment and torture at the hands of the hated Slorc.

Nineteen ninety-one ended with Aung San Suu Kyi, still under house arrest in Rangoon, receiving the Nobel Peace Prize. She has become the symbol of the courage of a captive land.

Ne Win lives on. His Tatmadaw specializes in the death march: driving village populations from place to place until they die off; moving half a million people out of Rangoon to malarial wastelands; creating a rootless mass of expendable slaves. Tens of thousands of refugees from Burma are in Thailand, thousands in China and India, even the bleak hills of western Laos. More than 300,000 Moslem refugees from Burma have crept onto the mud flats of Bangladesh in the past year alone, fleeing the Slorc's systematic religious persecution and the network of slave labor camps known as the Buthidaung Gulag.

The governments of Bangladesh, India, Europe, and the United States (democracies) oppose the Slorc, but the governments of China and Thailand condone and profit from the Burmese junta. Chinese and Thai political operatives are engaged in lucrative deals with the Slorc, particularly in the timber and narcotics trades. China and Thailand have imitated the Slorc way of crushing dissent in Beijing's Tiananmen Square and Bangkok's May 1992 demonstrations. The overlords of Burma, China, and Thailand have shown that their preferred method for quelling their peoples' calls for democracy is to use live ammunition.

Manerplaw is now headquarters for a government in refuge formed by some winners of the 1990 election, as well as the head-quarters of the Karen revolutionaries and the National Democratic Front. During the early dry season months of 1992, the Slorc made an all out attempt to seize Manerplaw with human wave assaults of intoxicated teenage soldiers, aerial bombardment, and Carl Gustaf cluster-bomb rockets. The Karens stood their ground and Man-erplaw held. The rains came in May (lighter than they used to be, due to deforestation) and the Tatmadaw guns have been silenced for now along Kawthoolei's front line.

Five brave gentlemen who figured in *Burmese Looking Glass* have since died: Chao Eric Nor Fah, Skaw Ler Taw, Nai Non La, Saw Benny Htoo, and Mo Heing. They are greatly missed as revolution-aries and as my friends, and I regret that they did not live to see Burma liberated, as it yet shall be.

GLOSSARY

Ethnic Groups

Akha: A tribe that lives in the mountains of northern Thailand, northeastern Burma, and southern China.

Apa Tani: A tribe that lives in northeastern India.

Arakanese: Buddhist and Moslem people of Arakan, on the western coast of Burma, which was once a trading empire.

Bengali: The people of Bangladesh, and the region of India around Calcutta; many people of Bengali ancestry live in Burma's cities. Also may refer to Moslem people from Arakan, who call themselves Rohingyas.

Burmese: Also known as Burman, they are the largest ethnic group in Burma, living mainly in the country's central plains and cities.

Cambodian: Refers to the people of Cambodia, who speak the Khmer language.

Chinese: Many people of Chinese ancestry live in the towns and cities of Burma and Thailand. Also, in the mountainous, rural north of Burma and Thailand, there are sizable populations of Chinese from Yunnan Province.

Dai: A branch of the Tai ethnic group, living mainly in an area of Yunnan called Sipsongbanna.

Indian: Many people of Indian ancestry, primarily Bengali, live in Burma.

331

Kachin: A group of related tribes living in the far north of Burma, and Yunnan.

Karen: A large tribal group living in Burma and Thailand.

Karenni: The "Red Karen" tribe, which lives in eastern Burma, and in Thailand.

Lahu: A tribe that lives in the mountains of Burma, Thailand, and Yunnan.

Laotian: Refers to the Lao people, a branch of the Tai ethnic group living in Laos; there is also a large Lao population in Thailand.

Lisu: A Kachin-related tribe living in the mountains of Burma, Thailand, and Yunnan.

Mon: A Buddhist people whose ancestors ruled much of Burma, Thailand, and Cambodia.

Padaung: A tribe of eastern Burma.

Palaung: A Mon-related tribe of northeastern Burma.

Pa-O: A Karen-related Buddhist tribe of Burma.

Shan: A branch of the Tai ethnic group, living mainly in northeast Burma.

Tai: An ethnic group, speaking similar Sino-Tai languages and having common cultural attributes, including Buddhism, living in Burma, Thailand, Laos, Yunnan, and other areas of Southeast and sub-Himalayan Asia.

Tavoyan: Refers to a Burmese-related group, living in coastal southern Burma.

Thai: A branch of the Tai ethnic group, living in Thailand; also known as Siamese.

Wa: A Mon-related tribe, living mainly in mountainous areas of northeast Burma, and Yunnan.

Yunnanese: Refers to Chinese from Yunnan Province, many of whom live in northern Burma and Thailand.

Armed Forces

Tatmadaw: The central government army of Burma.

Ka Kwe Ye: A Burmese government militia, including warlord groups.

National Democratic Front (NDF): Alliance of frontier ethnic rebel groups (Karen, Karenni, Kachin, Pa-O, Palaung, Wa, Shan, Arakanese, Mon, Lahu, Chin).

Burmese Communist Party (BCP): Hard-line communist rebel force with tribal troops.

Kuomintang (KMT): Remnants of Chinese Nationalist forces that fled the communist takeover of China to northern Burma and Thailand in the 1950s.

Shan forces:
- Shan United Revolutionary Army (Sura), led by Mo Heing
- Shan United Army (SUA), led by Khun Sa
- Shan State Army (SSA), an NDF member group
- Tailand Revolutionary Council (TRC), formed in 1984–85 by merger of Sura, SUA, and some elements of SSA

Border Patrol Police (BPP) and *Rangers:* Thailand's security and paramilitary forces stationed on the Burma border.

Drug Enforcement Administration (DEA): United States government antinarcotics agents.